THE
TRADITION
OF
POLITICAL
HEDONISM

THE TRADITION OF
POLITICAL HEDONISM
FROM HOBBES
TO J. S. MILL

FREDERICK VAUGHAN

1907

New York
FORDHAM UNIVERSITY PRESS
1982

Printed in the United States of America

Contents

Preface

My purpose in the present work is to give an account of the underlying unity that the modern liberal–democratic tradition assumed in the sixteenth and seventeenth centuries as a reaction against the long-dominant Aristotelian–Scholastic tradition of moral and political philosophy. C. B. Macpherson has identified that unity as "possessive individualism."[1] I am attempting here to go beyond Macpherson's valuable contribution in order to show how the founders of modern political philosophy consciously appropriated the principles of ancient hedonism and transformed them into political principles, making hedonism the major motive force in the rise of the modern liberal–democratic state. Several contemporary scholars have alluded to this peculiar character of modern liberalism;[2] but no one has up to now provided a thematic discussion of its origins and development from the seventeenth century to the present. The two recent works which come the closest to providing guidance in this matter are: James H. Nichols, Jr., *Epicurean Political Philosophy*,[3] and Albert O. Hirschman, *The Interest and the Passions*.[4]

Nichols' book is primarily an analysis of Lucretius' *De rerum natura*; it is a sensitive and scholarly presentation of Lucretius' political philosophy. The book also contains a brief discussion of the Lucretian legacy in such modern writers as Hobbes, Montesquieu, Locke, and Rousseau. I found this book especially helpful for understanding Lucretius and for confirming several aspects of the influence of ancient hedonism on the development of modern political philosophy.

Hirschman's book is a valuable study of the principles of hedonism which lie at the roots of modern economic thought. The author is especially perceptive when treating Hume and Bentham.

I wish to thank the Canada Council for its generous assistance on two occasions—during the winter of 1971 and the fall of 1974. That assistance permitted me to pursue research at the British Library, London, and the Bodleian Library, Oxford, where I was able to examine the Locke manuscripts in the Lovelace collection, as well as numerous sixteenth- and seventeenth-century books relating to the subject of this study. Without that help, this book would not have been possible.

I should like also to thank the Relm Foundation, Ann Arbor, Michigan, for supporting those aspects of research which I undertook in the United States. As well, I am also grateful to the Relm Foundation for bearing the cost of typing the final manuscript.

I wish also to thank the Librarian of the Royal Society of Edinburgh for the courtesy extended to me during my visit in November 1974 to review the Hume manuscripts in their possession.

Few people have been more helpful to me in this project than Sir Isaiah Berlin. It was he who as President of Wolfson College, Oxford, invited me to spend a pleasant and profitable period as a Visiting Fellow at Wolfson College during Hilary term 1971 and Michaelmas term 1974. And despite his reservations with what I am presenting here, he has urged me to pursue it to the end. Needless to say, I do not wish or intend to implicate him in this study. All errors of fact and interpretation are my own.

I am especially indebted to Gary Glenn, Northern Illinois University, for reviewing the draft manuscript. His careful and critical reading of the manuscript resulted in many improvements; not as many, alas, as he might have wished.

A number of other scholars read all or portions of the manuscript and I should like to express my gratitude to them: Thomas Schrock, University of California, Santa Barbara; C. B. Macpherson, University of Toronto; J. A. W. Gunn, Queen's University, Kingston; John Seaman, McMaster University; Patrick Kyba and William Christian, the University of Guelph; and Douglas Long, the University of Western Ontario. (Professor Long was especially helpful with the section on Bentham. He kindly permitted me to read the manuscript of his book on Bentham; as well, he provided me with access to Bentham manuscript material in his possession.) I do not wish to implicate these scholars in the deficiencies of the study.

Anyone who has written a book knows how important the secretarial assistance is to the final outcome. I wish to thank Diane Love for typing the draft manuscript and for suffering in patience the many revisions. I should also like to thank in this connection my former secretary, Jean Edmiston. Her attentive supervision reduced the typographical errors to a minimum. I owe a special debt of gratitude to Joanne Robinson for typing the final manuscript.

And finally to my wife, Carol, and two young sons, I must acknowledge my gratitude. My wife has had to listen to the numerous accounts of progress and non-progress over the past years; she did so with patience and encouragement. My sons, Geoffrey and Kevin, gave all the help consistent with their young ages. To them I dedicate this book.

Guelph, Ontario, Canada   FREDERICK VAUGHAN
Winter 1982

NOTES

1. *The Political Theory of Possessive Individualism* (Oxford: Clarendon Press, 1962).

2. See, for example, Leo Strauss, *Natural Right and History* (Chicago: The University of Chicago Press, 1953); also, Norman F. Cantor and Peter L. Klein, *Seventeenth Century Rationalism: Bacon and Descartes* (Waltham: Blaisdell, 1969); Basil Willey, *The Seventeenth Century Background* (New York: Columbia University Press, 1934); Paul Hazard, *The European Mind* (New York: Meridian Books, 1963).

3. (Ithaca: Cornell University Press, 1976).

4. (Princeton: Princeton University Press, 1974).

THE
TRADITION
OF
POLITICAL
HEDONISM

Introduction

> For whoever is willing to turn back his eyes and trace a tradition
> to its very source must necessarily come to a stand somewhere and
> in the end recognize someone as the first author of this tradition.
> JOHN LOCKE, *Essays on the Law of Nature*

LORD ACTON ONCE WROTE that "Few discoveries are more irritating than those which expose the pedigree of ideas." This is, of course, especially true when the ancestry of our major principles of action turn out to be dishonorable or base. An unquestioning faith in the soundness of the fundamental principles, along with a supreme confidence in the distinction between facts and values, has led the social-science disciplines to abandon philosophic reflection on the historic origins of those fundamental principles.

The conscious disregard of the historic origins of our intellectual principles is fraught with danger when we observe that the major contemporary influences on public policy are the least capable of assessing the roots of the principles they are employing in recommending public objectives. The indisposition among social-science disciplines to historic studies which bare the pedigree of major ideas and their development has blinded them to the undesirable consequences of those ideas.

This book is intended to be an essay in the pedigree of ideas; its purpose is to trace the origins and development of the central principles which have come to infuse modern political philosophy beginning with the enunciation of the new conception of nature as the norm in human affairs; beginning, that is, with the great founders of "the new natural philosophy," Bacon and Boyle.

This development, called either *modernity* or *the modern project*, emerged in the sixteenth and seventeenth centuries when the great philosophers of that period successfully undermined the old principles of political philosophy—drawn principally from Plato and Aristotle—and replaced them with new ones. The essential accord among these founders and their influential successors as to what constitutes the human good and the ends of human government has come to constitute a tradition whose influence on our times has become powerful if not dominant. A tradition can be said to exist where a central coherent and consistent set of principles infuses a movement and gives it direction. In order for a tradition in the proper sense of the term to emerge—as in the Christian tradition—there must be a central core of specific fundamental principles which constitute the motive force and which give it a unity. It is precisely in this sense that the principles of hedonism have come to infuse the Western liberal–democratic state.

Since the principles of modernity prompted the emergence of republican government, it is essential that we understand that those principles are today working themselves out in the United States, the oldest and most successful modern republic. Small wonder that Daniel Bell has recently concluded that "by the 1950's American culture had become primarily hedonistic, concerned with play, fun, display, and pleasure—and, typical of things in America, in a compulsive way."[1]

The movement toward republican government emerged as a decisive event in Western history after almost a millennium of monarchy. The new basis for consent in modern republican government forcibly replaced the old doctrine of natural right and natural law with a new doctrine of natural right (to self-preservation, understood as *comfortable* self-preservation) and natural law (as the extension into public law of the new natural right). Hence the old concept of the priority of the common good over the private good leading to duty (arising out of Aristotle and Aquinas) was replaced by the priority of the private good and the claim to individual rights. The new natural right led, as C. B. Macpherson has demonstrated,[2] to the powerful liberal spirit of "possessive individualism."

In order to uncover the basic unifying thread of the tradition of possessive individualism, or political hedonism, we must penetrate to the central or core principles, that is to say, identify what constitutes the nature of *the just* and *the good* among the recognized proponents of that tradition. That is not to ignore or to minimize their important differences. It is, however, to give more weight than is commonly given to what unites them in central principle rather than to what distinguishes them. The failure to recognize the common central commitment of the leading proponents of modern political philosophy to hedonism has denied us a clarity of vision as to where those principles, which we constantly reaffirm, are leading us. In short, we have become unwittingly committed to the principles of hedonism without being aware of the consequences.

The rejection of classical natural right led not only to profound philosophical consequences; it led to profound theological consequences as well. For where one "by most-firm reasons demonstrate[s] that there are no authentical doctrines concerning right and wrong, good and evil, besides the constituted laws in each realm,"[3] there one effectively eliminates the theological claim to instruct and to enjoin the compliance of citizens in such matters on the authority of the Bible. Transcendent theological appeal becomes as untenable as transcendent philosophical appeal. The scriptural preoccupation of the modern philosophers was, therefore, an essential aspect of the modern project of reconstruction; it was one thing to uproot and to replace the legacy of Plato and Aristotle as presented in a decayed scholasticism, but quite another thing to undermine the powerful revealed Christian theology, for the Bible commanded enormous private and public endorsement at the dawn of the modern period.

The "separation of church and state" taken for granted today (and ensconced in the Constitution of the United States) must be understood to be the consequence of the more fundamental conflict between the new political philosophy and Christian theology which took place in the seventeenth century. That conflict was resolved with the victory of the new political philosophy over Biblical theology.

Finally, where the new natural philosophy promised a more commodious life through the invention of useful devices (technology), the new political philosophy promised a greater (if not permanent) condition of civil peace—the fundamental or necessary condition for the pursuit of commodious living (political hedonism).

In order to understand how the quiet triumph of hedonism occurred we must begin at the beginning of the modern period and understand how the emergence of the new natural philosophy was the necessary condition for the establishment of the modern tradition of political hedonism.

NOTES

1. Daniel Bell, *The Cultural Contradictions of Capitalism* (New York: Basic Books, 1975), p. 70.

2. C. B. Macpherson, *The Political Theory of Possessive Individualism* (Oxford: Clarendon Press, 1962).

3. Thomas Hobbes, *De Cive* (New York: Appleton-Century-Crofts, 1949), "Preface to the Reader," p. 10.

1

The Rise of the
New Natural Philosophy

GALILEO GALILEI STANDS OUT in our consciousness both as a victim and as a symbol of the great revolution in science which occurred in the sixteenth and seventeenth centuries. He became a victim of the entrenched and established scientific world view because he openly challenged the scientific orthodoxy with his bold telescopic confirmation of the Copernican thesis; the thesis that affirmed that the sun, not the earth, is the center of the cosmos. The scientific revolution thus arose out of the conscious rejection of the old science.[1]

Galileo has remained ever since as a symbol of the scientific spirit because he stands as a constant reminder that the old scientific views must give way to the ever-increasing confirmation of new hypotheses, as the Newtonian physics was forced to give way to the Einsteinian physics, and as Einstein's theses have begun to give way to more recent views. What we sometimes forget, however, is that a similar revolt in philosophy occurred hand-in-glove with the new and bold science. The revolt in philosophy was perhaps less dramatic but no less resounding in its impact upon the course of Western civilization than was Galileo's revolt. The new natural or mechanical philosophy emerged as a handmaiden of the new science and necessitated as complete a rejection of the old philosophy—principally Aristotle—as did Galileo's new cosmology. As Francis Bacon affirmed at the early stage of the great revolt in philosophy:

> It is idle to expect any great advancement in science from the super-inducing and engrafting of new things upon old. We must begin anew from the very foundations, unless we would revolve forever in a circle with mean and contemptible progress [*Advancement of Learning* xxxi].

But, as we shall see, the great founders of the new philosophy were disciples of a philosophic tradition which reached back to Democritus. This tradition had its adherents throughout Renaissance and medieval times but it remained an "underground movement"; it was never able to assert its presence too boldly, especially after Thomas Aquinas made Aristotle the ancient philosophic basis of Christian philosophical and theological orthodoxy. Once the pillars of Aristotelian philosophy were successfully assailed by the rise of the new science in the sixteenth century, the proponents of Democritean philosophy or science became boldly defiant and eventually succeeded in gaining the philosophic dominance. The new natural philosophy eventually drove the old Aristotelian philosophy "underground" where it remains, to all intents and purposes, to this day; at least it is safe to say that contemporary philosophy shares more with the new natural philosophy of the early modern philosophers than with Thomas Aquinas or Aristotle. And one thing is beyond dispute: Aristotelianism is not the dominant philosophy in this or the previous three centuries.

The new natural philosophy was similar to the old philosophy of nature founded by Socrates in that it took its bearing from nature; but the similarity begins and ends there. The philosophy of nature propounded by Socrates and his disciples was rooted in the understanding of nature as teleological. According to this understanding all things in nature are ordered to their proper end; all things find their perfection in the attainment of their end by nature. Man's proper end by nature in this view is found in moral virtue—in justice and magnanimity. The universe is viewed as a *cosmos*, an ordered whole.

The new natural philosophy rejected the teleological view of nature and affirmed that nature could be properly understood only in terms of its physical properties—those properties which could be weighed and measured; this applied to man as well as other things in nature. In the Socratic view nature established the norm; in the new view of nature (which took its bearings from Democritus) man ascribed the norm in a world which was viewed as fundamentally purposeless and even hostile.

Modern political philosophy must accordingly be viewed as an extension of the new natural philosophy to moral and political matters; this was initiated principally by Bacon, Descartes, Boyle, and Locke. It becomes necessary, therefore, to turn our attention to the efforts of Bacon, Descartes, Boyle, and Locke to establish the new natural philosophy.

The effectiveness or success of modern political philosophy was due in large measure to the success of the application of this new natural philosophy to moral and political matters. The history of philosophy since the seventeenth century attests the effectiveness of the new natural philosophy in replacing the old Aristotelian philosophy and in establishing new directions in both science and philosophy. There can be no disputing the claim that the work of Bacon, Boyle, and their successors has profoundly shaped the course of modern natural science and philosophy.

The effectiveness of the new philosophy stemmed not from the fierceness of the rejection of medieval Aristotelian scholasticism, but from the positive force of that which its founders established in its place. The founders of modern philosophy prepared the project of redirection by attacking the fundamental pillars of the old philosophy and by replacing them with new ones.[2] Their attention was, accordingly, directed to three central issues: the conception of nature; the limits and power of the human intellect; and the need for a method which would make up for the deficiencies of human reason and assure access to the new understanding of nature.

I

One of the leading figures in this early modern project was Francis Bacon (1561–1626). Thomas Sprat wrote that to Francis Bacon must go the high praise as founder of the new philosophy. For, says Sprat, in his "books there are every where scattered the best arguments that can be produced for the defence of experimental philosophy; and the best directions that are needful to promote it."[3] This commendation is more than amply justified when one reviews Bacon's major writings. For Bacon's ambition was to re-constitute the entire range of human knowledge by a total and un-equivocal rejection of the old scholastic Aristotelianism.[4] "Our only remaining hope and salvation is," he concluded after review-ing the prevailing intellectual climate, "to begin the whole labour of the mind again; not leaving it to itself, but directing it perpetu-ally from the very first and attaining our end as it were by me-chanical aid."[5] The new philosophy was to be established on the basis of the "method employed by the school of Democritus, which made greater progress in penetrating nature than the rest."[6] Ba-con's ambition was to take his readers on an intellectual voyage of discovery not unlike that other voyage depicted in his *New At-lantis.* The intellectual voyage begins by discarding the Aristotelian logic which, he alleged, corrupted natural philosophy by forming the world of categories and by superimposing innumerable arbi-trary distinctions upon the nature of things. As a corrective he counseled a turn to the works of Anaxagorus, Democritus, and Leucippus because they "exhibited some sprinkling of natural phi-losophy, whilst Aristotle's physics are mere logical terms."[7] Once Aristotle was discarded Bacon set out with the aid of the ancient natural philosophers "to lay down the true way of interpreting nature."[8] He makes it clear that his discovery is much like the dis-covery of "lost" continents—they were not really lost; they merely had to be rediscovered by a world which had forgotten that they were there.[9] In the *New Organon* Bacon traces the history of man's failure to discover the true philosophy in the following terms:

> It is well known that after the Christian religion had been acknowl-edged and arrived at maturity, by far the best wits were busied upon theology where the highest rewards offered themselves and every species of assistance was abundantly supplied, and the study of which was the principal occupation of the western European nations during the third epoch. In the preceding ages, during the second epoch, that of the Roman philosophical meditation and labour was chiefly occu-pied and wasted in moral philosophy (the theology of the heathens). The age during which natural philosophy appeared principally to flourish among the Greeks was but a short period, since in the more

ancient times the seven sages . . . applied themselves to moral philosophy and politics, and at a later period after Socrates had brought down philosophy from heaven to earth, moral philosophy became more prevalent, and diverted men's attention from natural philosophy. . . . Since, therefore, during these three epochs, natural philosophy had been materially neglected or impeded, it is not at all surprising that men should have made but little progress in it, seeing they were attending to entirely different matters.[10]

Bacon accordingly set about to redirect men's minds back to the natural world of matter and motion in the belief that such a focus alone would "relieve man's estate" and lead him to the conquest of nature and thereby ensure progress.[11] There could be no genuine progress in the sciences unless there was first a commitment to natural philosophy. "For want of this, astronomy, optics, music, many mechanical arts, medicine itself, and (what is perhaps more wonderful) moral and political philosophy, and the logical sciences have no depth, but only glide over the surface and variety of things."[12] Bacon explicitly envisaged progress in moral and political philosophy through the application of the new natural philosophy.

Bacon's great promise was the control of nature issuing in new mechanical inventions. In order to achieve this, he counseled, one must unravel nature's secrets "for nature is only commanded by obeying her."[13] The grand result will be an "increase in power over nature."[14] The modern period was thus founded in the determination to command nature in the interest of power.[15] Bacon expounded at length on this theme in the *New Organon*. He announced early in this work that it was necessary "to penetrate the more secret and remote parts of nature, in order to abstract both notions and axioms from things, by a more certain and guarded method."[16] But he said that it is futile to introduce men to this proper method of understanding before the necessary preliminary work of removing the mental obstacles which inhibit its assimilation. The source of the obstacles is twofold: first, the human mind itself; and second, the influence of learning and association with men.

Before presenting the new method, Bacon accordingly dwelt at length on these "idols" which prevent men from philosophizing correctly. He identified four species of idols which beset the human mind. Elaborating on each in turn, Bacon said that the first set of idols, the idols of the tribe, are those that are proper or inherent in the race or nature of men. The human mind is like an "uneven mirror," he said, "which import their own properties to different objects, from which rays are emitted and distort and disfigure them."[17] This characteristic of the human mind is a fundamental obstacle to right reasoning and it is inherent in all men.

The second set of idols, the idols of the den, are those which are peculiar to each individual. In addition to the distortions which impede all men generally, each has "his own individual race or cavern, which interprets and corrupts the light of nature."[18] These are acquired from a wide variety of formal and informal influences upon each individual; prejudices and disposition based on temperament are their main source.

The third set of idols, the idols of the market, are those which stem from "the commerce and association of men with each other."[19] This association takes place through speech, and speech employs words—hence the imprecise and faulty use of language employed in formal and informal association or intercourse with men leads to faulty terms and, thus, distorted or imprecise thinking.

The final set of idols are those of the theatre, by which Bacon meant those distortions of thought which we absorb from our instruction in "the various dogmas of peculiar systems of philosophy."[20] He believed that the Aristotelian school of philosophy had been a major cause of these idols and therefore constituted the main obstacle to the new natural philosophy.

In addition to these intellectual sources of error is that which Bacon said is "by far the greatest impediment and aberration of the human understanding"[21]—i.e., "the dullness, incompetency, and errors of the senses."[22] In other words he claims that not only is the human intellect beset with numerous impediments to accurate knowledge, but that the senses—the avenues which provide human access to the material world—are "weak and erring." But it is clear that he did not despair of the possibility of attaining accurate human knowledge. Nor indeed did he suggest that we "deny the authority of the human senses and understanding, although weak, but rather to furnish them with assistance."[23] He insisted, however, that this assistance, this discovery of the "true way of interpreting nature," cannot be undertaken before "the above expiatory process and purification of the mind" is completed.[24]

As the human understanding is prone to flights of fancy, the solution must be found in a sure and steady method, one which will force the mind down—literally down to earth. "We must not then add wings, but rather lead and ballast to the understanding, to prevent its jumping or flying."[25] In short, what was needed is a method which will keep men's minds focused on the "general structure of things,"[26] one which will assist them to "penetrate the simplicity of nature."[27] It is better to dissect than to abstract nature, he said; "such was the method employed by the school of Democritus which made greater progress in penetrating nature than the rest."[28]

It becomes clear that Bacon called for a rediscovery of the ancient atomic approach to nature. He gives a sketch of the history of philosophy at one point and laments the loss of "natural philosophy, the mother of the sciences."[29] He then called for a return to the ancient natural philosophy because "no one can expect any great progress in the sciences (especially the operative part) unless natural philosophy be applied to particular sciences."[30] Bacon was especially insistent that there can be no progress in moral and political philosophy without the aid of natural philosophy.[31]

The new method Bacon proposed consists of the process of establishing axioms by applying the new induction. Unlike the old Aristotelian induction, which Bacon viewed as a progression of logical propositions, the new induction would set down the results of observation and experimentation as sure and steady axioms which in turn would lead to better axioms. He wrote that there must be an ascent by "a true scale and successive steps without interruption

or breach from particulars to lesser axioms, thence to the inter-
mediate (rising one above the other) and lastly to the most general."[32] He promised that the new induction would be useful in
the demonstration of the arts as well as the sciences. It would also
"separate nature by proper rejections and exclusions, and then conclude for the affirmative after collecting a sufficient number of
negatives."[33]

Bacon's new method was designed to keep the human intellect
down to earth in the interest of improving man's estate in this
world through the invention of useful devices. This transforma-
tion would put philosophy and science at the disposal of the people
in the interest of power and empire over the physical world which
is properly man's according to Bacon. Of this he wrote: "Our
method of discovering the sciences is such as to leave little to the
acuteness and strength of wit, and indeed rather to level wit and
intellect. For as the drawing of a straight line, or accurate circle
by the hand, much depends on its steadiness and practice, but if a
ruler or a compass be employed there is little occasion for either;
so it is with our method."[34] Bacon was thus determined to reduce
human dependence on wisdom (or wit), which is always the preserve of the few, and replace it with a mechanical method which
most men could apply with profit. His was a clear call to technological inventiveness. Bacon compares the future results of the
application of his new method to that of the inventions of printing,
gunpowder, and the compass.[35] And as no one can deny that these
have changed the course of human history through literature,
warfare, and navigation, no one can deny the great "successes" of
modern technological science. "No star seems to have exerted
greater power and influence in human affairs than these mechanical discoveries," Bacon concluded.[36]

In the final sentence of the *New Organon* Bacon mused over
man's lot in this world: "For man, by the fall, lost at once his state
of innocence, and his empire over creation, both of which can be
partially recovered even in this life, the first by religion and faith,
the second by the arts and sciences."[37] The "arts and sciences,"
through the new mechanical or natural philosophy, will assist man

to recapture not only his control over nature, lost at the fall, but it will help restore his lost innocence. We shall see in a later chapter that this great promise is an explicit challenge to the orthodox Christian doctrine regarding grace. As Christopher Hill has observed: "Bacon unfurled the philosophic banner of the Moderns, not only against the Ancients and their defenders in the universities, but also against the theologians."[38]

II

René Descartes (1596–1650) was, no less than Francis Bacon, preoccupied with the quest for the new natural philosophy and the conquest of nature. In the *Discourse on Method* (1637) Descartes showed that he was concerned with discovering a method that would replace the prevailing scholastic philosophy.[39] After recounting how difficult it is to undermine the widespread and popular myth that all men are equally endowed with the ability to reason well, Descartes proceeded to state that "it is not enough to have good faculties, but the principal is, to apply them well. The greatest souls are as capable of the greatest vices, as of the most eminent virtues: and those who move but very slowly, may advance much farther, if they always follow the right way, than those who run and struggle on."[40]

Descartes became a prominent pioneer in the development of the new natural philosophy. However much he and Bacon were to disagree over the method and details of the new philosophy, they shared a common ambition: to replace the old "speculative philosophy" with a useful one rooted in experience. As Descartes said in the *Discourse*:

> I perceived it to be possible to arrive at a knowledge highly useful in life; and in room of the speculative philosophy usually taught in the schools, to discover a practical philosophy, by means of which, knowing the force and action of fire, water, air, the stars, the heavens, and all the other bodies that surround us, as distinctly as we know the various crafts of our artisans, one might also apply them in the same way to all the uses to which they are adapted, and thus render ourselves the lords and possessors of nature.[41]

Both Bacon and Descartes began their quest for the correct method by first purging themselves of the old philosophy.[42] What Bacon did through the idols, Descartes did through his *Regulae ad directionem ingenii*. Descartes began with a rejection of the haphazard tendency to guess at the right way of reasoning; this was an unmethodical and lazy way. "We ought," on the contrary, Descartes affirmed, "to train ourselves first in those easier matters, but *methodically*. Thereby we shall accustom ourselves to proceed always by easy and familiar paths, and so, as easily as though we were at play, to penetrate ever more deeply into the truth of things."[43] Descartes' celebrated "methodical doubt," by which he arrived at the undoubtable *ego cogito*, became the foundation of his philosophy and the starting point of reconstruction in philosophy. As he wrote: "Those who have learned the least of all that hitherto has been distinguished by the name of philosophy are the most fitted for the apprehension of truth."[44]

But, unlike Bacon, mathematics was for Descartes "the firm and solid foundation" of the new philosophy because it aided in the acquisition of useful knowledge. Mathematics provides indisputable knowledge; above all it owes nothing to the senses or to the body: it is a pure mental construct which transcends opinion. This is the basis of his disagreement with Bacon, for whom the correct method was to be found in empirical experimentation. Philosophy for Descartes becomes indistinguishable from the quest for knowledge of the mathematical laws of physics. Such a knowledge alone leads to the effective mastery of nature. In this way only can philosophy become useful to men. Philosophy thus understood can provide "an infinity of artifices that would enable us to enjoy, without any pain, the fruits of the earth, and all the comforts that are to be found there."[45] Bacon most assuredly condoned such a view of the end of philosophy.

Human happiness has nothing to do with the traditional quest for moral and political principles; rather does the science of medicine lead to happiness because health of the body is the fundamental prerequisite of happiness. That is why Descartes' *Treatise of Man*[46] is a materialistic and mechanistic study of the functions of the human body and not, as one would expect from the title, a moral treatise. Descartes refers to "the machine of our body" in the *Passions of the Soul* (1649) and to himself as a "physicist."[47]

Descartes believed that Bacon failed to see that the new method must be mathematical in order to be both certain and systematic. But he was in complete agreement with Bacon as to the purpose or end of the new philosophy: the conquest of nature in the interest of useful "discoveries" which would "relieve man's estate."

III

No one played a more important role in undermining the Aristotelian conception of nature than Robert Boyle. Indeed, Boyle can be said to have led the modern effort to uproot and replace the Aristotelian conception of nature. In a work entitled *A Free Inquiry into the Vulgarly Received Notion of Nature* (1685/6),[48] Boyle drew attention not only to the error of the old conception but also to its dangers. The "vulgar" notion of nature was, of course, the Aristotelian conception and was viewed as totally useless as a means of understanding the universe and all its forms, animate and inanimate. Boyle claimed that it was nothing but a word used by Aristotelians to explain what is beyond their comprehension; it was another of those useless categories imposed by Aristotle.[49]

For Aristotle nature contains both a physical and a moral connotation. On the physical level it connotes that the object exists through power inherent in itself and not from an external source. As the cow exists by nature and the shoe exists by human contrivance.[50] On the moral or ethical level, nature provides the inherent capacity to attain virtue. The moral virtues are not engendered by nature: the conscious habit of performing the moral virtues renders man virtuous, nature provides the capacity.[51]

The most important aspect of the Aristotelian conception of nature is that everything, man included, possesses an end or perfection by nature; man can attain his proper end (or perfection) under the guidance of right reason.[52]

Boyle went so far as to suggest that the Aristotelian notion of nature was dangerous because it "defrauds the True God of divers Acts of Veneration and Gratitude, that are due to Him from men, upon the account of the Visible World and diverts them to that imaginary being they call nature which has no title to them."[53] The old conception of nature was, in sum, a usurper which led men away from the true source of events, i.e., God. Thus did Boyle place the matter in a theological context from the very beginning.

Despite his open support for and faith in the "new mechanical principles," Boyle claimed that in its early stage of development the new natural philosophy could not be expected to answer all the questions. But, he insisted, "we must not therefore necessarily recur to, and acquiesce in, that principle that men call nature, since neither will that intelligibly explain them: But in that case we should ingeniously confess, that we are yet at a loss, how they are performed; and that this ignorance proceeds, rather from the natural imperfection of our understandings than from our not preferring nature (in the vulgar notion of it) to the mechanical principles, in the explication of the phenomena of the universe."[54]

In other words, he predicted that while the new philosophy might not as yet be able to provide a total explanation of the universe, it will someday if it is pursued faithfully starting with the most observable phenomenon and proceeding step by step until an understanding of the whole is at last obtained. One thing was established, Boyle said, and that was that the mechanical hypothesis shows that the universe is "like a rare clock, such as may be that at Strasbourg, where all things are so skilfully contrived that the engine being once set a moving all things proceed according to the artificers first design, and the motions of the little statues, that at such hours perform these or those things, do not require like those of puppets the peculiar interposing of the artificer."[55] The way to understand nature is to understand the motions of the clock and how each part interlocks and contributes to the working of the whole. This can only be done by approaching the whole with the principles of the new natural philosophy.

In short, Boyle saw the Aristotelian concept of nature as an impediment to scientific advancement. "For to vouch nature as a cause, is an expedient, that can scarce be wanting for to any man, upon any occasion, to seem to know what he can indeed render no good account of."[56] The proper understanding of nature prompts a more appropriate mode of inquiry. Since nature is as a large machine, the mechanical approach alone will reveal her secrets. Returning to the image of the clock, Boyle says: "So, if he can explain it mechanically, he has no more need to think, or (unless for brevity's sake) to say that nature brought it to pass, than he, that observes the motions of a clock, has to say, that tis not the engine but tis art, that shows the hour; whereas, without considering that general and uninstructive name, he sufficiently understands how the parts, that make up the engine, are determined by their construction, and the series of their motions, to produce the effect that is brought to pass."[57]

Boyle did not simply replace the term nature with such terms as "cosmical mechanism"; he rejected the understanding of nature as good or disposing all things toward their proper end—i.e., he denied that nature was teleological. "If nature be so provident and watchful for the good of men and other animals, and of that part of the world, wherein they live; how comes it to pass, that from time to time, she destroys such multitudes of men and beasts, by earthquakes, pestilences, famine, and other anomolies?"[58] Nature cannot be considered a friend to whom man must conform his actions any more than he can afford to entrust to his physical well-being. The skillful physician is more a friend to man than nature, for "a great part of the physician's work is to appease the fury, and to correct the errors of nature. . . . if she were wise and watchful of its welfare, she would have been as careful to prevent, as the physicians to remedy them."[59]

In his *Excellency and Grounds of the Mechanical Hypothesis* (1674),[60] Boyle related at length the possibilities for mankind if the old philosophy were replaced by the new natural philosophy. He suggested that we begin by taking the real world as given, avoiding the useless discussions of the scholastics and other disciples of Aristotle as to the origin of the universe. It is appropriate, he affirmed, for the Christian to assume that God created it; the philosopher's or scientist's task was to get on with the business of understanding it and turning its forces to his own ends. "I plead only for such a philosophy as reaches but to things purely corporeal, and distinguishing between the first original of things and the subsequent course of nature, teaches, concerning the former, not only that God gave motion and matter, but that in the beginning he so guided the various motions of the parts of it as to continue them into the world he designed they should compose, (furnished with the seminal principles and structures or models of living creatures) and establish those rules of motion and that order amongst things corporeal which we are wont to call the laws of nature."[61] If this philosophy were adopted he was confident that even "unprejudiced persons" would see its value and adopt it.[62]

It is important to understand that what Bacon and Boyle prompt by redirecting philosophy to the physical world of matter and motion is an account of human nature (i.e., the ground of moral and political philosophy) radically different from that proposed by Plato, Aristotle, and the scholastic disciples of Thomas Aquinas. The new natural philosophy spurned the quest for a knowledge of the nature of things such as the Aristotelians sought; it taught that only the results of the physical actions (motions) of things were scientifically knowable and hence significant.

The new natural philosophy ushered the experimental method into political life, which abstracts from questions of morality (the *ought*). The only standard by which to claim an ought according to this method is the way men actually do things, that is, in the way men agree to act (i.e., convention). To impose a code of conduct from an understanding of what man by nature ought to do—as the Aristotelians did—was to Bacon and Boyle to prescribe a code of conduct for human beings in defiance of the true (physical) nature of man, which is revealed in what he actually does.

IV

Of all the founders of modernity, no one did more to ensure that men's minds were restricted to the "physical parcel of the world" or the empirical world than John Locke. He shared with Bacon and Hobbes the determination to rescue philosophy from the stultifying philosophy of the scholastics, which had contributed nothing but "the art of wrangling."[63] He began his *Essay on Human Understanding* with a rejection of innate theoretical and practical principles.[64] The mind is not, he insisted, stamped from birth with certain innate principles; it is, instead, a "white paper, void of all characters, without any ideas."[65] Experience is the major source of all ideas: "in that all our knowledge is founded, and from that it ultimately derives itself. Our observation, employed either about external sensible objects, or about the internal operations of our minds, perceived and reflected on by ourselves, is that which supplies our understanding with all the materials of thinking. These two are the foundations of knowledge, from whence all the ideas we have, or can naturally have, do spring. Most of our ideas come from the evidence or material presented by the senses. This source is called sensation."[66]

In addition to this major source of ideas is the internal "perception of the operations of our minds within us."[67] This source, called reflection, produces such ideas as perception, thinking, doubting, believing, reasoning, knowing, willing, and all the different acts of our own minds. It is wholly within each man.

These two sources—sensation and reflection—are, said Locke, "the only originals from whence all our ideas take their beginnings."[68] There is nothing in the human mind which does not proceed from one or other (or both) of these sources. Knowledge is accordingly defined as "the perception of the connection and agreement, or disagreement and repugnancy of any of our ideas."[69] But knowledge can be either intuitive or demonstrative. The former occurs when the agreement or disagreement of two ideas is seen immediately and without any assistance or intervention of another idea. Locke gave as an example of this the comprehension that a circle is not a square. "This kind of knowledge," he said, "is the clearest and most certain that human frailty is capable of."

On the other hand, demonstrative knowledge requires the assistance of one or more other ideas before the mind grasps the agreement or disagreement. This kind of knowledge, or manner of knowing, is called reasoning.[70]

It follows, said Locke, from this understanding of knowledge, that we can have knowledge no further than we can have ideas.[71] Knowledge is, therefore, either intuitive, demonstrative, or sensate. The conclusion is that "we cannot have an intuitive knowledge that shall extend itself to all our ideas, and all that we would know about them."[72]

It is important to observe that Locke included moral and political knowledge among those capable of demonstration.[73] He affirmed that there is no reason why the certainty in both morals and government cannot be attained with the same degree of accuracy as those in mathematics "if due methods were thought on to examine or pursue their agreement or disagreement."[74]

Thus does Locke prepare himself for the most important task— the reconstitution of political philosophy upon principles diametrically opposed to those of the Socratic tradition. We shall see later in this study how successful his efforts were.

v

Finally, there can be little doubt that Bacon, Boyle, and the other founders of the new natural philosophy—such as Isaac Newton— were influenced and inspired by the ancient Atomists. Robert Boyle frequently refers to "that great and ancient Sect of Philosophers, the Atomists";[75] and Francis Bacon openly asserted that "no man shall enter into the inquisition of nature, but shall pass by that opinion of Democritus."[76] Bacon elaborated on this theme in the *Advancement of Learning* where he writes that:

> The natural philosophies of Democritus and others, who allow no God or mind in the frame of things but attribute the structure of the universe to infinite essays and trials of nature, or what they call fate or fortune, and assigned the causes of particular things to the necessity of matter without any admixture of final causes, seem, so far as we can judge from the remains of their philosophy, much more solid, and to have gone deeper into nature, with regard to physical causes than the philosophy of Aristotle or Plato.[77]

Thus, the ancient atomists—as opposed to the ancient moral philosophers—provided the method of access to the true understanding of nature, according to Bacon.[78] And Bacon assured the extension of this method to include man as a part of the physical order as a corrective to the Platonic–Aristotelian understanding of the unique human (moral) order. Machiavelli had proposed prior to Bacon that the moral and political be brought down out of the realm of the *ought* and be placed in the real world of the *is*. In *The Prince* he counseled, with Plato and Aristotle in mind, that

> it seemed to me more profitable to go behind to the effectual truth of the thing, than to the imagination thereof. And many have imagined republics and principates that have never been seen or known to be in truth; because there is such a distance between how one lives and how one should live that he who lets go that which is done for that which ought to be done learns his ruin rather than his preservation—for a man who wishes to profess the good in everything needs must fall among so many who are not good.[79]

The key word which permeates Machiavelli's writings is "new"; whether it be a "wholly new Prince," or a "wholly new regime," or "new modes and orders," there can be no doubt that Machiavelli understood himself to be involved in the great task of a new founding, a new beginning. What is equally clear is that he understood the prevailing Aristotelian–Thomistic philosophy to be a decadent philosophy prompting men to take their bearings from fantasies and not from the way men actually live. Machiavelli accordingly rejected the old (Socratic) moral imperative and replaced it with a new one. For that tradition, stretching from Socrates to Aquinas, man is by nature directed to a life of virtue by nature; men ought to do what nature indicates as just, noble, and good; nature, in short, was the source of the moral imperative governing men and states.

The new moral imperative, the one which leads to "the effectual truth of things" as proclaimed in the *Prince*, the new "ought," is found in the way men in fact act, not in the way they should act. What men ought to do is what they actually do. And what men actually do is recorded in history, especially of war.

Machiavelli subtly and cleverly undermines the prevailing religious orthodoxy, Christianity, which he viewed as leading men into decadence, by quietly replacing God's role in the creation and preservation of the universe with *chance*. This is why Machiavelli's effort to establish new beginnings prompted him to turn back to pre-Christian—i.e., pagan—sources. Machiavelli accordingly has more in common with Democritus and Epicurus than most scholars are prepared to allow. The Bible (and hence religious orthodoxy) is called before the bar of history—i.e., the history of science—and it is found deficient. There is, hence, a close parallel between the way Epicurus defused the fear of the angry gods and the manner in which Machiavelli defused the authority of the Christian church.

In politics it is especially clear that Machiavelli replaces nature by chance (*fortuna*) in which *virtù* (manly ingenuity) becomes the conqueror. By contrast, for Aristotle the polis existed by nature and the just city was by nature: "it has definite limits and a definite order which serve as guides for men to follow." For Machiavelli, on the other hand, "nature herself presents men with an order capable of being understood and followed. But the state is whatever is willed by the prince—it is whatever he pleases. No natural order guides that pleasure. . . . The state is limitless; its only limits are due to circumstance and therefore to accident; due, as Machiavelli says, to fortune."[80]

It should come as no surprise to learn that Machiavelli was a hedonist; but he was a hedonist of a different nature from Epicurus. For Machiavelli "the pleasure deriving from honor and glory is genuine and perhaps the highest pleasure."[81] Since the founding and preserving of wholly new states by wholly new princes is the highest and surest route to glory, it is the supreme pleasure, because it survives beyond one's lifetime; in short, it renders one immortal.

Nowhere are the themes of the modern drama more cleverly or more subtly presented than in the writings of Niccolò Machiavelli: a new conception of nature; self-preservation; the rejection of the

Socratic moral imperative and the adoption of a new pagan-inspired morality; hedonism; a critique of Biblical religion; chance and the power of man over nature through *virtù*.

Small wonder that the founder of modern technology, Francis Bacon, should express his indebtedness to Machiavelli. Indeed, said Bacon, "we are much beholden to Machiavelli and others who taught us to study man as he is and not as he ought to be."[82] Taking his bearings from Machiavelli and the ancient atomic hypothesis, Bacon laid the solid foundations for the new political and moral philosophy which shaped the course of history from his time to the present.

CONCLUSION

However apparent the influence of the ancient atomists was on the rise of the new natural philosophy, there is no basis for claiming that atomism provided the moral and political foundation of the movement. It is clear, however, that when the new science ousted the old science it ousted the foundations of the old moral and political basis of public and private life. The new natural philosophy had to find a replacement for the old moral and political principles, which were clearly rooted in the Aristotelian–Thomistic view of the whole. But the new moral and political principles had to be compatible with the new natural philosophy.

The only ancient philosopher who provided an alternative to the Aristotelian–Thomistic view of nature and morality on the basis of the atomic view of nature was Epicurus. And, as we shall see in the following chapter, disciples of Epicurus proliferated in the seventeenth century and were successful in their attempt to provide just such a new moral and political foundation.

Finally, to ascribe this paramount importance principally to Epicurus is not to forget that two of the great founders of the modern tradition, René Descartes and Thomas Hobbes, claimed Plato, not Epicurus, as the ancient philosopher they most admired. They admired Plato because he ascribed a place of prime importance to mathematics.[83] But this admiration for Plato should not obscure the fact that Epicurus was profoundly important in the formation of Hobbes's moral and political philosophy.[84] Indeed as Michael Oakeshott has observed, we cannot understand Hobbes apart from his Epicurean roots and how he shaped this essentially apolitical philosophy into a powerful political philosophy.[85]

We must now turn, therefore, to a discussion of Epicurus' moral philosophy and determine the influence of that philosophy on Hobbes and his successors.

NOTES

1. For a good discussion of the rise of the new natural philosophy, see A. Rupert Hall, *The Scientific Revolution 1500–1800: The Foundation of the Modern Scientific Attitude* (London: Longmans, 1962). See also Charles Webster, ed., *The Intellectual Revolution of the Seventeenth Century* (London: Routledge and Kegan Paul, 1974). See also Francis Bacon, *Of the Advancement of Learning*, where he says that Luther, "finding his own solitude, being no ways aided by the opinions of his own time, was enforced to awake all antiquity, and to call former times to his succours to make a party against the present time," Bk. I, iv.2 (Oxford: Clarendon Press, 1974), p. 25.

2. See, for general background, Paul Hazard, *The European Mind, 1680–1715* (Cleveland and New York: Meridian Books, 1960), especially Part II, "The War on Tradition," and Part III, "The Task of Reconstruction."

3. Thomas Sprat, *The History of the Royal Society* (London, 1667), p. 25. The new natural philosophy was also called "experimental philosophy" or "mechanical philosophy." See Marie Roas, "The Establishment of the Mechanical Philosophy," *Osiris* 10 (1953), 413–524, especially Ch. III, "The Reintroduction of Ancient Atomism," 422–33, and Ch. IV, "The Early Mechanical Philosophers," 433–42.

4. Bacon was not entirely successful in his own time or for some years later. As John Tulloch writes: "The old scholasticism held its ground at Cambridge for at least twenty years after the publication of *Novum Organum*" (*Rational Theology and Christian Philosophy in England in the Seventeenth Century* [Edinburgh, 1872] II, 15). *Novum Organum* was published in 1620; in 1659 John Wallis was writing to Christian Huygens complaining that "our Leviathan is furiously attacking and destroying our universities." Cited by J. Scott, *The Mathematical Works of John Wallis, F.R.S. (1616–1703)* (London: Taylor and Francis, 1938),

pp. 170–71. See also R. Metz, "Bacon's Part in the Intellectual Movement of his Time," in *Seventeenth Century Studies Presented to Sir Herbert Grierson* (Oxford: Clarendon Press, 1938), pp. 21–32.

5. *Novum Organum*, preface. All references to Bacon's *Works* are to the Spedding, Ellis, and Heath edition (Boston, 1862). See Charles T. Harrison, "Bacon, Boyle and the Ancient Atomists," *Harvard Studies and Notes in Philology and Literature*, 15 (1933), 191–218. Also, G. B. Stones, "The Atomic View of Matter in the XVth, XVIth and XVIIth Centuries," *Isis* 10 (1928), 447–65.

6. Ibid., LI.

7. Ibid., LXIII.

8. Ibid., LXIX.

9. See Ibid., CXXIX, where Bacon develops the concept of "discovery" and its importance: "the reformation of a state in civil matters is seldom brought in without violence and confusion; but discoveries carry blessings with them, and confer benefits without causing harm or sorrow to any."

10. Ibid., LXXIX; see also *Filum labyrinthi*, in *Works* VI, 400 and 402, where Bacon says that the seeking of moral knowledge was the cause of man's fall.

11. See Christopher Hill, *Intellectual Origins of the English Revolution* (Oxford: Clarendon Press, 1965).

12. *Novum Organum*, LXXX.

13. Ibid., CXXIX.

14. Ibid., last paragraph of Book II.

15. For a good discussion of this issue, see Alexandre Koyré, *From Closed World to Infinite Universe* (New York: Harper Torchbook, 1957).

16. *Novum Organum*, XVIII.

17. Ibid., XLI.

18. Ibid., XLII.

19. Ibid., XLIII.

20. Ibid., XLIV.

21. Ibid., L.

22. Ibid., LXVII.

23. Ibid., LXIX.

24. Ibid., CIV.

25. Ibid., LVII.

26. Ibid., LVII.

27. Ibid., LI.

28. Ibid., LIX.

29. Ibid., LXXX.

30. Ibid., CIV.

31. For a concise discussion of this issue, see Jacob Klein, *Greek Mathematical Thought and the Origin of Algebra*, trans. Eva Bran (Cambridge: M.I.T. Press,

1968). Klein shows how the new natural philosophy "returns to the sources of the Greek science, which had been neglected by scholastic science, although it integrates both the presuppositions and the sources from a basis which is utterly foreign to ancient science" (p. 120).

32. *Novum Organum,* cv.

33. Ibid., lxi.

34. Ibid., cxxix.

35. Ibid., cxxx.

36. Ibid., cxxix.

37. An English translation by Thomas Newcombe appeared in 1649.

38. *Novum Organum,* xc.

39. Descartes directed his scorn at the "school" philosophy with the claim that "the monks have supplied the opportunity for all sects and heresies through their theology, that is to say, their scholasticism." Adams and Tannery, V, p. 176. Unless otherwise noted, all references to the collected works of Descartes will be to the *Oeuvres de Descartes,* edd. Charles Adam and Paul Tannery (Paris: Vrin, 1964; I–XI, Paris, 1897–1913).

40. Ibid., IV, p. 67; VI, p. 531; X, p. 32.

41. *Discourse on Method,* VI, para. 2.

42. For a good discussion of Bacon and Descartes on method, see Sheldon S. Wolin, "Political Theory as a Vocation," *American Political Science Review,* 63 No. 4 (December 1969), 1062–82.

43. *Descartes: Philosophical Writings,* trans. N. Kemp Smith (New York: Random House, 1956), Rule XI, p. 47. Italics in the original.

44. "Preface" to the Principles of Philosophy, *Oeuvres,* Adam and Tannery, XI, p. 11.

45. *Descartes: Oeuvres et Lettres,* ed. A. Bridoux (Paris: Pléiade, 1952), p. 168.

46. René Descartes, *Treatise of Man,* trans. and commentary by Thomas Steele Hall (Cambridge: Harvard University Press, 1972).

47. *Oeuvres,* Adam and Tannery, XI, p. 326.

48. This work was written about 1666 but was not published until 1685/6. See the preface where Boyle claims that he was the first to write explicitly on nature. See also J. E. McGuire, "Boyle's Conception of Nature," *Journal of the History of Ideas,* 33 (1972), 523–42.

49. Ibid., p. 133.

50. *Rhetoric,* I.x.13 (Loeb ed.).

51. *Nicomachean Ethics,* II, i–7 (Loeb ed.).

52. *Politics,* I.1252B–1253A1; *Physics,* II, 194A27–33.

53. Ibid., p. 132. See also p. 11 and p. 12 where he says that to deny the re-

ceived notion of nature is not to deny providence; far from it, he says that the old notion makes the world eternal.

54. Ibid., p. 375.

55. Ibid., p. 11.

56. Ibid., p. 20.

57. Ibid., pp. 67–68.

58. Ibid., pp. 287–88.

59. Ibid., p. 287.

60. Robert Boyle, *The Excellency and Grounds of the Mathematical Hypothesis* (London, 1674).

61. Ibid., pp. 3–4.

62. Ibid., p. 37.

63. John Locke, *Essay Concerning Human Understanding*, 2nd ed. (London, 1694), IV, 7.11.

64. Ibid., I, 2, and 3.

65. Ibid., II, 1.2.

66. Ibid., II, 1.2, and 1.4.

67. Ibid., II, 1.4.

68. Ibid., II, 1.4.

69. Ibid., IV, 1.2.

70. Ibid., IV, 2.2.

71. Ibid., IV, 3.1.

72. Ibid., IV, 3.3.

73. Ibid., IV, 3.18.

74. Ibid., IV, 3.18.

75. Robert Boyle, *A Free Inquiry into the Vulgarly Received Notion of Nature* (London, 1685), p. 218.

76. *Filum labyrinthi*, in *Works* VI, 428; see also "Cupid or the Atom" in *De Sapientia veterum*, in *Works*, XIII, 122–25.

77. *Of the Advancement of Learning*, Bk. II, vii.7, p. 94.

78. As Jacob Klein has written: "Now that which especially characterizes the 'new' science and influences its development is *the conception which it has of its own activity*. It conceives of itself as again taking up and further developing Greek science, i.e. as a recovery and elaboration of 'natural' cognition. It sees itself not only as the science of *nature*, but as *'natural'* science—in opposition to school science. Whereas the 'naturalness' of Greek science is determined precisely by the fact that it arises out of 'natural' foundations, so that it is defined at the same time in terms of its distinction from, and its origins in, those foundations, the 'naturalness' of modern science is an expression of its polemical attitude toward school science." *Op. cit.*, p. 120. Italics in the original.

79. *The Prince*, translation, introduction and notes by Leo Paul S. de Alvarez (Dallas: University of Dallas Press, 1980), Ch. XV, p. 93.

80. Ibid., p. x.

81. Leo Strauss, *Thoughts on Machiavelli* (Glencoe, Illinois: Free Press, 1958), p. 291. For an excellent study of Machiavelli, see Harvey C. Mansfield, Jr., *Machiavelli's New Modes and Orders* (Ithaca: Cornell University Press, 1979).

82. *Of the Advancement of Learning*, Bk. II, xxi.9, p. 157.

83. For a good discussion of the importance of Plato to Hobbes, see Leo Strauss, *The Political Philosophy of Hobbes* (Chicago: The University of Chicago Press, 1952), pp. 139–51.

84. See James H. Nichols, Jr., *Epicurean Political Philosophy* (Ithaca: Cornell University Press, 1976), Ch. V: "Lucretius and Modernity," pp. 179–210.

85. "Dr. Leo Strauss on Hobbes," *Politica* 11 (1937), 379.

2

The Revival of Hedonism

EVERY DISCUSSION OF EPICURUS (341–271 B.C.) must begin with a statement of how little survives of his writings.[1] As so little of his writings remains there is a tendency to equate him with his disciples, especially with Lucretius, whose *De rerum natura*[2] is a major source of information on Epicurean atomism and moral philosophy. Indeed, some scholars believe that the influence of Epicurus is synonymous with the influence of Lucretius.[3] Yet despite the paucity of extant works, a revival of interest in Epicurus' teachings took place in the seventeenth century. More frequently than not, however, he is discussed in the context of the influence which the ancient atomists had on the rise of modern natural philosophy and science.

We possess only fragments of Epicurus' actual words over and above three letters, which Diogenes Laertius has preserved in his *Lives of Eminent Philosophers*.[4] The first letter, addressed to Herodotus, contains a summary of Epicurus' teaching regarding nature. The second letter is addressed to Pythocles and consists of a brief discourse on the celestial phenomena. The third and final letter is addressed to Menoeceus and contains a résumé of Epicurus' moral teaching. In addition to these letters Laertius relates the "Forty Sovran Maxims" which Epicurus apparently wished his disciples to commit to memory. It is, of course, unfortunate that none of the many works of Epicurus which Laertius lists has survived him; or that none has yet been uncovered. It would be of considerable benefit, for example, to have access to Epicurus' treatises *On the Ethical End*, and *On Human Life*. When one considers how little there is of Epicurus' writings available, one cannot help being impressed at the impact he has had on the course of philosophy. As we shall see, the paucity of extant writings did not prevent a long series of dedicated disciples from emerging.

Before turning to the disciples of Epicurus we must first attempt to understand what Epicurus himself taught. We will not dwell too long on Epicurus' atomism, for, as we shall see, his influence stemmed more from his moral or ethical philosophy than from his atomism. In fact, it appears that Democritus exercised a more profound influence through his atomism than did Epicurus. It is, indeed, more than likely that the teaching of Democritus alone would have been sufficient to advance the cause of atomism. And just as Democritean atomism has had a profound impact on the development of modern natural science, so too has Epicurean moral philosophy as the main conduit of hedonism had a profound influence on the development of modern moral and political philosophy. We shall attempt to establish that bold proposition throughout the remainder of this essay.

Since atomism plays a central role in Epicurus' philosophy we must see what he taught on this matter and how it relates to his moral philosophy. Taking his general direction from Democritus and Leucippus,[5] Epicurus taught that all things were composed of atoms and that a knowledge of nature, i.e., a knowledge of the course of atoms, was indispensable to man in his pursuit of happiness. He taught that all bodies are composites of the fundamental elements called atoms. "These elements are indivisible and unchangeable and necessarily so, if things are not all to be destroyed and pass into non-existence but are to be strong enough to endure when the composite bodies are broken up, because they possess a solid nature and are incapable of being anywhere or anyhow destroyed. It follows that the first beginnings must be indivisible, corporeal entities."[6] But not only have these incorruptible elements or atoms existed from all eternity; they have been in continual motion from all eternity.[7] The constant motion and fortuitous combination of atoms accounts for the multiplicity of natural phenomena including the stars, the sun, and the terrestrial elements.

And what is true of the natural order is also true of the human

order. The human motive force—the soul—is corporeal, composed
of atomic elements dispersed throughout the entire body.[8] But
Epicurus was strenuously opposed to the natural philosophers of
his day who attempted to subject men to the blind force of fatalism.
"It were better to follow the myths concerning the gods," he says,
"than to be a slave to the Necessity of the physicists for the former
presumes some hope of appeasement through worship of the gods
while the latter presume an inexorable Necessity."[9] The physicists
denied the possibility of free will, which Epicurus was not disposed
to do. He rejected both determinism and chance. As Diogenes
Laertius relates: "he sees that necessity destroys responsibility and
that chance or fortune is inconstant; whereas our own actions are
free and it is to them that praise and blame are naturally attached."[10] Epicurus presented a frontal attack on determinism and
chance by showing that if a man is the victim of either the one or
the other then he cannot be praised or blamed for his actions; in
short, he is not a free agent. Epicurus explained and defended free
will in humans by means of the doctrine of the swerve.[11] By this
theory Epicurus taught that atoms were not inescapable victims of
linear and vibratory motion but that they were capable of veering
ever so slightly from a straight course. This theory is not found in
Democritus but was introduced by Epicurus in order to explain the
multiplicity of existing combinations or composites of atoms. Furthermore, Epicurus was determined to resist determinism. If atoms
were not capable of swerving then their course could be predeter-
mined with irrevocable accuracy. And however close to such pre-
determination one might claim it is possible for the physicist to
come, the presence of human volition and choice rendered an appropriate hypothesis necessary. It is imperative to understand,
therefore, that Epicurus' main concern was with man; his atomism
or natural philosophy is an indispensable prerequisite or foundation for his moral philosophy.[12] Unlike Socrates, who rejected the
study of the natural phenomena as distracting man's attention from
his more proper human or moral considerations, Epicurus established his moral philosophy in physical science. But even in his
letter to Herodotus Epicurus makes it clear that his purpose for

embarking on a study of the natural phenomena was in the interest of freeing men's minds from the tyranny of false physical and theological opinion, which he considered conspired to rob men of happiness. "We must hold that to arrive at an accurate knowledge of the cause of things of most moment is the objective of the study of nature and that happiness depends on this and upon knowing what the heavenly bodies really are and any kindred facts contributing to exact knowledge in this respect."[13]

No one knew better than Epicurus that it was an easier matter to undermine the physical basis of fatalism than it was to undermine the theological or religious basis of the belief in a divinity which spoke harshly to men through the roar of thunder and through other alleged manifestations of divine wrath such as floods and famines.[14] The prevailing religious practices were rooted in fear of the divinity, which seemed to demand endless offerings and sacrifices; the dreadful possibility of punishment after death at the hands of the angry gods propelled men's fears beyond this life into the next. Such a concept of divinity kept men in a permanent condition of anxiety and fear, robbing them of all possibility of earthly peace-and-happiness. These fears were all-placed, Epicurus asserted without impiety; the harsh acts of nature could be explained, he claimed, by natural causes and not by an angry divinity.

> There is yet one more point to seize namely that the greatest anxiety of the human soul arises through the belief that the heavenly bodies are blessed and indestructible and that at the same time they have volitions and actions and causality inconsistent with this belief; and through expecting or apprehending some everlasting evil, either because of the myths, or because we are in dread of the mere insensibility of death as if it had to do with us; and through being reduced to this state not by conviction but by a certain irrational perversity, so that, if men do not set bounds to their terror, they endure as much or even more intense anxiety than the man whose views on these matters are quite vague. But mental tranquility means being released from all these troubles and cherishing a continual rememberance of the highest and most important truths.[15]

The means by which men were to rid themselves of such unreasonable and unsettling opinions was through reflecting on sense
perceptions and feeling. "Hence we must attend to present feelings
peculiar to the individual, and also attend to all the clear evidence
available, as given by each of the standards of truth. For by study-
ing them we shall rightly trace to its cause and banish the source
of disturbance and dread, accounting for celestial phenomena and
for all alarm to the rest of mankind."[16] The whole of philosophy
must, above all else, Epicurus proclaimed, relieve the course of
human suffering. Epicurus defines philosophy, accordingly, as "an
activity which by words and arguments secures the happy life."[17]

But this does not mean that Epicurus taught impiety or disre-
spect for the gods. Indeed he openly counseled religious practices
but urged an end to the false belief in a divinity lurking behind
every dark cloud or storm ready to pounce on unsuspecting men;
the gods lived in a separate and distinct world above the human
and were incapable of harming men. And men could not influence
the gods by sacrifice or exotic rites. Epicurus even attributed the
highest form of happiness to the gods.[18] One of the greatest benefits
of religion, according to Epicurus, was that it could well be a cause
of considerable pleasure. As Philip Merlan states, the Epicureans
not only participated fully in religious ceremonies but they "probably prided themselves that they were the only ones to do it in the
right spirit—worshipping gods not because they hoped to influence
them or to thank them for benefits which they by their actions con-
ferred on men, but simply because they were perfect."[19]

The first important result of the new concept of the physical
order and the new theology was felt in moral philosophy. As
Diogenes Laertius makes clear in the list of works written by Epicurus, the main concern of Epicurus was to turn philosophy toward the human concerns in the interest of making human life
more pleasant; to rid it of the drudgery to which it seemed to have
been relegated by the old physics and superstitious religion. Once
he established the futility of sacrificing to remote gods, Epicurus
set about to redefine the character of the good life. In his letter to
Menoeceus, he began by reminding Menoeceus that there is no

basis for the fear of death—especially a death in which the angry gods would inflict severe punishment upon wayward mortals. "Accustom thyself to believe that death is nothing to us, for good and evil imply sentience, and death is the privation of all sentience; therefore a right understanding that death is nothing to us makes the mortality of life enjoyable."[20] But Epicurus reminded Menoeceus that an indispensable prerequisite for the life of pleasure is the rejection of the quest for immortality, which is such a great cause of anxiety and unhappiness. Man's proper occupation and concern ought to be with the present life and how to live it with as much pleasure as possible.

The definition of the good life in terms of pleasure (ἡδονή) has earned for Epicurus the epithet of hedonist, which is, with rare exception, used in a pejorative sense.[21] The presentation of Epicurean hedonism as base, as being equivalent to the injunction "let us eat and drink, for tomorrow we die," was not unknown to Epicurus.[22] He tells Menoeceus that "when we say, that pleasure is the end and aim, we do not mean the pleasure of the prodigal or the pleasure of sensuality, as we are understood to do by some through ignorance, prejudice or willful misrepresentation."[23] On the contrary, insists Epicurus, the pleasure to which man has an inclination by nature does not consist of drinking bouts or revelry and the like. One could never seek the life of genuine pleasure by letting one's base inclinations rule unchecked. Prudence must always enter and guide men to prefer the higher to the lower pleasure. At times prudence will counsel men to forgo pleasure in the short run in the interest of long-term or more permanent future pleasure. "By pleasure we mean the absence of pain in the body and of trouble in the soul; [the] avoidance, and banishing of those beliefs through which the greatest tumults take possession of the soul. Of all this the beginning and the greatest good is prudence."[24] Prudence is, therefore, for Epicurus the most precious of all possessions because it is the source of all other virtues; "for it teaches that we cannot lead a life of pleasure which is not also a life of prudence, honour, and justice; nor lead a life of prudence, honour or justice which is not also a life of pleasure."[25] Unlike Aristotle, who taught that virtue was its own justification and reward, desirable for its own sake, Epicurus taught that "we choose the virtues too on account of pleasure and not for their own sake, as we take medicine for the sake of health."[26]

For Epicurus man is by nature prompted toward the life of pleasure both of the body and of the mind. He talks of man being "by nature"[27] destined for the life of pleasure; of ends being "fixed by nature"[28] and the like, all of which points to an underlying teleology. There can be no question that man is free according to Epicurus; free, that is, to seek that which is according to his nature. However liberating Epicurus' philosophy may have been he never once taught that man could determine his own nature. Epicurus does not raise the question of who designed man as he is; he takes the evidence as presented and does not concern himself with the origin of nature.

Despite this nod in the direction of teleology of human nature in Epicurus, there can be no doubt but that man is by nature destined to ends which do not transcend the physical world. Epicurus' teleology is physically rooted and oriented. As William Wallace says, "the very animals which are found upon the earth have been made what they are by slow processes of selection or adaptation. . . . Plants and animals have the same source as rocks and sands. It is from the seeds or elements contained in the earth that the animals have in some strange maternal throes . . . been evolved in their season."[29]

Epicurus counseled serious reflection upon the human appetites and desires—both physical and mental. Such reflection will lead, he asserted, to the conclusion that "of desire some are natural, others are groundless; and that of the natural some are necessary as well as natural, and some natural only. And of the necessary desires some are necessary if we are to be happy, some if the body is to be rid of uneasiness, some if we are even to live. He who has a clear and certain understanding of these things will direct every preference and aversion towards securing health of body and tranquility of mind, seeing that this is the sum and end (τέλος) of a blessed life."[30] And again: "Pleasure is our first and kindred good.

It is the starting point of every choice and of every aversion, and to it we come back, inasmuch as we make feeling the rule by which to judge of every good thing."[31] Thus for Epicurus philosophy must be radically empirical; it must begin with reflection upon sense data and never go beyond that which sense dictates. And the end of philosophy must be, as Francis Bacon was later to assert, "to relieve man's estate."

Epicurus' reflection on man led him to the conclusion that man is by nature oriented toward bodily and mental pleasure. His reflections also led him to the conclusion that at times these two levels of human desire would come in conflict. Prudence must come to the assistance in such cases and direct each man toward the solution. At times prudence will even counsel that pleasure be set aside and pain endured. "Oft-times we consider pains superior to pleasures when submission to the pains for a long time brings us as a consequence a greater pleasure. While, therefore, all pleasure because it is naturally akin to us is good, not all pleasure is choiceworthy, just as all pain is an evil and yet not all pain is to be shunned,"[32] Man through prudence, or the act of "measuring one against another, and by looking at the conveniences and inconveniences," must be the judge in such cases.[33]

One of the most important aspects of Epicurus' doctrine, for our purposes, is his teaching on justice and injustice. As one might expect from what we have seen already, Epicurus does not acknowledge a concept of natural right or natural justice. Justice is nothing more or less than the expedient procedures agreed upon by men to further agreeable social relations. All agreements which cease to lead to agreeable or convenient relations are no longer just. As Epicurus puts it: "Among the things accounted just by convention, whatever in the needs of mutual intercourse is attested to be expedient, is thereby stamped as just, whether or not it be the same for all; and in case any law is made and does not prove suitable to the expediencies of mutual intercourse, then this is no longer just. And should the expediency which is expressed by the law vary and only for a time correspond with the prior conception, nevertheless

for the time being it was just, so long as we do not trouble ourselves about empty words, but look simply at the facts."[34]

The closest Epicurus comes to acknowledging a concept of natural justice is in the Thirty-first Sovran Maxim. Here he says that
"natural justice is a symbol of expedience to prevent one from
harming another, or one from being harmed by another."[35] In
other words there seems to be a natural desire among men to enter
into arrangements for their mutual convenience. But he makes it
clear that it is relative to time and place. "Taken generally," he
concludes at one point, "justice is the same for all, to wit, something found expedient in mutual intercourse, but in its application
to particular cases of locality, or conditions of whatever kind, it
varies under different circumstances."[36]

In the final analysis, justice for Epicurus is strictly conventional
and based on utility. In many respects we learn more about Epicurus' conception of justice in what he says about injustice. The
first thing he makes clear is that injustice is not a vice or even in
itself bad. It is an evil only because it is a source of pain: "Injustice
is not an evil in itself, but only in consequence of the fear which
attaches to the apprehension of being unable to escape those appointed to punish such actions."[37] Epicurus even says that no matter
how many times a man may successfully violate the law he will always carry with him the fear of being caught.[38]

Finally, one of the most contentious aspects of Epicurus' philosophy is his advice to flee all political involvement. We are frequently told that his philosophy is apolitical. More often than not
this judgment is based on the comment found in the fragments
where Epicurus says: "We must release ourselves from the prison
of affairs and politics."[39] This is the most explicit reference in his
own words. On the other hand, he constantly speaks as if civil society and government are a major part of the life of most people.
His comments on justice and injustice lead one to conclude that he
was concerned with at least designating the minimal conditions of
political life. There is no question that he did not appear to have
written on forms of government or other major political issues.

Despite the existence of a fully developed moral philosophy in Epicurus, it is not easily made the foundation for a political philosophy. The primary difficulty arises out of the fact of individualism and the privacy of pleasure and pain. Later disciples of Epicurus, as we shall see, surmounted these difficulties by a utilitarian conception of law and justice. The only way one can conceivably meld a collection of individuals who are motivated by pleasure and pain into a reasonably harmonious social and political unity is through the bond of mutual advantage. It is not difficult to understand how a social contract tradition arose out of this foundation, which asserts that men are not by nature social and political animals.

Epicurean Hedonism

There have been many efforts to rescue Epicurus from the dark recesses of history. But in spite of these efforts the popular mind as well as the scholarly persists in attributing to Epicurus a base and reprehensible hedonism. One of the most recent scholarly efforts to rescue Epicurus from opprobrium merits our attention here. In his *Studies in Epicurus and Aristotle*,[40] Philip Merlan begins by drawing attention to the important distinction which Epicurus makes between katastematic hedonism (ἡδονὴ καταστηματιχή) and kinetic hedonism (ἡδονὴ κατακίνησιν). The former variety is, says Merlan, identical to *voluptas* as used by Cicero.[41] This variety of pleasure is the quiet which the organism feels once pain is removed. The pleasure which thus accrues in this type of ἡδονή is not caused by a positive external force; it is the pleasure the organism itself provides by experiencing a release from pain, the pleasure which accompanies the proper functioning of the organism.

Kinetic pleasure is the product of an external stimulus which heightens the natural disposition of the organism for pleasure.[42] Epicurus, according to Merlan, recognised both varieties of pleasure and taught that "either of these could take place in the mind or in the body."[43] According to Diogenes Laertius, an example of katastematic ἡδονή would be ἀπονία (freedom from bodily pain) and ἀταραξία (freedom from passion, or calmness); examples of kinetic ἡδονή would be εὐφροσύνη (cheerfulness) and χαρά (delight).[44]

Merlan argues that a proper understanding of Epicurean ἡδονή leads to the conclusion that it is best understood or translated as the philosophy of joy.[45] Joy is proper only to human beings, a point which Epicurus emphasized when he stated that ἡδονή is not possible among animals because they lack the faculty of reason by which alone one can be freed from the tyranny of fears. Nor are animals capable of prudence; they lack, that is, the faculty by which to discern between higher and lower, ephemeral and permanent delights. As far as we can determine, however, Epicurus believed that even animals experienced the two varieties of pleasure. The absence of the intellectual faculty, however, deprived them of the pursuit of "joy" which is, according to Epicurus, the highest good. This understanding of ἡδονή is not unlike that of Aristotle's as Merlan points out. The important difference is, however, that the highest ἡδονή for Aristotle is σοφία, and it is not desirable because it is pleasurable but for its own sake. According to Aristotle this is man's *summum bonum* and is only incidentally pleasurable.[46] Aristotle also agrees that ἡδονή is natural to animals as well as men. It is this acknowledgment in both Aristotle and Epicurus (but especially the latter because he does not acknowledge σοφία as a man's highest good) which had led so many to conclude that hedonism is base. There can be no question that Epicurus leaves himself open to be understood in this manner. The paucity of extant works of Epicurus and the long train of base hedonists who claim Epicurus as their mentor has led many (with the assistance of Aristotle and his later disciples) to conclude that Epicurus taught a base hedonism. Merlan's thesis, which is persuasive, is that the evidence presented in Diogenes Laertius does not support the popular misunderstanding. Merlan concludes: "Whether it occurs in Epicurus or in Aristotle, the term ἡδονή can mean anything between gross sensual 'pleasure' and entirely spiritual 'joy.' . . . ancient hedonism is richer and more subtle than current definitions of hedonism would lead us to assume."[47] Without concurring in this possibility for Aristotle, we must agree that it is true of Epicurus. Furthermore, Epicurean ἡδονή can lead to base hedonism especially among those disciples who are unable or unwilling to act prudently in the manner suggested by Epicurus. In other words, despite his commitment to a noble or high hedonism, Epicurus prepared the way for base hedonism.

Lucretius (ca. 99–55 B.C.)

The most famous disciple of Epicurus was Titus Lucretius Carus, who presented a comprehensive account of his master's doctrine in a poem entitled *De rerum natura*.[48] This poem was the chief means by which the Epicurean doctrine was transmitted through the centuries, and therefore it occupies a place of special importance. It consists of six books addressed to the Roman Memmius, and presents a full account of the atomic and moral philosophy of Epicurus and how that can be the basis of a life free of fear and oppressive anxiety. It begins with an invocation to Venus—the beautiful goddess of nature "by whose power all animals are generated, by whose charms all nature is governed"[49]—that is to say, on a note of joy and hope. But it soon becomes clear to the reader that Lucretius' message is far from being one of joy; the true scientific account of the human condition prevents it from being so. As Lucretius himself says:

> For first, I teach great things in Lofty strains,
> And loose Men from Religions grievous Chains,
> Next, tho' my Subject's dark, my Verse is clear,
> And sweet, with Fancy flowing every where:
> And this design'd: For as Physicians use,
> In giving Children Draughts of bitter Juice,
> To make them take it, tinge the Cup with Sweet,
> To cheat the Lip; this first they eager meet,
> And then drink on, and take the bitter Draught,
> And so are harmlessly deceiv'd, not caught:
> For by this Means they get their Health, their Ease,
> Their Vigour, Strength, and baffle the Disease.
> So since our Methods of Philosophy
> Seem harsh to some; since most our Maxims fly,

I thought it was the fittest way to dress
In pleasing Verse, these rigid Principles,
With Fancy sweet'ning them; to bribe thy Mind
To read my Books, and lead it on to find
The Nature of the World, the Rise of things
And what vast Profit too that Knowledge brings.[50]

Lucretius sets down clearly here that his message will be useful to men but that it contains "rigid Principles." That is to say, the human condition without the knowledge presented by a scientific understanding of the course of atoms and the place of man in the scheme of nature is a harsh and fearful one; it is above all harsh and fearful because of the false ideas of the gods with their ability to inflict eternal punishment on men. The true understanding of nature, Lucretius promises, will liberate men from this bondage. But he is quick to warn that the true understanding of nature does not lead to a life of unmitigated joy; rather does it lead to knowledge of the life of nature as harsh and barely tolerable. Unlike the philosophies of others, his will not hold out false hopes for men. He begins, therefore, by attempting to show that a great deal of the misery which men suffer is due to the unlimited desires and unfounded fears which were the products of their ignorance. Lucretius set out to liberate men from this condition by showing them that the course of nature (especially man's place in it) is ruled by laws which can be understood by men but not altered by them. (Unlike Francis Bacon, man's lot does not consist in attempting to conquer nature by a knowledge of her laws; nor does philosophy lead to the redirection of the course of nature by science and technology. Any such efforts, Lucretius taught, would lead to more misery by adding to men's irrational desires and powers to reap destruction, for such ambitions are based on false hope.) The human condition can be rendered happy, Lucretius teaches, by first removing the fears through a knowledge of nature, a knowledge of the atomic structure of the world, of the infinity of the universe, and second, by resigning oneself to one's lot. Little wonder that Lucretius ends his long poem with a terrifying account of the plague at Athens; he brings the reader a long way from the earlier delightful account of nature in all her beauty to an account of the cruelty of nature without a semblance of hope. In short, nature is not benevolent but the indifferent source of frightful tremors and volcanic destruction; of unrelenting floods and indiscriminate lightning.

Unlike some moderns, however, Lucretius does not counsel a flight from nature; rather does he counsel a life in accordance with nature—a life free of unnatural desires and irrational fears. Lucretius presents his views clearly at the opening of Book III. He writes:

> 'Tis Pleasant, when the Seas are rough, to stand
> And view another's Danger, safe at hand:
> Not 'caused his troubled, but 'tis sweet to see
> Those Cares and Fears, from which our selves are free.
> 'Tis also pleasant to behold from far
> How Troops engage, secure our Selves from War.
> But above all, 'tis pleasant to get
> The Top of high Philosophy, and sit
> On the calm, peaceful, flourishing Head of it.
> Whence we may view deep, wondrous deep below,
> How poor mistaken Mortals wand'ring go,
> Seeking the Path to Happiness: some aim
> At Learning, Wit, Nobility, or Fame:
> Others with Cares and Dangers vex each Hour
> To reach the Top of Wealth and Sov'reign Power:
> Blind wretched Man! In what dark Paths of Strife
> We walk this little Journey of our Life!
> While frugal Nature seeks for only Ease;
> A Body free from Pains, free from Disease;
> A Mind from Cares and Jealousies at Peace.[51]

The life according to nature is the life in which "We may enjoy the sweet Delights of Sense."[52] The secret to this way of life is to flee from the world of false ambitions and false opinions as to the nature and power of the gods. The truly wise man will acknowledge the limitations of his nature and will seek his happiness—bleak and restricted though it may be—in accordance with his nature without unreasonable fears or impossible hopes.

HEDONISM IN FRANCE

The presence and influence of Epicurus was nowhere more evident in the seventeenth and eighteenth centuries than in France. Some would have us believe that were it not for the French disciples of Epicurus, hedonism would not have entered England. While we make no pretense to settle that point, we cannot deny the importance of Epicureans in France nor their influence on their English contemporaries. We shall, however, reserve judgment on the matter of influence until the next section of this chapter, where we shall discuss the presence of Epicureans in England during this period and the extent to which they are indebted to the French.

No European country, not even Italy, openly espoused hedonism with as much public acclaim as did France. For the better part of the sixteenth and seventeenth centuries, France was the undisputed haven of Epicureans. Its most famous French Epicureans were Pierre Gassendi and François Bernier. The reception of Epicurus into France was prepared by the climate of free-thought and unorthodox inquiry which preceded Gassendi. "In sixteenth-century France," Virgil Topazio relates, "Corneille Agrippa contributed to this movement by renouncing the divine origin of law, and he was followed by the humanists Rabelais and Montaigne. The former's anti-clerical satire and lusty zest for life combined with the latter's scepticism gave an added impetus to the growing tide of Epicureanism and free thought destined to dominate the seventeenth and eighteenth centuries."[53] As Agrippa complains in his most popular English work, *Of the Vanitie and Uncertaintie of Artes and Sciences*, published in London in 1575, "the Philosophers with great advantage doe search out the causes and the beginnings of things, but God the Creator of all things they neglect and know not. Among Princes and Magistrates there is no peace, and one for a light gaine seeketh anothers destruction. The Phisitions cure the bodies of the sicke, and neglect their owne soules. The lawyers verie diligent in the lawes of men, do transgress Gods commandments."[54]

The main inspiration or source of what has come to be called "free-thought" was "the growing tide of Epicureanism."[55] And despite the efforts to minimize the influence of the Italian humanists on the rise of the "free-thought" in France, one cannot deny the impact made by Julio Cesare Vanini (1585–1619). Not only did he cause a flurry of intellectual excitement throughout learned circles in France during his lifetime (which led to his burning at the stake in Toulouse in 1619) but a debate raged for at least a century over his teaching and alleged unorthodoxy.[56] D. C. Allen claims that "the last great defender of Epicurus before it became correct to discuss his philosophy in polite circles is J. C. Vanini."[57] There were many efforts to perpetuate the teaching of Epicurus all through the Renaissance. The French were not unfamiliar with the works of the Italian Epicureans such as Lorenzo Valla or Coluccio Salutati, or Francesco Filelfo. The academics of France were not oblivious to the storm which raged around the Italian efforts to rehabilitate Epicurus. Petrarch had condemned Epicureanism in his "Triumph of Fame," and Marsilio Ficino wrote at length in his *De Voluptate* of the need to rescue the philosophy of pleasure from the Epicureans.

It is clearly impossible to date the point at which an interest in Epicurus arose or when his impact was first felt. But surely Vanini must be accorded a place of prominence in the eventual successful emergence of Epicureanism. This defrocked Carmelite monk had traveled widely throughout Italy, France, Germany, and England and found disciples wherever he went. And under a contrived or veiled orthodoxy, Vanini taught a quite unorthodox philosophy with profound theological ramifications. His two major works are *Amphitheatrum aeternae Providentiae divino-magicum, Christiano-physicum, nec non astrologo-catholicum, adversus veteres philosophos, atheos, epicureos, peripateticos et stoicos* (1615) and the *De Admirandis naturae reginae deaeque mortalium arcanis* (1616). Vanini's heterodoxy emerges from these works only after a careful reading; his approach was to contrast the orthodox and atheistic (Epicurean) views and permit the orthodox view to win. The stronger arguments clearly belong to the "defeated" as Vanini apparently made obvious to his young disciples. The subtlety of style and contrived ambiguity was not missed by later disciples who were denied the oral version of the master. David Durand was concerned in his *The Life of Lucillio Vanini* (1730), which included an "Abstract of his Writings," that readers of the "Abstract" not miss Vanini's subtle nuances. "Vanini in his life time was famous all over Europe for his philosophical writings. . . . They were written in a good Latin style, and so artfully contrived, that under the pretext of defending Christianity and Morality, he slily [sic] insinuated the rankest atheistical Principles, aiming at nothing less, than to destroy all Religion, even the Natural not excepted."[58]

The presence of so many Epicureans in Italy and the storm which raged around the efforts to rehabilitate Epicurus among later Renaissance writers makes it beyond dispute that the excitement was felt strongly throughout Europe. To say that the Italian Epicureans did not influence profoundly the thought of the sixteenth and seventeenth centuries would be equivalent to saying that the emergence of modern science cannot in some measure be attributed to Galileo.

However much influenced or prompted by the Italians to turn toward Epicurus, the French spent little time reading the Italian authors; they went directly to Diogenes Laertius and Lucretius. As a result, they produced some of the most outstanding disciples of Epicurus. Names such as Pierre Gassendi, Baron d'Holbach, la Mettrie, Bernier, and "Les philosophes" in general, conspired to ensure that Epicureanism would flourish as it had never done in the past—not even during the lifetime of Epicurus himself. It is to these that we must now turn.

Of Pierre Gassendi's works, the most important for our purpose is entitled *Syntagma philosophiae Epicuri*[59] but it was long preceded by his first book, which appeared in 1624 under the title *Exercitationes paradoxicae adversus Aristotelos libri septem*[60] and which constituted an attack on the philosophy of Aristotle and can be said to have prepared the way for his later writings.[61] The *Syntagma* was incomplete and published posthumously in 1658; a later edition published in Amsterdam in 1684 contains a preface by Samuel Sorberius which is entitled "De vita et moribus Petri

Gassendi." This book consists of three sections treating the three
major aspects of the thought of Epicurus. In the first part, Gassendi discussed the Epicurean canons in which Epicurus presents
his empirical basis of knowledge. Gassendi concurred fully in Epicurus' claim that sense experience is the exclusive source of knowledge. The second part contains an account of Epicurean and
Lucretian atomism, with which Gassendi takes partial exception.
In this part of the *Syntagma* Gassendi, a priest, showed his determination to make Epicureanism consistent with Catholic theological orthodoxy. He distinguishes the two categories of causes, primary and secondary, and claims that God is the author of the
former and that our knowledge is properly restricted to the latter.
Gassendi's efforts at this point are to explain how one can know if
there are no innate ideas and if all of one's knowledge must come
through sense perception. He argued in the following way: as God
is the first cause of all things, knowledge (or at least *acknowledgment*) of his existence becomes the prerequisite of all speculation or
philosophy. But since Gassendi concurs with the Epicurean doctrine
regarding sense as the basis of all knowledge, how can one come to
know of God's existence? Gassendi readily acknowledged that the
idea of God is not innate and that it cannot come merely by sense
experience. His reply to the question is that man possesses a natural
desire to know God, and that the testimony of other men (i.e., the
belief in God transmitted over the ages on the authority of human
testimony) combined with the experience of order and harmony in
the universe lead men to the idea of God. It is quite clear that such
a proposition, which appears to follow the scholastic philosophers
more closely than Epicurus, does not answer the important questions. But in fairness to Gassendi, it must be said that his efforts to
make Epicureanism compatible with Christian theology prompted
him to go beyond his master Epicurus and attempt to construct a
positive theology, or at least the basis for a theology, upon the
premisses provided by Epicurus. There can be no doubt that Epicurus leaves one in complete ignorance of the divinity and does not
present a complete theology. His posture was clearly one of ag-

nosticism.[62] It is very unlikely that he would have agreed with Gassendi's description of God as the first cause.

Gassendi's theology led him to reply to Epicurus' and especially to Lucretius' teaching that fear is the basis of the belief in the divinity. No orthodox Christian could accept such a premiss. Gassendi accordingly rejected Epicurus' denial of providence, which is the same as to say, the influence of the primary over the secondary causes. Epicurus was at pains to refute just this proposition as it was the foundation of fear of the unplacated gods.[63] This led Epicurus to claim that "God exercises neither a general care over the whole world nor a special care over men."[64] Such an unfortunate attitude will, said Gassendi, have to be refuted not only by religious evidence but also by natural reason.[65]

Before discussing the third and final section of the *Syntagma*, we should observe that Gassendi published in 1647 a work on Epicurus, entitled *De vita et moribus Epicuri*, which consisted of an effort to rehabilitate and rescue the philosophy of Epicurus not only from historical obscurity but also from the disrepute into which it had been consigned for so many centuries by the disciples of Aristotle. The fact that Gassendi was partially successful can be seen in the fact that this work was greeted with public acclaim. This book concentrated on the moral philosophy or ethics of Epicurus and in all probability constitutes the basis for the third section of the *Syntagma*, which treats the ethics of Epicurus. In this section Gassendi presents a clear account of Epicurean hedonism. In the first instance his statement on the character of the good life is little more than a paraphrase of Epicurus. Gassendi says that the happy life consists in a tranquil mind and a body free from pain and that philosophy is like medicine to the extent that its chief objective is to ensure a tranquil mind.[66] There can be no mistake about Gassendi's agreement as to the importance of pleasure or *voluptas* as the first principle of the good life. "Pleasure appears everywhere to be the beginning and indeed the end of a happy life, since we comprehend it to be by nature our first good and the good of all animals; and it is that by which we determine all choice and rejection and that towards which we move; by the use of this affection all good must be assessed by a rule."[67]

In the *De vita et moribus Epicuri*, Gassendi is at pains to show that Epicurus "spurned base pleasure."[68] This work deals almost exclusively with Epicurus' ethical philosophy. He barely notes in passing that "Epicurus honoured and followed Democritus."[69] Gassendi concurs completely in Epicurus' judgment that all men are by nature led toward pleasure and drawn away from pain;[70] and the highest forms of pleasure are to be preferred over the lowest forms. True pleasure does not consist in the act itself, as Aristippus contended, says Gassendi, but "in a state or condition in which the body is free of pain and the mind free of anxiety."[71] Gassendi deplored the efforts of those who for so long had presented Epicurean hedonism as base.[72]

There were many French writers who turned to Epicurus at this time either to praise or to blame him. Among those who wrote in French were Jean-François Sarasin, who wrote his *Discours de morale sur Épicure* in 1645/6. This was reprinted in 1651 under the title *Apologie pour Épicure*. Sarasin makes the point that the modern prejudice against Epicurus was due solely to the jealousy the moderns bore against the ancients for having been so great. Sarasin's book is an unequivocal defense of Epicureanism.[73] Jacques Parrain Baron des Coutures published his *Morale d'Épicure* in 1685 and translated into French Lucretius' *De rerum natura*, the great Latin work which had much to do with the spread of Epicureanism in the seventeenth century. Jacques du Rondelle (1630–1675) was later to publish a work in French called *La vie d'Épicure* (1679) on the life and morals of Epicurus. In the later Latin edition (published in Amsterdam, 1693), du Rondelle praises Gassendi as "most learned" and "the most illustrious of philosophers."[74]

The great disciple of Gassendi was François Bernier, who published an eight-volume work in 1678 entitled *Abrégé de la philosophie de Gassendi*.

In a widely read volume published in England in 1699 as *Three Discourses of Happiness, Virtue and Liberty*, Bernier openly espoused the moral philosophy of Epicurus and of his own master Pierre Gassendi. Bernier began by sweeping aside the long-uncontested claim that Socrates was the founder of moral philosophy. There were many wise men prior to Socrates, such as Pythagoras, he claimed, who can rightfully claim the title of moral philosophers. The greatest test of Socrates' claim (or rather of the claim made on his behalf by his disciples) was reflection upon how useful the Socratic moral teaching had been. It is clear, for all to see, said Bernier, that the world is still filled with unhappy and anxious people. Quoting Epicurus, Bernier concluded: "That the Discourses of a Philosopher, that cures not the Mind of some Passion, is vain and useless; as the Physick that drives not away the Distemper from the Body, is insignificant."[75] And as with so many of the disciples of Epicurus, Bernier attempted by resorting to Epicurus' own words, as reported in Diogenes Laertius, to rescue Epicureanism from its ill repute by explaining that for Epicurus pleasure ought to be the end of our life, and the chief good. " 'The end of a Happy life,' saith he, 'is nothing else but the Health of the Body, and the Tranquility of the Soul'."[76] Bernier readily admits that a great deal of the misunderstanding surrounding what Epicurus meant by pleasure can be traced to the use of the word ἡδονή which, he says, "is certain that this word comprehends the honest pleasures, as well as the loose and debauch'd."[77] But Bernier protests at length that Epicurus did not countenance or espouse the "mean and sordid pleasures of the body."[78] He dwells at length in his discussion of pleasure on the fact that it is sought for its own sake and that its enjoyment was to be governed by prudence and wisdom, which are subordinate to the good life of pleasure and not sought for their own sake.[79]

In large measure this work contains a paraphrase of the writings of Gassendi. Indeed, Bernier's great contribution to the cause of the Epicurean revival in the seventeenth century is to have kept Gassendi's, and hence Epicurus', thought alive. One important difference between Gassendi and Bernier seems to be that Bernier makes no effort to ensure the compatibility of Epicurus and orthodox Christian theology. He does refer in one place to the "Great Creator and Author of Nature,"[80] but this is sufficiently vague as to be safe from the charges of heterodoxy.

Most important for our purposes is the fact that Bernier was one of the first Epicureans to attempt to make his subscription to the teachings of Epicurus compatible with political involvement. The second most frequently misunderstood aspect of Epicurus' teaching (second only to the widespread misunderstanding of his concept of hedonism) was his allegedly apolitical teaching. Bernier addresses himself explicitly to this question by first acknowledging that Epicurus did indeed say that a wise man ought not to "intermeddle with the Affairs of Government." But he says that this advice must not be understood "absolutely without Exception." "He designs to advise us plainly, that a wise man ought to concern himself with the Affairs of Government only when an occasion shall be offered, where his Wisdom and Council are required and needful, but otherwise he need not engage himself; and that Ambition, the desire of Riches, Offices and Dignities, should not draw him out of his private Station."[81]

Despite Bernier's importance in the revival of hedonism, it is not as important in France as the efforts of that cluster of "philosophes" known at times as the "d'Holbachian clique." This group included the likes of La Mettrie, d'Holbach, Diderot, and Voltaire. La Mettrie wrote several works, the most important of which was *L'Homme machine* in which he reduced man to a machine, eliminating any need for a spiritual element.[82] In the *Art de jouir*, La Mettrie presented a picture of hedonism which did little to rehabilitate it from the depths to which it had been consigned by the enemies of Epicurus. "Let us enjoy the little time that remains," wrote La Mettrie; "let us drink, let us sing, let us love those who love us; may joy and laughter follow our footsteps; may all pleasures be ours, one after another, to amuse us and to enchant our souls; and however short life may be, we shall have lived."[83] La Mettrie can be said to have set the cause of Epicureanism back by a long stride except for those who wished to see in Epicureanism an open invitation to debauchery and riotous living. Obviously unmindful of the master's words on the role of wisdom and prudence,

La Mettrie concludes with a prayer to pleasure: "Pleasure, sovereign master of men and gods, before whom all else vanishes, including reason itself, you know how much my heart adores you, and all the sacrifices it has made at your altar."[84] It should come as no surprise to learn that, rather than assist the revival of a respectable Epicureanism, La Mettrie's *La système d'Épicure* contributed to the attempt to turn Epicurean hedonism into what Epicurus, Lucretius, and later Gassendi and Bernier, were at pains to prevent.

Conclusion

A fuller account of the activities and writings of French Epicureans is beyond the scope of this study. Our purpose is merely to indicate the existence of the major French disciples of Epicurus in the seventeenth century and present a brief outline of their main doctrines. We are more concerned with identifying the presence and influence of Epicureans in England during the seventeenth century. Let us therefore now turn to England.

HEDONISM IN ENGLAND

As Robert Hugh Kargon has demonstrated convincingly, atomism took firm root in England in the seventeenth century and became the most powerful force in the development of English philosophy and science.[85] As Kargon writes: "Through Thomas Hobbes and a group of English *emigrés*—the Newcastle Circle—atomism again became, in the 1640s, a living issue in English natural philosophy. The center of this *emigré* activity was Paris; the leading figures of the group (Hobbes, Charles Cavendish, William Cavendish, then Marquis of Newcastle, and John Pell who was in the Netherlands) were in close contact with the French giants of the mechanical philosophy—Descartes and Gessend."[86] Kargon goes on to show how seriously these *emigrés* studied the atomism of the French masters; and despite his tendency to minimize the moral dimensions of Epicureanism, which the *emigrés* also imbibed during their sojourn in France, Kargon does confirm that they were

strongly influenced by the hedonism which accompanied the revival of atomism in the seventeenth century. In England the proponents of the new natural philosophy tended to emphasize Democritus and minimize the importance of Epicurus who was known
to have taught a theological and moral doctrine which ran counter
to the established theological orthodoxy of the English Church.[87]
There were, nevertheless, avowed disciples of Epicurus in England; unlike that of their French counterparts, however, the interest in Epicurus in England was in the first instance or primarily
centered upon his contribution to atomism. As well, many of the
English scientific disciples of atomism openly repudiated Epicurean atheism and morality.[88] It is important to realize, however,
that, to a certain extent, one must say that because of the close contact with the intellectual circles of both France and Holland, the
presence of Epicurus on the Continent can in a certain sense be said
to imply the presence of Epicurus in England. The philosophers in
England knew about and read the works of the French Epicureans.
No better example of this can be found than Robert Boyle, who
openly acknowledged his indebtedness to Pierre Gassendi in his
Origin of Forms and Qualities.[89] The impact made by Descartes'
mechanical philosophy on English philosophy was also an important event. As Marjorie Nicholson says, "the French Philosopher's
cool and impersonal disregard of the past, his break with history
and tradition, offered valuable ammunition to those who were
coming more and more to place emphasis upon the future rather
than on the past and were thus developing in England the idea of
progress."[90] But in addition to this there did exist in seventeenth-
and eighteenth-century England an influential coterie of avowed
and outspoken Epicureans. But unlike the French and the Dutch,
the English writers were under the strong injunction to meet the
demands of theological orthodoxy. It was never a crime in England to attack the scholastic disciples of Aquinas but it was quite
another matter to lay the foundations of a philosophy which could
be identified as Epicurean and hence atheistical. Since "English
clerics rallied in force to assault Epicureanism,"[91] many English
writers sought refuge in the ancient device of ironic ambiguity. A

large part of the writing about this period tends to focus on the impact of ancient atomism on English scientific and philosophic thought and to denigrate the moral or ethical impact of Epicureanism. There can be little doubt that the major interest of English philosophers and scientists was in what Joseph Glanvill at the time called "the more excellent Hypothesis of Democritus and Epicurus."[92] Glanvill lamented that "the Aristotelian Philosophy hath prevailed; while the more excellent Hypotheses of Democritus and Epicurus have long lain buried under neglect and obliquy: and for ought I know might have slept for ever, had not the ingenuity of this age recall'd them from the Urne."[93]

Thomas Franklin Mayo relates that "between 1650 and 1700 no less than 13 books appeared in England dealing specifically with Epicurus himself or with such classical Epicureans as Lucretius and Petronius."[94] It is regrettable, however, that Mayo does not accord importance to the early writings of Walter Charleton in which he expounded the moral or ethical philosophy of Epicurus. No one, however, played a more important role in the dissemination of the Epicurean moral philosophy in England than the great Oxford classicist Meric Casaubon, who exclaimed in his *Translations of the Six Books of Manilius* that "The Philosophy of Epicurus is now too well known to need Explication."[95] Thomas Creech was the first to translate the *De rerum natura* of Lucretius into English (1682), thus making the major ancient disciple of Epicurus more readily available to English readers. Creech's work contains not only a translation of Lucretius but a commentary on those sections of the *De rerum natura* which are not compatible with Christian orthodoxy. "If any man considers the inconsistencies that are in the Epicurean Notion of a Deity, how the Attributes disagree and how the very being thwarts all their other Philosophy, he will easily agree with Tully, and admit his censure to be true, *Verbis ponunt, Re tollunt Deos*: In words they assent, but in effect they deny a God."[96] Causaubon says in his *Of Credulity and Incredulity in Things Natural, Civil and Divine*, that "Epicurus, who generally, in former ages, among all accounted sober and wise, by Heathens and Christians, learned and unlearned, for his life; but more for his impious doctrine, and outrageous opposition whatsoever pretended to God, or godliness, was a name of horror and detestation; is now become the saint of many Christians."[97] It is difficult to know to whom Casaubon is referring here as he does not name those Christians. Perhaps he was merely attempting to draw attention to the traditional unorthodoxy ascribed to Epicurus for the benefit of those among his contemporaries who openly flirted with Epicureanism. One thing is clear: he had Gassendi and his English disciples such as Boyle in mind and wished to proffer a caveat lest their enthusiasm for Epicurean atomism lead them into atheism. Casaubon refers to Gassendi as "the great reviver and abettor of Epicureanism, in this unhappy age."[98] The works of Gassendi's major disciple, François Bernier (whom Locke knew and admired), were known in England and helped to disseminate the unique blend of Epicureanism and Christianity Gassendi sought to pass on to posterity. Bernier's *Three Discourses of Happiness, Virtue, and Liberty*, in which he expounded Epicurean hedonism, became available in English as early as 1699. And although he makes every effort to rescue Epicurean hedonism from sordid sensuality, he makes little or no effort to show how it could be compatible with Christian orthodoxy. Casaubon must have been pleased to see Boyle's *Some Considerations About the Reconsileableness of Reason and Religion* (1675) where the author acknowledged that philosophy must be compatible with theological truth.

Casaubon appears to have understood better than most of his contemporaries that, despite the efforts of Gassendi or even Erasmus,[99] the moral philosophy of Epicurus was hostile to the predominant understanding of right and wrong, justice and injustice. In his view, Epicurus and Gassendi would have us believe that

> what men call right and wrong, justice and injustice, vertue and vice, were but fancies, and empty sounds; nothing truly real, and worthy our pursuit, but what was pleasant and delightful, which also was profitable. Is not this impious? Can anything be more? ... But I know it will be said: Did not the same man explain himself, that by pleasure, he did understand chiefly, a vertuous life, without which there

could be no true pleasure? And again, Doth not the same, though he acknowledged no Divine Providence, yet acknowledge and proffers to believe, that there is a God; and that he thought it very convenient, that God (whether one or more) for the excellency of his nature, should be reverenced and worshipped by Men.[100]

The clearest and fullest English exposition of Epicurean moral philosophy was written by Walter Charleton.[101] Indeed, Charleton's *Epicurus's Morals* (1655) was the first major work in English on Epicurus. It opens with a lengthy "Apologie for Epicurus" in which Charleton attempted to persuade a "person of Honour" that Epicurus has been misrepresented by "such learned men as either did not rightly understand, or would not rightly represent his opinion."[102] So far as Charleton was concerned, a correct understanding of Epicurus would reveal a "sublime Witt, a profound Judgement, and a great Master of Temperance, Sobriety, Continence, Fortitude and all other Vertues, not a Patron of Impiety, Gluttony, Drunkenness, Luxury and all kinds of Intemperance."[103]

Charleton proceeded to assert that Epicurus held three fundamental tenets which are incompatible with the Christian faith. (He claims that he gets his information from Epicurus' "Treatise Concerning Ethicks." But it has always been presumed that this treatise was lost. This remains a puzzle.)[104] In his *Natural History of the Passions*, Charleton says: "For being of opinion, that the *Ethicks* of Epicurus are [after Holy Writ] the best Dispensatory I have hitherto read of Natural medicines for all distempers incident to the mind of Man. . . . This therefore, I now do; not doubting but that in the Morals of that grave and profound Philosopher, you will find as good Precepts for the moderating your Passions, as Human wisdom can give."[105] He summarized those tenets as: "(1) that the Souls of Men are mortall, and so uncapable of all either happiness or misery after death; (2) That Man is not obliged to honour, revere, and worship God, in respect of his beneficences, or out of the hope of any Good or feare of any evill at his hands, but meerly in respect of the transcendent Excellencies of his Nature, Immortality, and Beatitude; (3) That self-homicide is an

Act of Heroick Fortitude in case of intollerable or otherwise inevitable Calamity."[106] However disagreeable the first proposition
might be to the Christian faith, Charleton asked his readers to re-
frain from condemning the honest efforts of a "meere naturalist,
borne and educated in times of no small Pagan darknesse."[107]
Charleton confessed that he has studied all the writings of those
who have tried to prove the immortality of the human soul and
found none convincing. The point he makes here is that unassisted
human reason cannot provide the basis for belief in the immortality
of the human soul and all that flows from that. "I have observed
many learned men, Divines, and others, who have long laboured
their thought in the same Disquisition, to concurre with me in
opinion. That to believe the soul of Man to be immortall, upon
Principles supernaturall, is much more easie, than to demonstrate
the same by Reasons purely Naturall."[108] Christians have long had
the support, Charleton argued, of divine revelation; they have
long been "illuminated by a brighter light than that of Nature."[109]
Whereas those who condemn Epicurus, who lacked this essential
assistance, do him and divine revelation a grave injustice. How
could it have been otherwise for Epicurus? He was, after all,
ignorant through no fault of his own of "that unattainable Truth,
when he could steer the course of his judgment and beliefs by no
other Starre, but that remote and pale one of the Light of Nature;
that bright North-Starre of Holy Scripture appearing not at all to
the Horizon of Greece, till many Ages after his death."[110]

As for the second tenet regarding the obligation to honor or
worship God, Charleton defended Epicurus in a similar manner.
Epicurus lived in a time "when there was scarce any Religion, but
sottish Idolatory, where there were more Gods than Nations, yea,
than Temples; and when all Devotion was absurd and ridiculous
Superstition."[111] In such circumstances Epicurus ought to be honoured rather than condemned "for having so clear and genuine an
apprehension of some of the Divine Attributes, than reproached
for not comprehending them all."[112] To place the basis of worship
on the foundation of respect for the excellency of the divine nature

is closer to the Christian foundation than the then prevailing practices of idolatry, concludes Charleton.

Charleton made a very strong point when he reminded his Christian friends that a fundamental tenet of Judaeo-Christian orthodoxy is that God revealed himself to man. This being so, he continued, it is "highly unreasonable . . . for any man [i.e., Jew or Christian] to expect, from Epicurus, the knowledge of the true and legitimate worship of God, when that was by God himselfe praescribed only to the ancient Hebrews, and professed only by their Posterity, and no other Nation in the world."[113] None of the ancient philosophers (Plato, Aristotle, the Stoics) fared any better than Epicurus, so why should he be more severely condemned than they? "Besides, Human Justice will hardly permit, that any man should suffer meerly for wanting that, which, *without supernatural means*, was impossible for him to obtain."[114]

There can be no doubt, says Charleton, that suicide, the third tenet, is a "bloody and detestable opinion" and completely incompatible with the Christian religion. But even in this instance Charleton exonerates Epicurus of blame. "This, as a Christian, I hold to be a bloody and detestable opinion, because expressly repugnant to the Law of God; and yet in the person of a meer Philosopher, I might, without being unreasonably Paradoxicall, adventure to dispute, whether it be so highly repugnant to the Law of Nature, as men have generally conceived."[115] Charleton gives the clear impression that the law of God and the law of nature are distinct and that the former is superior to the latter. He was sufficiently concerned with the question to devote an entire treatise to it. In *Epicurus's Morals*, he argued that if you take the stoic view of the law of nature, a "meer Philosopher" has "no very easie task . . . to prove, that in case of insupportable distresse, and where all other hopes of evading, or ending that misery (then which there can be no greater Evill) for a man to free himselfe from that extremity of Evill, and seek the Good of ease and quiet, by taking away his own life . . . is an infringement of the Law of Nature."[116]

The natural law as understood and presented by Hobbes is of no use in this dilemma, Charleton claimed: "if we understand Self-preservation (which all men allow to be the foundation of Natural Law in Generall) to be no other, but an innate love or Naturall affection to life, as a Good, when life ceaseth to be a Good, and degenerates into an Evill, as commonly it doth to men, in cruel torments of the body, or high discontent of minds . . . and when all the Stars of hope and comfort are set in the West of black despair, why should not the force on obligation of that Law also, cease at the same time?"[117] Indeed, said Charleton, one could even make the case that the law of nature on the foundation of self-preservation could oblige one in extreme circumstances of mind or body to commit suicide. However wrong Epicurus may have been in counseling suicide, Charleton concluded that he was not alone nor indeed the most vehement supporter of it. He then proceeded to relate how Cicero and the Stoics, as well as more ancient writers such as Demosthenes, Democles, Cleanthes, Chrysippus, and Empedocles all countenanced suicide. Indeed, he even cites Augustine (i.e., a Christian) as supporting it "when no Calamity urged him."[118]

Charleton's final conclusion is very interesting if for no other reason than its weakness. After a lengthy discussion of the question of suicide and how the natural law (of either the Stoic or Hobbesian variety) was insufficiently strong to persuade against it, he concluded: "But lest we seem to give any encouragement to that which God, the Church, and the Civill Power so highly condemn; let us grant, that self-murther, in whatever case, is a violation of the Law of Nature."[119] One would have expected Charleton to conclude that suicide was a violation of the divine law or the law of God. But he does not, at least not in this work.

In a later work entitled *The Harmony of Natural and Positive Divine Laws* (1682), Charleton does very little to help one conclude that the harmony of the natural and divine laws is easily achieved. At times he appears close to John Locke and at other times close to the Stoics, or a blend of both.

By Nature all Wise Men understand the Order, Method and Oeconomy instituted and established by God from the beginning or Creation for Government and Conservation of the World. All the Laws of Nature therefore are the Laws of God: And that which is called Natural, and Moral, is also Divine Law; as well because Reason, which is the very Law of Nature, is given by God to every man for a rule of his Actions; and because the Precepts of living, which are thence deriv'd, are the very same that are promulgated by the Divine Majesty for Laws of the Kingdom of Heaven, by our most blessed Lord Jesus Christ, and by the Holy Prophets, and Apostles; nor is there in Truth any one Branch of Nature or Moral Law, which may not be plainly and fully confirm'd by the Divine Laws delivered in Holy Scripture: as will soon appear to any man who shall attentively read and consider what our Master Hobbes hath with singular judgment written in the 4th Chapter of his Book *de Cive*.[120]

Apart from the fact that the reference to Hobbes renders the subject more difficult to resolve (since Hobbes's natural-law teaching can in no way be said to be compatible with Christian orthodoxy), what Charleton says here is clearly undermined by what he said in *Epicurus's Morals*. Charleton exonerated Epicurus from all blame since he was required to depend entirely on human reason, which leads into theological error without the assistance of divine revelation and into moral errors because not even the natural law can be ascertained without the aid of divine assistance. If we accept the testimony of the *Harmony of Natural and Divine Positive Law* as the authoritative expression of Charleton's thoughts on this question, then we can only conclude that his laconic remarks at the end of his "Apologia" in which he concludes that suicide is contrary, not to the Law of God, but to the law of nature, are deliberately evasive. The case as presented in *The Harmony* is far too carefully and closely reasoned to permit one to say that Charleton simply "nodded" in *Epicurus's Morals* and that later in *The Harmony* he changed his mind. It is more likely that he was fully conscious of his unorthodoxy and that he was more cautious in presenting the moral philosophy of Epicurus. One thing is beyond dispute: Charleton's book on Epicurus' moral philosophy is a clear and forceful presentation of Epicurean hedonism. And when one compares the forcefulness of his presentation of Epicurean moral phi-

losophy with the weakness of his rejoinders to Epicurus' unorthodox theological conclusions, one cannot escape the suspicion that
Charleton permits Epicurus to make the stronger case. In his *Enquiries into Human Nature* (1680) Charleton states clearly that
man cannot have knowledge of God's eternity, power, wisdom, and
so forth, "for how can a finite have an adequate notion of an infinite?"[121] This posture of skepticism is closer to Epicurus than to
Gassendi.

In *Epicurus's Morals* Charleton made available in the English
language for all England to read and to ponder an excellent summary of Epicurus' hedonistic philosophy. He showed for example
that Epicurus was not a base hedonist and that "the Pleasure,
wherein Felicity doth consist, is the Indolency of the Body and
tranquility of Minde";[122] that "Prudence, Temperance and Fortitude are inseparably conjoyned to Pleasure";[123] and that it is "the
Office, or Duty of Prudence, to order and compose all the accidents
and actions of a man's life, so as that they may conduce only to
Felicity."[124] And, finally, since injustice would bring remorse of
conscience, the life of pleasure is also just.[125]

Charleton gave a good deal of attention to the concept of justice
in this work. He began by restating the Epicurean belief that justice, as all virtues, is not a virtue "to be wished for, embraced, and
pursued, immediately for itself, but mediately, or for the great
Pleasure it brings with it."[126] Under the obvious inspiration or
guidance of Lucretius, Charleton traces the concept of right and
justice back to the first beginnings of human society.[127] In the beginning or the "first age of the World," wrote Charleton, "men
lived wandering up and down, like wild Beasts, and suffered many
incommodities, both from the fury of Wild Beasts, and the inclemency of the Air; till, Reason advising them thereunto, they con-
vened and conjoyned themselves in certain Companies or Societies,
that so they might the better provide against those incommodities,
by building themselves Huts or Cottages, and furnishing themselves with other Defensatives against the fury of Wild beasts, and
against the injuries of weather."[128]

Civil society and laws emerged out of the mutual needs of these peoples thus banded together. But for the inclemency of the weather and the ferocity of the other "Wild Beasts," there would have been no inclination to join together: civil society is not natural; it arose out of mutual need or utility. In time, order or laws were imposed upon these bands of people by the more powerful of their numbers. Conditions became oppressive and the people inevitably rose up against their harsh masters. The prudent citizen, observed Charleton, saw the benefit of the laws while the "vulgar men" had to be coerced.[129] The coercive force of law became necessary because there was no other "remedy for the Cure of the peoples ignorance of the Utility of those laws, than that of their own Fear of the Punishments prescribed by the Lawes: because even in our daies, it is Fear alone which contains Vulgar men within the bounds of their duty, and hinders them from committing anything against either the publick or private Commodity."[130] Charleton expressed the regret that all men do not know the advantage of seeking their own utility; "if all men could equally both understand, and bear in mind, what is truly Profitable; they would need no Lawes at all."[131] Civil society is thus not only the product of the external force of insecurity or "incommodities" of life, but the laws which govern men in society are the product of their weaknesses, their incapacity to perceive and understand that which is "truly Profitable."

CONCLUSION

It is one thing to establish the presence of minor disciples of Epicurus and Lucretius in England and France throughout the seventeenth century; it is quite another matter to contend that the major founders of the principal philosophic movement, such as Hobbes and Locke, were influenced by the emergence of hedonism at this time. Even the explicit association of Hobbes and Locke with the leading French Epicureans such as Gassendi and Bernier, respectively, is not sufficient to warrant one to conclude that Hobbes and Locke were Epicurean or even hedonists. There are too many aspects of their philosophies which have nothing in common with Epicureanism to permit a simple coincidence.

The major task therefore will be to prove that hedonism, however refined or reformulated, became the central moving force of the modern moral and political philosophies of the giants of the British tradition. The extent to which the revival of hedonism infiltrated the thinking of the major English political philosophers, Hobbes and Locke, will accordingly be the chief concern of the next chapters.

NOTES

1. The best available English source book on Epicurus is still Cyril Bailey, *Epicurus: The Extant Remains* (Oxford: Clarendon Press, 1926); see also his *The Greek Atomists and Epicurus* (London: Oxford University Press, 1928); see also N. W. DeWitt, *Epicurus and His Philosophy* (Minneapolis: University of Minnesota Press, 1954); see also J. M. Rist, *Epicurus: An Introduction* (Cambridge: Cambridge University Press, 1972).

2. References are to *Of the Nature of Things*, trans. Thomas Creech, 2 vols. (London, 1714).

3. See G. D. Hadzsits, *Lucretius and His Influence* (New York: Longmans, 1935).

4. References are to Diogenes Laertius, *Lives of Eminent Philosophers*, trans. Hicks, Loeb Classical Library ed., 2 vols. Vol. II, Book X, "Epicurus."

5. Epicurus does not follow either Democritus or Leucippus in many important matters. The crucial Epicurean doctrine of the swerve is an example of such a matter. See J. M. Rist, *Epicurus* (Cambridge: Cambridge University Press, 1972); also see Karl Marx's doctoral dissertation, *The Difference Between the Democritean and Epicurean Philosophy of Nature in General* (Moscow: Progress Publishers, 1975).

6. Diogenes Laertius, p. 571.

7. Ibid., p. 573.

8. Ibid., p. 593.

9. Ibid., p. 659.

10. Ibid., p. 659.

11. For a good account of the concept of swerve in Epicurus, see David J. Furley, *Two Studies in the Greek Atomists* (Princeton: Princeton University Press, 1967), pp. 227–36; also Rist, *op. cit.*, pp. 48 ff.

12. As Rist says, Epicurus "always [subordinated] natural philosophy to ethics," *op. cit.*, p. 164.

13. Diogenes Laertius, p. 607.

14. Ibid., on thunder and lightning, see pp. 629–30.

15. Ibid., p. 611.

16. Ibid.

17. Sextus Empiricus, *Adv. Math.* XI no. 169; cf. Epicurus Fragment 222V.

18. Diogenes Laertius, "Letter to Pythocles," p. 647.

19. Philip Merlan, *Studies in Epicurus and Aristotle*, 40–50; see also *De rerum natura* VI, 75, where Lucretius speaks of the Epicurean's "placidum pectus." Also A. J. Festugière, *Epicurus and His Gods* (London: Oxford University Press, 1955).

20. Diogenes Laertius, "Letter to Menoeceus," p. 651.

21. For a good discussion of the Epicurean doctrine of pleasure, see Rist, *op. cit.*, Ch. VI, pp. 100–26.

22. For an eighteenth-century portrayal of Epicureanism as base hedonism, see Jeremy Taylor, *A Course of Sermons for all the Sundays of the Year*, sermon XV, "The House of Feasting: or the Epicurean Measures," pp. 191 ff.

23. Diogenes Laertius, "Letter to Menoeceus," p. 657.

24. Ibid., p. 656.

25. Ibid., p. 657. It is a major oversight in Rist's otherwise useful study of Epicurus that he does not treat the role of prudence.

26. Ibid., p. 663.

27. Ibid., p. 659.

28. Ibid.

29. William Wallace, *Epicureanism*, Chief Ancient Philosophers (London, 1880), p. 115.

30. Diogenes Laertius, p. 653.

31. Ibid., p. 655.

32. Ibid.

33. Ibid.

34. Ibid., "Sovran Maxims," XXXVII, p. 675.

35. Ibid., XXXI, pp. 673–75.

36. Ibid., XXXVI, p. 675. As Rist says: "It is that we properly use the word 'justice' to mean a pledge of mutual advantage between men by which they agree not to harm one another so that they may not be harmed themselves," *op. cit.*, p. 124.

37. Ibid., XXXV, p. 675.

38. Ibid.

39. "Fragments," LVIII, p. 115, in Cyril Bailey, *Epicurus: The Extant Remains*.

40. Philip Merlan, *Studies in Epicurus and Aristotle* (Wiesbaden: Harrasso-witz, 1960), p. 4.

41. Ibid.

42. On the subsidiary role of kinetic pleasure, see Rist, *op. cit.*, p. 109.

43. Merlan, *op. cit.*, p. 5.

44. Ibid., p. 6.

45. See Rist for arguments against this interpretation; *op. cit.*, pp. 101ff.

46. See Aristotle, *Nicomachean Ethics*, 1153B25; 1153B29–31; 1154B8.

47. Merlan, *op. cit.*, p. 37.

48. For an excellent study of *De rerum natura*, see James H. Nichols, Jr., *Epicurean Political Philosophy* (Ithaca: Cornell University Press, 1976); also Leo Strauss, "Notes on Lucretius," *Liberalism: Ancient and Modern* (New York: Basic Books, 1968).

49. *De rerum natura*, Bk. I, p. 3.

50. Ibid., 1.939–959, pp. 73–74.

51. Ibid., 1.1–20, pp. 3–5.

52. Ibid., 1.36, p. 6.

53. Virgil Topazio, *D'Holbach's Moral Philosophy* (Geneva: Institut et Musée Voltaire, 1956).

54. Cornelius Agrippa, *Of the Vanitie and Uncertaintie of Artes and Sciences*, trans. James Sandfor (London, 1569), p. 179.

55. See a discussion of this issue in T. S. Spink, *French Free-Thought from Gassendi to Voltaire* (London: Athlone Press, 1960).

56. For an account of the life and troubles of Vanini, see B. de Grammont, *Historiarum Galliae ab execessu Henrici IV, libri XVIII* (Toulouse, 1643).

57. D. C. Allen, "The Rehabilitation of Epicurus and His Theory of Pleasure in the Early Renaissance," *Studies in Philosophy*, 41 (1944), 13.

58. David Durand, *The Life of Lucilio Vanini* (London, 1730), "To the Reader," p. iv.

59. The full title of the work is: *Syntagma philosophiae Epicuri cum refutationibus dogmatum quae contra fidem Christianam ab eo asserta sunt* (Amsterdam, 1684).

60. (Grenoble, 1624).

61. G. S. Brett's *The Philosophy of Gassendi* (London: Macmillan, 1908) is still one of the best English accounts of Gassendi's thoughts.

62. A. J. Festugière, *Epicurus and His Gods*, trans. C. W. Chilton (Oxford: Blackwell, 1955); see also Benjamin Farrington, *The Faith of Epicurus* (New York: Basic Books, 1962).

63. Gassendi called Epicurus' denial of providence "gravissimus lapsus," *De vita et moribus Epicuri*, p. 91.

64. Ibid., "Deus non gerere nec generalem totius mundi, nec specialem hominum curam."

65. Ibid., p. 92, "Tamquam non religione modo sed naturali etiam rationi penitus adversum."

66. Gassendi, *Syntagma*, p. 3; see also, "De Felicitate," pp. 417ff.

67. Ibid., p. 422.

68. *De Vita*, pp. 175–76; Index, s.v. "Voluptates impuras spernit Epicurus."

69. Ibid., p. 131.

70. Ibid., pp. 81–82.

71. Ibid.

72. Ibid., p. 83; he deplores the "perpetuum erga Epicurum concepêre odium."

73. See *Discours* in *Oeuvres de Jean-François Sarasin*, ed. Paul Festugière, Tome II, pp. 37–74 (Paris, 1926).

74. Jacques du Rondelle, p. 135, "Doctissimus"; and p. 3, "praegloriossimus Philosophorum."

75. François Bernier, *Three Discourses of Happiness, Virtue, and Liberty* (London, 1699), p. 3.

76. Ibid., p. 45.

77. Ibid., p. 44.

78. Ibid., p. 46.

79. Ibid., pp. 86ff. See pp. 26–27 for Bernier's synonyms for pleasure.

80. Ibid., p. 90.

81. Ibid., p. 251.

82. La Mettrie, *Oeuvres philosophiques* (Amsterdam, 1764).

83. *L'Art de jouir*, II, 322 (Paris, 1921).

84. Ibid.

85. Robert Hugh Kargon, *Atomism in England from Hariot to Newton* (Oxford: Clarendon Press, 1966).

86. Ibid., p. 63.

87. Ibid., pp. 75–76.

88. See, e.g., Robert Boyle, *Some Considerations about the Reconcileableness of Reason and Religion* (London, 1675). See also Kargon, *op. cit.*, Ch. VIII, "Walter Charleton and the Acceptance of Atomism in England," pp. 77–92.

89. See Milič Čapek, "Was Gassendi a Predecessor of Newton?" *Ithica*, The Proceedings of the Tenth International Congress of the History of Science (1962).

90. Marjorie Nicholson, "The Early Stage of Cartesianism in England," *Studies in Philology*, 26 (1929), 369. See also Sterling Lamprecht, "The Role of Descartes in Seventeenth-Century England," *Studies in the History of Ideas*, 3 (1935). Also Robert Kargon, "Walter Charleton, Robert Boyle, and the Acceptance of Epicurean Atomism in England," *Isis* 55 (1964).

91. Ralph Horne, "The Atomic Tradition in England," *Ithica* (1962), p. 721.

92. Joseph Glanvill, *The Vanity of Dogmatizing* (London, 1661), p. 146.

93. Ibid.

94. Thomas Franklin Mayo, *Epicurus in England* (Dallas: Southwest Press, 1934), p. xi.

95. Meric Casaubon, *Translations of the Six Books of Manilius* (London, 1697).

96. Note that Cicero says "gods." Thomas Creech, *Titus Lucretius Carus, His Six Books of Epicurean Philosophy* (London, 1682), p. 2.

97. Meric Casaubon, *Of Credulity and Incredulity* (London, 1668), p. 201.

98. Ibid., p. 206.

99. Erasmus' *The Epicurean* appeared in 1545. Erasmus presents Jesus here as the first genuine "Epicurean."

100. Ibid., p. 203.

101. Walter Charleton (1619–1707) was educated at Oxford where he matriculated in 1635. In 1643 he was appointed physician to Charles I; Charles II appointed him Royal Physician in 1653. He was elected to the Royal College of Physicians in 1689–1691. See Humphrey Rolleston, "Walter Charleton, D.M., F.R.C.P., F.R.S." *Bulletin of the History of Medicine* 8 (1940), 403.

102. *Epicurus's Morals*, "Apologie."

103. Ibid.

104. Walter Charleton, *Natural History of the Passions* (London, 1674).

105. Ibid., p. 188.

106. *Loc. cit.*

107. *Loc. cit.*

108. *Loc. cit.*

109. Ibid., p. 189.

110. *Loc. cit.*

111. *Loc. cit.*

112. *Loc. cit.*

113. *Loc. cit.*

114. *Loc. cit.*

115. *Loc. cit.*

116. Walter Charleton, *op. cit.*, p. 191.

117. *Loc. cit.*

118. *Loc. cit.*

119. Walter Charleton, *op. cit.*, p. 194.

120. Walter Charleton, *Natural and Positive Divine Laws* (London, 1682), pp. 9–10.

121. Walter Charleton, *Enquiries into Human Nature* (London, 1680), p. 30. See his *Natural History of the Passions*, "Epistle Prefatory," where he refers to "the immortal Gassendus." He also refers here to "that Prince of Modern Philosophers, the Lord St. Albans."

122. *Epicurus's Morals*, p. 140.

123. Ibid.

124. Ibid., p. 45.

125. Ibid., p. 140.

126. Ibid., p. 142.

127. It is interesting to note that throughout his *Enquiries into Human Nature*, Charleton uses the expression "state of nature" in an anatomical sense, i.e., the condition before disease.

128. *Epicurus's Morals*, pp. 149–50.

129. Ibid., p. 155.

130. Ibid.

131. Ibid., p. 156.

3

The Formative Force
of Hedonism

As WITH A TARTAN, where it is most often possible to identify the predominant hue of the cloth, so too with major philosophical movements is it possible to identify the underlying force which gives it unity and momentum. In the following chapters we shall attempt to demonstrate that hedonism provided the inner formative force of political philosophy at the foundation of the modern period and that it has shaped the direction of political life in the West ever since.

We shall examine the principal writings of the major modern philosophers, beginning with Thomas Hobbes, with a view to uncovering the hedonistic character of their writings; we shall then attempt to understand what place it occupies in the context of the main features of their respective political philosophies.

If we emphasize a basic underlying proposition common to all the modern political philosophers it is individualism, reconfirming the discovery of C. B. Macpherson.[1] We shall argue, however, that modern individualism is the necessary consequence of the modern rejection of the classical claim that man is by nature a social and political animal. Individualism is the only alternative to natural sociality which modern political philosophers deny; man is by nature in the modern view radically selfish. It follows from that proposition that the state and all social arrangements leading to and sustaining the political order must be directed to fulfilling the individual's selfish desires. This means that the ends of both the individual and the state are determined by this new conception of human nature as radically selfish or possessive. It is obvious that within such circumstances the means of achieving consent as to the ends to be pursued in political action will emerge as an important political preoccupation and problem.

What emerges in this study as more important than the possessive character of individualism is the hedonistic character of modern possessiveness. The core of the desire to possess emerges as the need to satisfy the demands of pleasure and the aversion to pain. This fundamental characteristic of individualistic hedonism becomes transformed into "political hedonism" under the direction of the modern political philosophers, especially Hobbes and Locke. That is to say, the natural selfish individualism of men is made the basis for communal association in the interest of satisfying and securing the demands of individual hedonism in a condition of peace and safety, and where, for the most part, the basic human fact of individualism is preserved.

There can be little doubt as to the importance of this development, for as Leo Strauss has written, political hedonism is "a doctrine which has revolutionized human life everywhere on a scale never yet approached by any other teaching."[2] And since Hobbes was the principal formulator of this doctrine, we must first turn to him.

THOMAS HOBBES (1588–1679)

While one cannot say that Hobbes was the founder of modern political philosophy—that distinction belongs to Machiavelli—one can say that he was indispensable in the development of modern political hedonism. For, as Michael Oakeshott has said, "never before or since has the Epicurean tradition had so acute an exponent or received so masterly a statement" as in Hobbes.[3] However much one might disagree with the sweep of this claim, one cannot deny that Hobbes was a proponent of the hedonistic tradition. Not only did he know the writings of the leading Epicurean of his day—Pierre Gassendi—he spent some time with him in France. But more important than the actual contact with avowed Epicureans, Hobbes's doctrine, despite significant differences, is fundamentally compatible with Epicureanism.[4] It is one of the great paradoxes of history that this great modern political philosopher based his political philosophy on the foundations of Epicurean apolitical philosophy. As Leo Strauss has observed, "He gives that apolitical view a political meaning. He tries to instil the spirit of political idealism into the hedonistic tradition. He thus became the creator of political hedonism."[5] We shall explore this more fully, in a moment, but before doing so, we must say a word about Machiavelli, Bacon, and the new natural philosophy.

Machiavelli effected the major change in the political philosophy and practice of modern times by convincing his successors that the old Socratic political philosophy was useless because it aimed too high—i.e., because it aimed at moral virtue. He suggested in *The Prince* that men lower their sights and study man as he *is* (and presents himself in history) and not as he *ought* to be according to a set of transcendent standards. Look at the record of human affairs—the historical works—and there one will see human nature unfolding in the deeds of real men, he counseled. Above all, he asserted, do not look to the old political philosophers who construct an impossible goal for men and who claim that the best regime is that which they imagine and admit has never really existed.[6]

Hobbes, unlike the earlier founders of modernity such as Bacon, directed his attention to the means by which the modern project could become consolidated and embodied in political form. Bacon, Hobbes's earlier mentor, left incomplete his sole political tract— *New Atlantis*—but as a clear expression of his hope for the future.[7] Thomas Hobbes played no small role in making that hope a reality.

Hobbes acquired from Bacon a commitment to the new natural philosophy to which Bacon had contributed so much at the early stages of development. We do not wish to reopen the long-standing controversy as to whether Hobbes came late or early to the new philosophy,[8] for it can be demonstrated that in his maturity, when he wrote his major works, Hobbes was a thoroughgoing proponent of the new mechanical or natural philosophy. He believed that it was not being applied to civil matters; many were employing it in the interest of natural science, but none was bringing the results to bear upon politics. "Natural Philosophy is therefore but young; but civil philosophy yet much younger, as being no older . . . than my own book *De Cive*."[9] Hobbes believed that he was the true founder of the new political philosophy because he was the first to attempt to place it on the foundations of the new natural philosophy and thereby the first to make it useful to men.

Thomas A. Spragens has recently presented an account of the relationship of Hobbes's natural philosophy and his political theory. He concludes that "Hobbes's natural philosophy cannot provide the content of his political theory."[10] But Spragens attempts to find the basis for the content of Hobbes's political theory in "an Aristotelian residue" which persisted in Hobbes long after his acquaintance with the new natural philosophy. This hypothesis sets Spragens on a quest for "isomorphic" relations with the Aristotelian cosmology. The quest leads him in the final analysis to a highly speculative account of the similarities between the Hobbesian and Aristotelian cosmology.[11] Unfortunately his account fails entirely to take note of the major substantive differences between Hobbes and Aristotle. He fails to indicate that for Aristotle each being is determined by an inherent design to its complete fulfilment. Man for Aristotle is by nature ordered to the complete life of *moral virtue* (a concept never used by Spragens yet which is so important for Aristotle). For Aristotle man's *summum bonum* consists in substantive fulfillment, not merely the state of rest or satisfaction which accompanies requited desire. There is no *moral* τέλος in Hobbes as there is in Aristotle; there is no *summum bonum* in Hobbes as Spragens observes.[12] Rather do we find in Hobbes a conception of human nature as being moved (drawn and repelled) by pleasure and pain. That is to say, Hobbes's human nature is purely corporeal; it lacks moral content in the sense in which Aristotle's does not. For Hobbes the human good is identified with the pleasant,[13] while this is not true for Aristotle.

What is especially unfortunate in Spragens' account is that he never thinks to relate Hobbes's doctrine to Epicureanism as Oakeshott suggested. Spragens is correct in claiming that Hobbes's natural philosophy cannot provide the basis of the content for his political theory, but he would have found that content in Epicurus had he taken the trouble to look there.[14]

The first thing readily apparent in Hobbes, and which places him firmly in the Epicurean tradition, is that he accepts the proposition that man is by nature apolitical and even asocial. Hobbes was the first modern political philosopher to expound this conviction in the context of a prepolitical state of nature. And while one finds no equivalent of this in Plato or Aristotle, one finds a remarkably similar doctrine in Book V of the *De rerum natura* of Lucretius. But Hobbes does not simply accept the fact of man's apolitical character, for he believes that politics is not only inescapable but also desirable (as the only means of surviving). This determination placed him at odds with Epicurus, for whom politics was a cause of disquietude for some.

There can be no doubt that Hobbes was committed to the mechanical philosophy which had emerged under the influence of Bacon, Boyle, and others. His *Leviathan* presents a clear mechanical conception of man; he subscribes to the belief that the essential elements are matter and motion and that this applies to man as part of the natural or physical world. Accordingly, Hobbes set out to discover what *the* fundamental human motion was which determined all men's actions. His conclusion was: *fear*. The fear of violent death at the hands of another is, according to Hobbes, the most fundamental human fact, which is confirmed by observations of those around us as well as by history—i.e., by the evidence of the present and past actions of men. The positive expression of this fear is the desire for self-preservation. Hobbes concluded that the passion of fear is the fundamental human fact upon which all rules of association must rest. Furthermore, he says, if we take men back far enough in time we see that all men are by nature enemies. The prepolitical condition in which men lived before entering civil society was a "*bellum omnium contra omnes*," a war of all against all, where man was a wolf to other men. That is to say, men are by nature radically hostile to one another.

In this matter Hobbes is at odds with Epicurus; for him the

object of philosophy is to liberate men from all fears, especially the fear of death. Hobbes explicitly emphasizes the fear of violent death at the hands of another; in other words, threats to the person which appear to constitute for him the extreme in pain. In this respect Hobbes was more realistic than Epicurus.[15] Hobbes adopts the view of the common man on this matter and is therefore more egalitarian than either Epicurus or Lucretius.

Since the controlling human fact is fear, man cannot be restrained by reason but by passion. That is, all rule must be directed toward channeling the passions; all politics must therefore attempt to direct the passions. The condition of the state of nature, says Hobbes, could not endure because no one could possibly live in peace in such circumstances. Accordingly men formed political associations by contracting to make one of their members the sovereign. It was as if a great multitude of men living in foxholes, terrified of one another, equal in the capacity and the right to kill their neighbors, began to realize that they could not long endure in such a frightful condition. As a result they all gave their weapons to one man and in so doing contracted with one another to give him supreme power in exchange for a condition of peace wherein they could pursue the means to self-preservation free of the constant threat to their lives. It is important to note that according to Hobbes the sovereign does not make a contract with his people. Furthermore, he says that it is quite possible that a sovereign could come into existence by conquest as well as by consent.[16]

Since men could not hope to restrain their selfish natures but through the fear of reprisal, it was better in Hobbes's view to live under the potentially benign fear of a sovereign who was at least providing a condition of peace. The inclination to seek peace was the primary dictate of the true law of nature for Hobbes because it was the corollary which stems from the positive aspect of the fear of violent death, the desire for self-preservation. Thus for Hobbes the peaceful condition was one in which men had the protection to pursue the life of comfortable or commodious self-preservation. And the right of self-preservation included the right to the means to those things which contributed to the life of comfortable self-preservation. And since this is true of all men even in civil society, the laws enacted by the sovereign conduce in fact to man's safe condition. But unlike the laws of the old moral philosophers, these laws do not lead men to their highest end—their *finis ultimus*—because there is no such end for Hobbes; rather do they make it unprofitable for men to contravene the peace. But Hobbes understands obedience to the civil laws as essentially obedience to oneself because the laws flow from the fundamental social contract. One gives laws to oneself because there is no other source; injustice now becomes defined as disobeying oneself or the laws one gives to oneself.

It is clear from *Leviathan* and *De Cive* that, despite his acceptance of the basic Epicurean doctrine of radical individualism, Hobbes rejects the alleged apolitical consequences of Epicureanism. Hobbes agrees with most of Epicurus' moral philosophy except where it tends to imply a condition without political association. Furthermore, Hobbes transforms the right of self-preservation into a new doctrine of natural right; as far as one is able to discern, Epicurus did not have a corresponding doctrine. It is important to note, however, that Hobbes's solution to the problem is constructed on the premises provided by Epicurus. His conclusions do not contradict Epicurean principles of individualism. Hobbes believed that politics was necessary because the continuous condition of war in the state of nature rendered life in every sense impossible and death more desirable. He brings men out of the unbearable condition of war into a condition of peace by means of a free choice based on right (either to come in or to stay in), and they retain the right to self-preservation even in civil society. In other words, he never forsakes the individualism which underlies his philosophy.

By bringing men out of the endless war into a peaceful condition, Hobbes also renders man's natural hedonism political. That is to say, he not only institutionalizes it but gives greater scope to its potential achievement. There can be no doubt that for Hobbes pleasure was the motive factor permeating the desire for comfortable self-preservation. But he seems to reject Epicurus' contention that man's end was in a contented mind. Hobbes says, contrary to

Epicurus: "To which end we are to consider, that the felicity of this life, consisteth not in the repose of a mind satisfied. For there is no such *finis ultimus*, utmost end, nor *summum bonum*, greatest good, as is spoken of in the books of the old moral philosophers."[17]

Instead, there is a constant desire aided by hope and the expectation of gratification. Without this continuous striving for more and more a man might just as well be dead. "Felicity is a continual progress of the desire, from one object to another; the attaining of the former, being still but the way to the latter. . . . So that in the first place, I put for a general inclination of all mankind, a perpetual and restless desire of power after power, that ceaseth only in death."[18]

On the question of what constitutes good and evil, Hobbes is explicit in *Leviathan*. Early in the work Hobbes says: "But whatever is the object of any man's appetite or desire, that is it which he for his part calleth *good*: and the object of his hate and aversion, *evil*. . . . For these words of good and evil, and contemptible are ever used with relation to the person that useth them: there being nothing simply and absolutely so; nor any common rule of good and evil, to be taken from the nature of the objects themselves."[19] Hobbes is here in consort with Epicurus on this matter.

This sentiment is reinforced in the *Elements of Law* where Hobbes states that

> And forasmuch as necessity of nature maketh man to will and desire *bonum sibi*, that which is good for themselves, and to avoid that which is hurtful; but most of all, that terrible enemy of nature death, from whom we expect both the loss of all power, and also the greatest of bodily pains in the losing; it is not against reason, that a man doth all he can to preserve his own body and limbs both from death and pain. And that which is not against reason, men call *right*, or *jus*, or blameless liberty of using our own natural power and ability. It is therefore a right of nature, that every man may preserve his own life and limbs, with all the power he hath.[20]

What is instructive in these two passages is that man's hedonism is clearly an element of human nature—a "necessity of nature"—which leads him under the claim of "right or nature" to preserve himself from pain and death. Furthermore, man is free—if not compelled—to use all his power to preserve his life and limb. This right is an aspect of Hobbes's egalitarian doctrine of natural right of self-preservation and it continues to prevail in civil society; since man had no part in its origin he can have no part in its destruction. But Hobbes also makes it clear that the concept of self-preservation does not stop at mere existence. In *De Cive* he says that the duty of the ruler is "to study, as much as by good laws can be effected, to furnish the citizens abundantly . . . with all good things . . . which are conducive to delectation."[21] But this does not mean that Hobbes permits this rule of individual or private action to persist and guide the individual within civil society. He is emphatic to the contrary late in *Leviathan* where he says that: "This private measure of good, is a doctrine, not only vain, but also pernicious to the public state."[22] To permit the access to a private standard of judgment is, for Hobbes, to permit the Aristotelian evil to remain, and that would never do. "Aristotle and other heathen philosophers, define good and evil, by the appetite of men; and well enough, as long as we consider them governed every one *by his own law*; for in the condition of men that have no other law but their own appetites there can be no general rule of good and evil actions. But in a commonwealth this measure is false: not the appetite of private men, but the law, which is the will and appetite of the state is the measure."[23] Hobbes says in the *Elements of Law* that one precept of the new law of nature is "that every man divest himself of the right he hath to all things by nature."[24]

The laws of the commonwealth are designed to further the interest of the members who enter it; and this interest is the fulfillment of the desires (i.e., pleasures) of the members. The end of the state is identical with the end of the individuals comprising it; but the end of the individuals is private passions (pleasure), and therefore the duty of the state is to provide the public or institutional support for the pursuit of pleasure; private hedonism thus becomes political hedonism. The laws of the state become general rules by which man's right to the satisfaction of his desires—by all the power available to him—are coordinated so as to prevent a condition of war from emerging. This is clearly the basis of *laissez-faire* liberal economics. There will necessarily be competition for resources as long as they remain plentiful and unappropriated but when the resources become scarce then the competition will become more intense. For no man can claim them by right of nature: "Nature has given all things to all men."[25] The only way conflicting claims can be resolved is by competition. As Hobbes says, "Considering that many men's appetites carry them to one and the same end; which end sometimes can neither be enjoyed in common, nor divided, it followeth that the stronger must enjoy it alone, and that it be decided by battle who is the stronger."[26]

The right to possess flows necessarily from the basic inalienable right of self-preservation. "As a man's judgment, in right of nature, is to be employed for his own benefit, so also the strength, knowledge, and art of every man is then rightly employed, when he useth it for himself; else must not a man have the right to preserve himself."[27] The "civilized" human condition becomes, therefore, the competitive relations of the market economy. Man's natural hostility is not obliterated in civil society; it is moderated and restrained within rules, which he gives himself to his own eventual benefit. The hostile and warlike savage becomes the peaceful possessive individual of the competitive marketplace.

Hobbes makes it clear that the joy of achieving success is in the process of achieving. In the *Elements of Law* he says, "Felicity, therefore, (by which we mean continual delight) consisteth not in having prospered, but in prospering."[28] Hobbes emphasized this point with the claim "that as men attain to more riches, honours, or other power; so their appetite continually groweth more and more; and when they are come to the utmost degree of one kind of power, they pursue some other, as long as in any kind they think themselves behind any other."[29]

Hobbes not only alludes to the inherent competitiveness of men but sheds light upon his definition of power found in *Leviathan* and in so doing departs significantly from Epicurus. But, once again, Hobbes takes his bearings from the common man's view of life (as did Machiavelli). In *Leviathan* he says that power is a man's "present means to obtain some future apparent good."[30] And it is both natural and instrumental:

> *Natural* power, is the eminence of the faculties of body, or mind: as extraordinary strength, form, prudence, arts, eloquence, liberality, nobility. *Instrumental* are those powers, which acquired by these, or by fortune, are means and instruments to acquire more: as riches, reputation, friends, and the secret work of God, which men call good luck. For the nature of power, is in this point, like to fame, increasing, as it proceeds; or like the motion of heavy bodies, which the further they go, make still the more haste.[31] This restless quest of power after power ceases only in death.

It is not surprising to find that Hobbes's hedonism pervades his understanding of virtue and vice, justice and injustice. He defines virtue, after explicitly rejecting Aristotle's conception, as: "the habit of doing according to these and other laws of nature that tend to our preservation."[32] That is to say: peaceableness. And since the surest way to peace is to obey the laws, virtue becomes citizenship or patriotism. "The sum of virtue is to be sociable with them that will be sociable, and formidable to them that will not."[33] As a result justice is "that habit by which we stand to convenants," and injustice the contrary.[34]

Hobbes's hedonistic individualism leads necessarily to a new definition of the πόλις. It is: "a city, which may be defined to be a multitude of men, united as one person by a common power, for their common peace, defence and benefit."[35] This definition stands in sharp contrast to Aristotle's, for whom the city existed for the moral virtue of its citizens. One of the intriguing extensions of the new definition is that Hobbes specifically provides for the establishment within the new polis of corporations with subordinate governmental functions as well as for trade.

Hobbes's modification of Epicureanism implies that Epicurus was too unrealistic in thinking that there could be a peaceful condition without a political order to ensure it. And despite the differences, Hobbes did adopt all the major aspects of Epicurean moral philosophy and made it a central part of his political philosophy. The good is identical with the pleasant in Hobbes as in Epicurus;

virtue is not sought for its own sake but for the pleasure it brings; justice is based on the utility of agreement in both. Fear of powers invisible or the gods has the same disturbing results in both—except that for Hobbes it has unsettling political possibilities as well. They both believe that the way to undo these unsettling fears of the divinity is through scientific explanation of the phenomena which engender fear in the ignorant.

One must deduce from Hobbes the fact that his new political philosophy is based on a new conception of nature or human nature. He openly affirms: "I have derived the rights of sovereign power and the duty of subjects, hitherto from the principles of nature only. . . . that is to say, from the nature of man, known to us by experience, and from definitions of such words as the essential to all political reasoning, universally agreed on."[36]

Hobbes believed that he brought human reason out of the clouds of the tradition and down to earth; he gave it weights as Bacon had suggested, and discovered that reason led to the conclusion that man is essentially a passionate animal who more often than not has become the dupe of philosophers or theologians. That is to say that nature reveals man as being a captive of his physical or emotional nature. Hobbes considered as one of his major insights his claim that man is not by nature a social and political animal. This does not mean, as we have seen, that he can live for long out of a political order.

We must conclude by noting that Hobbes maintains that the natural hostility that men have toward one another remains even after they enter civil society. And despite the fact that the sovereign will take care of those who attempt to exercise this hostility in a violent form, there must be some means by which men can associate with one another on a day-to-day basis. Competition is the civil form of hostility—it is moderated by custom and education (and religion), but it must be viewed as the acceptable means of expressing one's natural hostility within civil society. There can be no escaping the push of hostility even in civil society. The direct market relation of bartering was the first acceptable expression of the "civilized" relationship. The market economy emerged, therefore, under the inspiration of the political hedonism which lies at the heart of modern political philosophy.

The important thing to note is that Hobbes introduced the basis for the emergence of the politics of hedonism. This achievement has influenced the political life of the West in a permanent way ever since. But this did not occur without the assistance of John Locke who, along with Hobbes, shaped the course of Western politics. We must turn now to John Locke's political philosophy and review it in the light of our understanding of the impact of Epicureanism on Hobbes.

JOHN LOCKE (1632–1704)

However important Thomas Hobbes was to the emergence of a political philosophy on the foundations of the new natural philosophy, John Locke was indispensable for its consolidation and eventual permanence. Laying the solid foundations for a political philosophy in man's passionate nature, Hobbes not only grounded political philosophy in the new natural philosophy, he adduced a new conception of human nature and law. Hobbes undertook to base politics on man understood as an apolitical being. He concentrated on men in their prepolitical condition and their first political acts. Although he does of course talk about the need for a strong sovereign and other matters relating to the relationship between subject and sovereign, his emphasis is more on the transition from the prepolitics of open hostility (the human condition without politics) than on the control of this natural hostility once men come together in political groups or states. Hobbes concentrates on the beginnings of political relationships and on what strains or threatens to end them.

Locke accepts with minor reservations the basic premisses of Hobbes and builds a political philosophy on those premisses. His chief concern, however, was with the relations of individuals to one another and the government *within* civil society. His *Two Treatises of Government* prescribes rules for men who have compacted to live in a civil society. *The Second Treatise* in particular implies precepts for the market relationships that conform to Hobbes's conception of human nature. Locke dwelt at length on the manner in which civil government should permit man's natural competitiveness to develop into formal market relations that transcend barter due to the emergence of money as a medium of exchange. For Locke, the emergence of money was a crucial factor in developing the competitive relations in civil society since it legitimized unlimited acquisition. According to Locke, man is prohibited by nature from acquiring more than he can use before it spoils; but since money (understood primarily as gold) does not spoil the prohibition is circumvented and man becomes free to accumulate as much as by his industry and ingenuity he is capable of accumulating. The natural forces of the market were understood as manifestations of the natural competitiveness (i.e., civilized hostility) which Locke said *in fact* governed men's lives. So that his political philosophy is an attempt to set out rules of civil relationship—one citizen with another and all with the sovereign—that are in accordance with man's acquisitive nature.

It will be useful to review at this point C. B. Macpherson's thesis regarding the possessive individualism of Hobbes and Locke because this study is a modification of Macpherson's thesis.

However accurate Macpherson's characterization of Hobbes's and Locke's political philosophies may be, the notion of possessive individualism does not take into account the moral principles which propel the possessive individual. When one articulates those moral principles, one sees that the possessive individual is a hedonist and that the political philosophies of Hobbes and Locke are best understood as hedonistic.

Nearly three decades ago, in the *Cambridge Journal*,[37] Macpherson summarized his thesis in the following three points:

> 1. Man, the individual, is seen as absolute natural proprietor of his own capacities, owing nothing to society for them. Man's essence is freedom to use his capabilities in search of satisfactions. This freedom is limited properly only by some principle of utility or utilitarian natural law which forbids harming others. Freedom therefore is restricted to, and comes to be identified with, domination over things,

not domination over men. The clearest form of domination over things is the relation of ownership or possession. Freedom is therefore possession. Everyone is free, for everyone possesses at least his own capacities. 2. Society is seen . . . as a lot of free and equal individuals related to each other through their possessions, that is, related as owners of their own capacities and of what they have produced and accumulated by the use of their capacities. The relation of exchange (the market relation) is seen as the fundamental relation of society. Finally, political society is seen as a rational device for the protection of property, including capacities; even life and liberty are considered as possessions, rather than as social rights with correlative duties.[38]

Both here and in the more fully developed account in *The Political Theory of Possessive Individualism: Hobbes to Locke*, Macpherson claims that Hobbes's and Locke's possessive individualism is the result of a conscious commitment to the "bourgeois vision" and the product of their absorption of the major assumptions regarding the nature of man that pervaded the seventeenth century.[39] In short, that Hobbes and Locke were more the products than the producers of fundamental principles of modern liberalism which emerged in the seventeenth century.[40] Macpherson gives the clear impression that Locke merely adopted the fundamental premises of Hobbes and amended them for his own narrow "bourgeois" purposes. However correct Macpherson is regarding the possessive individualism of the tradition beginning with Hobbes, he does not penetrate the character of individualism, which he correctly states is "the chief characteristic of the liberal tradition from Hobbes to Bentham."[41] He is prevented from identifying the character of individualism by an unwillingness to look for the roots of the modern tradition in Epicureanism and by the consequent reluctance to explore the moral teachings of Hobbes and Locke. Had he done so, he might have emerged with an understanding of the philosophies of Hobbes and Locke as the logical consequence of clear conceptions of human nature as hedonistic.[42] He would have found that the commitment of Hobbes and Locke to the "bourgeois society" is the result of their moral principles and constitutes the logical terminus of their articulate views of man as by nature a selfish, possessive individual.

Both Hobbes and Locke viewed man as by nature his own master and the sole proprietor of himself and of his labor. But this means that by nature man is radically apolitical because he has obligations only to himself. The only way individuals can come together into a political or social whole is through consent—i.e., through the free grant of legislative authority to another. But even here Hobbes and Locke make it clear that in granting such authority the individuals intend to achieve a condition which will redound to their own individual benefit. In obeying the laws they are obeying themselves. That is why in both Hobbes and Locke the individual in civil society retains the right to self-preservation; he is by nature incapable of giving it away.

In principle, at least, it is tautological to say that individualism is possessive because individualists are by definition concerned exclusively with their own well-being; their possessiveness flows from their individualism. The identification of the fundamental principles of men's possessive nature becomes important because those principles direct men's actions in civil society. Both Hobbes and Locke found those principles in hedonism.

One discovers in reading Locke's *Two Treatises of Government* that he subscribed to the doctrine regarding a prepolitical state of man espoused by Hobbes. But where Hobbes's state of nature is one of outright hostility, Locke's is not quite so violent, although in the final analysis, as Richard Cox argues persuasively,[43] there is very little difference between Locke's and Hobbes's state of nature. Both for Hobbes and for Locke man in the state of nature is radically independent. According to Locke, man in the state of nature is motivated solely by the desire for pleasure and the aversion to pain. He is a hedonist because he is by nature an individual driven by the desire to fulfill the needs of his passionate nature. As in Hobbes, Locke's natural man is not drawn to any *finis ultimus*, but driven from behind by his passionate nature. Virtue is not sought for its own sake but because of the pleasure it brings. In the *Essay*

Concerning Human Understanding, Locke says that good and evil are "good or evil, only in reference to pleasure or pain."[44] He continues in words reminiscent of Epicurus: "that we call good which is apt to cause or increase pleasure or diminish pain in us; or else to procure or preserve us the possessions of any other good, or absence of any evil. And on the contrary, we name that evil, which is apt to produce or increase any pain, or diminish any pleasure in us; or else to procure us any evil, or deprive us of any good."[45] Locke emphasizes that by pleasure and pain he means the mental as well as the physical pleasures and pains.

Since Locke was a cautious writer fully aware of the dangers that went with openly espousing hedonism, he did not publish his most explicit thoughts on morality. In the Lovelace collection at the Bodleian Library, Oxford, there are three documents in which Locke explicitly treats the principles of morals. Those documents are entitled: "Morality" (undated), "Ethica" (dated 1692), and "Of Ethick in General" (undated).[46] These documents are all explicitly hedonistic and confirm the guarded hedonism of the *Essay* and the *Two Treatises*. In "Morality" Locke claims that all men seek happiness and that happiness consists of pleasure and that misery consists of pain. And he clearly relates the matter to man's basic possessiveness and civil society. "Man made not himself nor any other man. Man made not the world which he found at his birth. Therefore no man at his birth can have no right to anything in the world more than an other. Men therefore must either enjoy all things in common or by compact determine their rights. If all things be left in common, want, rapine and force will unavoidably follow in which state as is evident happiness cannot be had which cannot consist without plenty and security." That is to say, man's competitiveness stems from his right to possess, which belongs equally to all men, and that the only way this natural right can be restricted or channeled is by compact or mutual consent.

Justice emerges from this as the *duty* to keep the compact designating right since the alternative is savage conflict and civil war. "Justice is established as a duty and will be the first and general rule of our happiness," says Locke.

In "Ethica" Locke defines in some detail the character of mental pleasure and its relation to bodily pleasure. After stating that every rational creature is moved to action by some good, he claims that "good is only pleasure or greater pleasure or the means to it." He then makes the claim that "pleasures are all of the mind, none of the body, but some consist in motions of the body, some in contemplations and satisfactions of the mind separate abstract and independent from any motions or affections of the body. And these later [sic] are both the greatest and more lasting. The former of these we call for shortness sake . . . pleasure of the senses, the other pleasures of soul or rather material and immaterial pleasures." Locke does not, as is evident from this document, reject sensual pleasures; but he does place them below mental pleasures because they are more ephemeral than mental pleasures. "Material pleasures last not beyond the present application of the object to the sense and make but a small part of the life of the most voluptious [sic] man." Locke emphasized that no matter how great sensual delight may be it cannot be compared with mental delight. And the reason is not because the rational faculty is higher than the sensual faculties, but because "even in those material sensual pleasures, contemplation makes up the greatest part and when the senses have done the mind by thought continues a pleasure wherein the senses have no share." Later in this document Locke writes: "Next pleasures of the mind are the greatest as well as more lasting. Who ever was so brutish as would not quit the greatest sensual pleasures to save a child's life whom he loved. What is this but pleasure of thought remote from any sensual delight." The human mental capacity to continue to recollect some past sensual experience clearly outreaches the actual sensual experience, but there is no denying that the continued recollection is a recollection of some specific sensual delight.

And despite Locke's claim that no man would continue to enjoy himself while a child was in extreme danger, the reason he responds is because the child is an object of his affections. After all, he says that the child is one "whom he loved," i.e., one's own or closely related so as to command affection. One cannot help asking, what would be the response of the same man to the plight of a child whom he did not love? [47]

Locke believed that charity was a means of pursuing one's own interest. He says: "If then happiness be our interest and business, 'tis evident the way to it is to love our neighbour as our self, for by that means we enlarge and secure our pleasures since then all the good we do to them redoubles upon our selves and gives us an undecaying and uninterrupted pleasure." Pleasures, even those which arise out of acts of charity, are sought because they constitute happiness and pains are avoided because they detract from happiness.

In "Of Ethick in General" Locke confirms his hedonism but distinguishes between moral and natural good and evil. "The difference between moral and natural good and evil is only this that we call that naturally good and evil which by its natural efficiency of the thing produces pleasure or pain in us, and that is morally good or evil which by the appointment of an intelligent Being that has power draws pleasure or pains after it not by any natural consequence but by the intervention of that power."[48] From this Locke draws the conclusion for the necessity of the "proper basis and . . . foundations" of morality. That is to say, a foundation which would carry with it a commanding obedience. In order to do this, he says, "we must first prove a law which always supposes a law maker, one which has a superiority and right to order everyone and also a power to reward and punish according to the terms of the law established by him." Locke adds that "God is the soverain law maker who has set rules and bounds to the actions of men."[49] This appears to lay the foundation for the claim that the law of nature is necessarily linked with the existence of God, as it was for Thomas Aquinas who defined the law of nature as "the law of God in rational creatures." Aquinas not only distinguishes the natural law (*lex naturalis*) from the other laws governing physical nature, but also indicated that the existence of God is necessarily prior to the natural law. From what Locke says here and in *The Reasonableness of Christianity*, one could be led to believe that his notion of the part played by God is similar to that which He plays in Aquinas.[50]

Locke's conception of God must be understood in the context of his law of nature; his teaching regarding the knowability of the law of nature is closely related to his theology. But this complicates rather than explicates the matter, for Locke presents the law of nature as knowable through the "proper use of the faculties" and only by those "few who, neither corrupted by vice nor carelessly indifferent, make a proper use of that right."[51] It is accessible to those few, those "studiers," such as himself, who explicate it—i.e., provide the authoritative interpretation for the guidance of those many who are not studiers or who have become corrupted by vice or careless indifference.

Furthermore, Locke set out to define a new natural law in order to locate a new foundation for civil law. This is why he says in the *Essays on the Law of Nature*, that "if the law of nature is not binding on men, neither can any human positive law be binding."[52] Locke's major or overriding concern was how to establish in practice that regime which is based on the understanding of human nature as presented in Hobbes. Since, according to Hobbes, all men are by nature enemies of one another, the chief political task is to bring such hostile men out of their brutish condition and into civil society ruled by law. But the foundations of civil law must be established in the law of nature, according to both Hobbes and Locke.

The *Essays on the Law of Nature*

An attentive reading of these eight essays reveals that Locke curiously avoids Scripture. From what he says in *The Reasonableness of Christianity*, it would appear that the law of nature is the "voice of God," and that it can accordingly be referred to as the "law of God," or "divine law." He even says in *The Reasonableness* that the entire law of nature is contained in the New Testament: "Such a law of morality Jesus Christ hath given us in the New Testament . . . by revelation."[53]

Yet despite this, Locke does not once appeal to Scripture in his most explicit account of the law of nature in the *Essays*. What is more puzzling is that he also avoids all obvious Biblical references. For example, on two occasions Locke refers to *"lapsu primi hominis"* and *"de primo homine aut illius lapsu."* Von Leyden translates these passages as "on account of the Fall," and "about Adam and his fall." But Locke avoids these Biblical terms. His effort to avoid using Biblical or even theological terms is carried further throughout the *Essays*. For example, Locke often refers to "god" and "God," and to the "author" of the laws of nature. Yet he only once refers to God as the "creator"; all other times he refers to God as the *"opifex,"* the maker (this term carries a mechanical connotation). When Locke writes: *"a sapientissimo authore,"* Leyden translated it as "by a most wise creator,"[54] giving the phrase a theological connotation lacking in the Latin text. Locke even goes so far as to refer to *"aliquem harum rerum omnium opificem,"* i.e., to "some maker of all these things."

Furthermore, Locke now appears to retract completely his remarks in *The Reasonableness*, for he says explicitly in the *Essays* that "the way in which we arrive at the knowledge of this law [i.e., the law of nature] is by the light of nature as opposed to other ways of knowing."[55] He deliberately excludes "supernatural and divine revelation" as a reliable source of knowledge of the law of nature. As we shall see shortly, this knowledge is only available through the human senses to men who use their reasoning powers correctly.

But Locke's efforts to dissociate himself from the Bible and the Christian conception of natural law (as presented by Aquinas or Hooker) is carried further in the *Essays*. In *Essay* II, "Can the Law of Nature be Known by the Light of Nature? Yes," Locke discusses the three ways in which the law of nature may be known: (*a*) from the common practices of men, (*b*) through tradition, (*c*) by sense knowledge. While he says that the first source is not adequate he claims that at times through education and custom an approximation of the law of nature may be attained in this manner. The third way, i.e., knowledge based on sense experience, is *the* sure and certain way. The only way he rejects completely is the second, i.e., tradition. The reasons he gives for rejecting tradition as a source of knowing the law of nature are: first, it is based on human testimony, which must be traced back in time to its source, which source then must be judged by reason as being trustworthy or reliable; second, the content of the tradition (in addition to the means by which it is transmitted) must be carefully sifted by those who use their reasoning faculties properly. But that, he says, is what is done in the third avenue of access to knowledge of the law of nature.

What complicates tradition as a source of knowledge of the law of nature is that it contains conflicting accounts. Who is to judge those accounts and by what standards? Reason, Locke says, cannot accept the testimony of tradition because that would be accepting it on trust and not by knowledge attained by human reason "since it would depend more on the authority of the giver of information than on the evidence of things themselves, and would therefore be a derived rather than an inborn law."[56]

One cannot read what Locke says here and not apply it to the New Testament as a source of knowledge of the law of nature. In one of the rare references to the divine law in the *Essays* Locke says: "if that first author of the tradition in question has laid down a law to the world, because he was instructed by some oracle or divine spirit, then a law of this kind and promulgated in this manner is *by no means* a law of nature but a positive law."[57]

The distinction between the law of nature and divine positive law which Locke makes here was made in *The Reasonableness*. And while it is true that Thomas Aquinas makes the same distinction, for him the divine positive law is compatible with the natural law. Such a doctrine does not emerge from what Locke has written on the law of nature. If anything, Locke begins his account of natural law in *The Reasonableness of Christianity* by giving the appearance that his teaching is not unlike the orthodox Christian conception as presented by Aquinas. As we progress through his accounts in *The Reasonableness* and in the *Essays* we find that he gradually opens up a distinction between the two and concludes by ruling out completely the divine positive law as forming a part of the law of nature.[58]

So far we have seen what Locke says cannot be the law of nature. We must now attempt to understand his positive thoughts on this matter. We shall proceed by examining, first, the way of knowing the law of nature, and, second, the content of the law of nature as presented in the *Essays on the Law of Nature*.

Of the eight *Essays*, four treat the three ways in which the law of nature is known. He argues in *Essays* II and IV that the law of nature can be known only by the light of nature and that the light of nature comes through sense perception. He rejects both the claim that natural law is written on the hearts of men and that it can be known through tradition. Locke rejects these two possible sources because they do not meet the test of reason. Hence, the epistemology presented in *Essays* II and IV makes them the controlling essays; they are crucial to the positive and negative aspects of his doctrine.[59] Locke says explicitly in *Essay* II: "it is clear that the law of nature is knowable by the light of nature. Since whatever among men has the force of law necessarily looks to God, or nature, or man as its author; yet whatever man has ordered or God commanded by oracle, all this is positive law; however, since the law of nature cannot be known by tradition, all that remains is that it becomes known to men by the sole light of reason."[60] But Locke makes it abundantly clear that knowledge of the law of nature is available only to those who use their faculties "*recte*," and they are few: "For most people are little concerned about their duty."[61] The law of nature, he repeats throughout the *Essays*, is "hidden," "obscure," like gold and silver, concealed in the bowels of nature. One must expend considerable mental energy in the effort to discover the law of nature by the light of nature and "there are only a few who, neither corrupted by vice nor carelessly negligent, make a right use of that light."[62] Locke surely considered himself one of the few.

In *Essay* IV Locke asks: "Can Reason Attain to the Knowledge of the Law of Nature through Sense-Knowledge?" His affirmative response is based on the following line of argument. He begins by

defining reason as "the discursive faculty of the mind which progresses from things known to things unknown and argues from one
thing to another in a definite and legitimate sequence of propositions."[63] The exercise of reason thus understood is the means by
which "mankind arrives at the knowledge of the law of nature."[64]
He then says that sense-knowledge provides the material for this
manner of reasoning. The first thing sense presents to the mind as
the material upon which it must operate is "that this visible world
is constructed with wonderful art and regularity, and of this world
we, the human race, are also a part."[65] In short, he says that sense
reveals order and motion in the universe. He then says that the
human mind "proceeds to an enquiry into their origin, to find out
what was the cause, and who was author of such an excellent
work."[66] From the recognition of design in the universe, Locke
says that there must undoubtedly be a "most powerful and wise
maker of all these things." He thus appears to make the traditional
argument for God's existence from design. But Locke is implying
here that the mind goes beyond the evidence provided by sense and
infers the existence of a creator. As he says, "These things having
been deduced by the testimony of the senses, reason dictates that
there is some superior power to whom we are rightly subject."[67]
This superior power is God, says Locke, "who has a just and in-
eluctable rule over us and at whose pleasure can raise us up or
throw us down, and make us by the same power happy or miser-
able."[68] Men emerge as the helpless playthings of a powerful and
arbitrary God; no image could be further from the orthodox image.

This doctrine is further obscured by the later statement that,
despite the existence of sense and reason throughout all mankind,
not all men attain to the idea of God. The weak excuse that this is
perhaps due more to the failure of those men to use their senses and
reasoning faculties is hardly compelling; it casts doubts on what
Locke says about the human capacity to know God and hence the
law of nature.

Locke's conclusion is that "it is clear that men can infer from the
senses that there exists some powerful superior who has right and
power over them."[69] This conclusion establishes the first pre-

requisite for a law of nature. That is to say, unless there is an author who wills the law there can be no law. Or as Locke says, "in order that anyone may understand that he is bound by a law, he must know beforehand that there is a law-maker, i.e., some superior power to which he is rightly subject."[70] But Locke fails to prove the existence of a *person* who might be called God. What he demonstrates is that there exists a *power* which imposes an order and design on all things. But it might just as easily be called *nature* as God. We cannot simply take for granted that he is referring to the orthodox God especially since he insists on using pagan terms— such as "*summi alicujus numinis*"[71]—for the author of nature.

From the alleged establishment of the existence of God the lawmaker, Locke proceeds to show that "he has not made this world in vain and without purpose."[72] This leads him to conclude that there exists "a superior power with respect to the things to be done by us; that is, God wills that we do something."[73] This is the closest Locke approaches the orthodox Christian view of God as the author of the natural law as expressed in Thomas Aquinas. But despite the appearances, Locke's doctrine of natural law is not grounded, as it is in Aquinas, in the recognition of a personal God.[74] Aquinas for example claims that one of the main precepts of the natural law is to know the truth about God.[75] Locke never says this; rather does he refer to a "certain propensity of nature" which propels man to seek life in society. He says that man "feels himself not only to be impelled by life's experience and pressing needs to procure and preserve a life in society with other men, but also to be urged to enter into society by a certain propensity of nature."[76]

What propels man to enter civil society are the "experience and pressing needs" of life and the obligation he is under "to preserve himself."[77] Thus, man is not by nature a social and political animal as he is in Aristotle and Aquinas. By nature man is propelled to preserve himself or to flee life's "experiences and pressing needs." This doctrine is consistent with the doctrine of the state of nature and its inconveniences which Locke presents in the *Second Treatise*.

We shall have occasion later to reflect further on Locke's understanding of God; let it suffice for the moment to say that from the

Essays on the Law of Nature God is a gratuitous inference and that the "superior power" can just as easily be understood as the operation of nature. Locke's ambiguous teaching makes it possible for those who are so disposed to conclude that the God to whom he refers is the orthodox God of tradition. This is because Locke was not only a cautious writer but a responsible man; the fact that he did not publish these essays must give rise to doubts about his own thoughts on their orthodoxy. If they can be understood easily as orthodox Christian, then why did he not publish them? No one can deny that he was under considerable pressure to prove his orthodoxy. These essays would certainly not have survived the scrutiny of such as Edward Stillingfleet.

The importance of natural law for Locke is crucial as we learn from *Essay* I. There he argues that unless there is a law of nature there can be no stable civil law: "certainly positive civil laws are not binding in themselves by their own force, or in any other way than by the power of the law of nature, which order obedience to superiors and the keeping of public peace."[78] It can hardly be true, therefore, as von Leyden suggests, that Locke does not accord any importance to the concept of the law of nature.[79] On the contrary, both the *Second Treatise* and the *Essays* confirm that the competitive relations among men in civil society are rooted in the law of nature.[80]

Having seen something about the foundation and importance of the law of nature, we must now explore its content. The eighth essay is the only one which deals explicitly with the content of the law of nature. It is entitled: "Is Each Man's Private Utility the Foundation of the Law of Nature?" The answer Locke gives is "No." As with most of what Locke has written, this *Essay* is more complex than one might expect on first reading. To begin with, Locke appears to refute those opponents of the natural law who claim that utility is the foundation of all civil laws and that utility differs from place to place. In short, he appears to refute the ancient proponents of the victory of conventional right over natural right. But when one follows Locke's line of argument carefully, one discovers that what he rejects is that view of conventional right which permits unrestricted access to *private* utility. In other words, "this very iniquitous opinion," as he calls it, destroys any basis for a conception of common good without which civil society is intolerable. But Locke does not reject utility as the foundation of the law of nature. He sets out in this essay to present the foundation of natural law in a conception of utility compatible with his view of man's nature and at the same time capable of providing the foundations of civil laws. He never once accepts classical natural right as the alternative to conventional right.

Locke says early in *Essay* VIII that:

> when we say that each man's private utility is not the basis of natural law, we do not wish to be understood to say that the common right of mankind and each man's private utility are opposed to one another, *for the greatest protection of each man's private property* is the law of nature, without the observance of which it is impossible for anybody to be master of his property and to pursue his own advantages. Hence it will be clear to anyone who rightly considers for himself the human race and the customs of men, that nothing contributes so much to the common benefit and utility of each and so effectively keeps men's possessions safe and secure as the observance of natural law.[81]

This important statement contains the main clues to the puzzles which surround this eighth essay. It is reasonable to assume that Locke is one of those who constitute "the more rational part of men," or one "who rightly considers for himself the human race and the customs of men."[82]

From the above one sees that *utility* plays some role in natural law, but not that private utility which permits each person the liberty to do what he himself, according to circumstances, judges to be of advantage to him. Locke continues: "You have certainly no reason for holding that each person's private utility is the standard of what is equitable and right unless you let every single person be judge in his own case and himself determine what is in his own interest; for no one can be a fair and just appraiser of another's convenience."[83]

The condition in which one has the right to be a judge in his own case is precisely the condition Locke describes in the *Two Trea-tises*[84] as the state of nature. It is the condition of unrestrained in-dividualism. The problem for Locke was how to bring radical in-dividuals into civil society without doing violence to the basic right of nature to be the judge of what is to the individual private advantage. By nature man is apolitical in the sense that by nature he has the right to determine what is to his benefit.

The main portion of *Essay* VIII consists of three arguments in response to the question which Locke says puts the problem suc-cinctly. That question is:

> Is it true that what each individual in the circumstances judges to be of advantage to himself and his affairs is in accordance with the law of nature, and on that account is not only permitted to him but also necessary, and that nothing in nature obliges except so far as it carries with it some immediate personal utility? [85]

Before proceeding to examine Locke's responses to this question, we must reflect on the question itself. It consists of three parts: first, whether whatever one judges to be to one's advantage is in ac-cordance with the law of nature. In other words, does the law of nature sanction at all times the radical selfish individualism of the state of nature? An affirmative response to this question implies that the law of nature is found simply in the fulfillment of one's private desires, i.e., that it is immediately and universally avail-able to all men through the satisfaction of their appetites. Such a proposition cannot be maintained, Locke implies here, and he ex-plicitly rejects it in the *Second Treatise*.[86] The law of nature is *not* simply the life according to our appetites; furthermore it is not known immediately by all men but only to those who have the capacity and who study human nature.

The second part of the question extends the first part but adds the important element of necessity or command. In other words, does the law of nature as understood in the first part of the ques-tion impose a command on each person to seek his private utility? If it does, then one must be reproved for *not* pursuing one's im-mediate private utility.

The third and final part of the question simply reverses the main point and implies that no man is under any obligation other than to seek his private utility. In other words, if something can be judged as to one's private utility then one is obliged to pursue it. If this were the proper understanding of the law of nature it would simply be what one judges to be to one's immediate advantages.

Locke's first response to this understanding of the law of nature is that it is not possible for something to be the foundation of the law of nature "which is not the foundation of the binding force of other, less universal, laws of the same nature."[87] Since there is ample evidence to show that people who have been called great and honourable have acted out of selfless generosity, the reverse of private utility can be said to be the foundation of the laws and actions of men.

In the second response Locke merely shows that it is humanly impossible to seek the private utility of all men because the human condition is one of limited resources. Indeed he says that "it is impossible for anyone to grow rich except at the expense of someone else."[88] If private utility were simply equated with the law of nature, Locke says, it would perpetuate the condition of war which exists in the state of nature. "What else indeed can human intercourse be than fraud, violence, hatred, robbery, murder, and such like, when every man not only may, but must, snatch from another by any and every means what the other in his turn is obliged to keep safe?"[89]

In the third and final response Locke argues that "it is not possible for that to be the foundation of the law of nature, which, once posited, all justice, friendship, and generosity are taken from life. For what kind of justice is there where neither personal property nor ownership exist, or what property where each may not only possess what is his, but that is his own whatever he possess because it is useful to him?"[90] Here he not only relates the law of nature to the possession of property, but also rejects the doctrine that the law of nature is simply equated with man's natural appetites and instincts. To pursue these would be to destroy the hope of peace and civil society. He insists that to live according to the dictates of one's natural appetites and desires is "contrary to reason, to human nature and to an honourable life."[91]

On the other hand, he says that to live in accordance with the law of nature gives rise to "peace, harmony, friendship, (impunity), security and possession of our property."[92] In other words, reason (which he says in the *Second Treatise* "*is* that law"[93]) dictates that a life in accordance with the natural appetites leads to self-destruction. Reason leads those who study human nature to conclude that if men seek the ingredients of happiness—those things bounded by peace and property—they will most assuredly attain their private utility. That is to say, by seeking the common utility one attains one's own utility. This is why Locke concludes that "the rightness of an action does not stem from its utility, but utility proceeds from its rightness."[94] So that, in the final analysis, private utility is indeed the end result of the law of nature.

Locke thus gives a qualified affirmative answer to the question posed in this essay: each person is the judge of what is to his advantage (directly in the state of nature, but only indirectly in civil society); he is under a necessity to pursue his private utility but only through pursuing the common utility; and, finally, he is under the obligation to seek his private utility. It is for these reasons that Locke said earlier that he did "not wish to be understood to say that the common right of mankind and each man's private utility are opposed to one another."

The law of nature of Locke is thus rooted in the command of nature to pursue the individual or private utility; but this is another way of saying that man is by nature commanded to preserve himself. Natural law turns the natural right to self-preservation into a command. But private utility cannot be obtained by each man's pursuing his own immediate private utility within civil society; it must be pursued by way of the common utility.

Thus does Locke bring the radical individuals of the primitive human condition into civil society but in doing so he does not do violence to man's radical (apolitical) individualism. Reason, which teaches men that they can establish a condition of peace through consenting to a political arrangement in which they can pursue their private utility, thus guides men out of the state of nature or the natural condition of war and rapine to a condition of peaceful accumulation and enjoyment of property—i.e., to a life of market hedonism.

The Market Hedonist

There is no doubt that for Locke man is driven by the desire for pleasure and the aversion to pain.[95] But this is not to be understood as a weakness—it is rather the source of man's productivity, of all his achievements. The restless pursuit of pleasure, or "uneasiness," is "the chief if not only spur to humane industry and action."[96] The role of government (since government is based on trust) is to provide the conditions in which man's "uneasiness" can flourish and thereby assist him toward greater progress. The role of the civil law is "to protect the lives, liberties, and possessions of those who live according to its laws."[97] And since the key to justice and injustice is property (i.e., "the right to anything"[98]) government must take care to protect that which is accumulated but can only do so without violation of man's possessive nature. The laws of the state must not violate that natural law which stems from man's radical individualism; they should, however, ameliorate the harshness of the competitive relations man has a right to even in civil society. After all, the only reason men compacted to enter into civil society was to pursue in peace the natural right to self-preservation (the "liberty" Locke refers to above), that is to say, to acquire possessions (understood as property and capital). The state or sovereign does not give these rights, nor has it any other function but to provide the circumstances in which the right can be exercised. Needless to say, undue restraint of the exercise of these rights to possession on the part of government is not tolerable.

On the question of virtue and vice, Locke says that they are determined by popular designation and are relative to peoples: "Virtue is everywhere that which is thought praiseworthy; and nothing else but that which has the allowance of public esteem is called virtue."[99] This formulation is clearly consistent with Epicurus' definitions of virtue and vice. In Locke's view virtue is therefore conventional and not by nature (as it was for Aristotle). Locke is affirming here that man's nature as such does not contain a conception of virtue as the perfection of his proper nature. Locke saw himself as one "skilled in nature or history of mankind."[100] And the study of nature and history shows, he says, that the quest for joy is the universal preoccupation of man—nature plants this sole motive force in him. And he defines joy as "the possession of some good which we have the power to use as we please."[101] But Locke explicitly rejects license ("A Liberty for everyone to do what he lists, to live as he pleases, and not to be tied by any laws"[102]) in favor of natural liberty. In the state of nature liberty allowed man "to be free from any Superior Power on Earth, and not to be under the Will or Legislative Authority of Man, but to have the Law of Nature for his Rule."[103] In civil society natural liberty consists of "a Liberty to follow my own Will in all things where the Rule prescribes not; and not to be subject to the inconstant, uncertain, unknown, Arbitrary Will of another Man. As *Freedom of Nature* is to be under no other restraint but the Law of Nature."[104] It is interesting to note that he says that "joy is a delight of the mind, from the consideration of the present or assured approaching possession of a good."[105] Nothing can assure the future possession of some good more certainly than money. Little wonder that Locke became the father of modern capitalism.

Locke is thus as much a hedonist as Hobbes and for both the state exists to serve man's hedonistic ambitions. Both start from the premiss that man is radically individualistic (i.e., by nature apolitical and an enemy of every person) and is driven by the desire for commodious self-preservation or pleasure; he enters civil society for the purpose of pursuing in peace the life of pleasure understood as the unlimited accumulation of goods. What has become known as the market economy emerges out of these premisses.

There is one important matter on which Hobbes and Locke disagree and that is the concept of the sovereign or sovereign power. In Hobbes, man's pride compels him to submit himself to the government[106] or sovereign control of *Leviathan*, king of the proud who rules with absolute power of life and death over his subjects.[107]

The sovereign makes no compact with his subjects but he is, says Hobbes, bound to obey certain laws of nature.[108] Furthermore, as we saw earlier, the subjects under *Leviathan* cannot change the form of government.[109] "And therefore they that are subjects to a monarch, cannot without his leave cast off monarchy, and return to the confusion of a disunited multitude; nor transfer their person from his that beareth it, to another man, or other assembly of men."[110] He defines injustice as the act by which one breaks one's convenant with the sovereign. Hobbes lists twelve aspects of the rights of supreme power of the sovereign.[111] The sovereign is bound only to provide the peaceful conditions. Hobbes adds that by safety or peaceful condition is "not meant a bare preservation, but also all other contentments of life, which every man by *lawful* industry, without danger, or hurt to the commonwealth, shall acquire to himself."[112]

For Hobbes the dissolution of the commonwealth and the subsequent return of all men to the wild condition of the state of nature "is the greatest evil that can happen in this life."[113] The sovereign is accordingly duty bound to prevent this from happening by ensuring that he is in full possession of all the power he needs to preserve the peace.[114]

In sum, Hobbes's sovereign is in every sense of the term absolute—with no human (or divine) authority above him. This contrasts strongly with Locke's conception of the civil sovereign. Locke thinks that Hobbes is not consistent when he grants such irrevocable power to the civil sovereign. Accordingly, he set out to render the concept of sovereignty compatible with the radical individualism of the human condition.

Locke's concept of sovereignty flows from his concept of the state of nature as a condition "not to be endured" and civil government as the proper remedy for the "inconveniences of the state of nature."[115] Furthermore, "the great and *chief end* therefore, of Mens uniting innto Commonwealths and putting themselves under Government *is the Preservation of their Property*."[116] Civil society is, as in Hobbes, designed to remedy these conditions of extreme danger and hardship. Men enter into civil society by way of a compact with one another and give all their power (that which they possess by right in the state of nature) "into the hands of the Community."[117] The civil legislature and executive powers are derived from the power each possesses in the state of nature. It is not created by the compact or given by the sovereign; it is given over by the individuals who possess it as a right in the state of nature. The prime objective is for the preservation and enlargement of property. In contradiction to Hobbes's doctrine of absolute sovereignty Locke says:

> Absolute Arbitrary Power, or Governing without *settled standing Laws*, can neither of them consist with the ends of Society and Government which Men would not quit the freedom of the state of Nature for, and tie themselves up under, were it not to preserve their Lives, Liberties, and Fortunes, and by *stated Rules* of Right and Property to secure their Peace and Quiet. It cannot be supposed that they should intend, had they a power so to do, to give to one or more *an absolute Arbitrary Power* over their Persons and Estates and put a force into the Magistrate's hand to execute his unlimited Will arbitrarily upon them.[118]

To do so would be "to put themselves into a worse condition than the state of Nature."[119] In the state of nature each man had at least the right to defend himself against the force of others; and all were equal in terms of force.

Starting as did Hobbes with the fundamental fact of the desire for individual self-preservation, Locke could not conclude (as did Hobbes) to the need of absolute power. Indeed, Locke saw it as a violation of the principle of individualism; to place one's right to self-preservation in the hands of absolute power would be equivalent to exchanging a harsh and intolerable state of nature for one not much better, and no rational creature could be supposed to have done that.[120]

Locke therefore subscribes to Hobbes's premisses but declines his conclusions as far as they relate to the character of civil government. Locke concludes to limited government based on consent of the governed; and he maintains that this conclusion is in keeping with the basic facts of man's natural, prepolitical condition.

Once civil society is entered into, says Locke, it assumes a nature and life of its own with a single purpose: "the preservation of the Community."[121] And it is governed by "the *first and fundamental natural Law*, which is to govern even the Legislative it self, is *the preservation of the Society* and (as far as will consist with the publick good) of every person in it."[122] This in turn means that those who contracted to enter into civil society must be committed to the preservation of the "peaceful and quiet" condition which conduces to the preservation and accumulation of property. Locke also says that the contract is irrevocable as long as the government survives. A citizen is "perpetually and indispensibly obliged to be and remain unalterably a Subject to it, and can never be again in the liberty of the state of Nature."[123]

Both Hobbes and Locke required unanimous consent to hand over all rights to the civil society; and both left to the majority the choice of the form of government. The difference between them, however, is that Hobbes made that choice a one-time, forever-binding, choice (so that the sovereignty of civil society was handed over to a self-perpetuating sovereign government body or person). Locke, on the other hand, left the sovereign civil society free to choose, by any future shifting majority, what governmental body should have fiduciary powers *pro tempore*. Locke explains the matter in the following way: "For when any number of Men have, by the consent of every individual, made a Community, they have thereby made that Community one Body, with a Power to Act as one Body, which is only by the will and determination of *majority*."[124] The reason for this is implicit in the use of the term "body" for the community. As no body can respond at the same time to conflicting commands, neither can the civil body respond if it is the victim of a divided command. Furthermore, since it is unreasonable to expect that a political community could always function in unanimity there must be found a way of continuing in those circumstances where a unanimous decision is not forthcoming. The solution is majority rule, which Locke feels is a reasonable approximation of unanimous rule. Furthermore, the majority command the allegiance of the entire community and not just the consenting (majority) part.

But Locke's doctrine of majority rule is far more complex than one is led to believe at first sight. An attentive reading of the *Second Treatise* reveals that Locke teaches that the majority will rule because it is the "greater force" in the community. But what of those times in a political community where a minority is in fact the greater force? Locke tends to imply that the minority will command the entire community.[125] But at the decisive early point when the community establishes a form of government—i.e., the specific moment in which legislature and executive power is to be exercised—then the majority has a decisive role to play; it is in such circumstances "the greatest force." And since as Locke says "the *first and fundamental positive Law* of all Commonwealths *is the establishing of the Legislative Power*,"[126] this initial act is crucial to the future of the community. At the founding period the simple majority determines the character and structure of the constitution.[127] The majority can and must decide whether to establish a monarchy,[128] by consigning the legislative power to one man; a democracy, by reserving the legislative power to the people; or an oligarchy, by entrusting the legislative powers to the few wealthy men. Unlike Hobbes, however, the legislative powers of government are not absolute but *fiduciary*.[129] They are given by the people to the government in trust for the purpose of preserving themselves and acquiring property in peace. This follows from the fact that men cannot give up their right of self-preservation. Furthermore, according to Locke the government once chosen exercises "supreme" and "sacred" power in unalterable hands.[130] This is to ensure against the idea (which worried Hobbes) that men might think it implies the right to alter the form of government from time to time at will. Despite Locke's insistence that government is rooted in consent it does not follow that this implies a ready rule or prescription for civil disobedience. Locke conceded a right of revolution (unlike Hobbes, who considers it a "disease") but he was not unmindful that such a right (which follows from the individual inalienable right of self-preservation) can be exercised only in the most extreme circumstances where life has become so intolerable as to make a return to the state of nature (which is what revolution does) more desirable. But Locke seems to say that such circumstances can only come about as a result of the default of a king. "When a King has Dethron'd himself, and put himself in a state of War with his People, what shall hinder them from prosecuting him who is no King, as they would any other Man, who has put himself into a state of War with them."[131] The clear implication is that the king alone can render the right of revolution appropriate by first violating his commitment to the natural law to preserve the community in peace and quiet. There is reason to believe that Locke did not believe that anything short of this abdication could justify the appeal to the right to revolution because it is a right (to self-preservation) one cannot give up. Since the abdication of rule is a declaration of war then each one must rise up against the king "as they would against any other man." That is to say, in "dethroning himself" the king ceases to be king—he is just another man who is threatening members of the community. Short of this condition of extreme oppression the people still do not have the right to rebel. Furthermore, Locke makes it clear that one who foments revolution is "guilty of the greatest Crime, I think, a Man is capable of."[132] He thus firmly closes the door to popular revolution.

One other area where Locke parts company with Hobbes is in the division or separation of powers. Locke tended to be more fearful of the possibility of abuse of political power than was Hobbes. He says that the powers of government must be separated "because it may be too great a temptation to human frailty apt to grasp at Power, for the same Persons who have the Power of making Laws, to have also in their hands the powers to execute them."[133] Locke thus distinguishes only two main powers—legislative and executive. He implies throughout that the judicial function is a proper part of the legislative function. The separation of the executive and legislative powers is consistent with his fear that power can be accumulated into one set of hands and thus become a threat to self-preservation.

Despite Locke's apparent insistence on legislative supremacy, he teaches that the executive may and indeed must under certain circumstances "act according to discretion, for the publick good, without the prescription of the Law, and sometimes even against it."[134] By positing such a prerogative power to wise or "godlike" princes, Locke makes room for the approximation of absolute monarchy; but since such princes cannot be assured at all times it is important to establish a government with a structure (separation of executive and legislative powers) so that it will be possible for the people through the legislative branch to control a prince who is not-so-wise or not-so-godlike. But Locke says explicitly that "a good Prince, who is mindful of the trust put into his hands and careful of the good of his People, cannot have too much Prerogative."[135] Locke's chief executive is thus strong and energetic.

CONCLUSION

Plato and Aristotle (and Aquinas) had taught that nature contains the standard of personal and public virtue, magnanimity and justice, and that both private and public morality were to be judged by reference to this transcendent and universal norm, not standards established by custom or consent. In other words, nature ($\phi\acute{\upsilon}\sigma\iota\varsigma$) was to give direction to custom ($\nu\acute{o}\mu\sigma\varsigma$) and rule over it. Hobbes begins *Leviathan* with the word *Nature* and makes it clear that he believes that the Socratic tradition was correct to the extent that nature provides the clue to personal and public morality. But Hobbes looked at man in his prepolitical condition and saw that by nature he was a hostile animal at war with his fellows. Hobbes taught that the true nature of man uncovered by the new natural philosophy reveals man to be a being who is pushed from behind by drives, the chief one being *fear*. Hobbes thus effected the triumph of νόμος over φύσις by the skillful redefinition of φύσις.

With this as the foundation, Hobbes enunciated a new natural law—one devoid of all theological content as in Thomas Aquinas and one which took full cognizance of man's selfish or individualistic nature. On the authority of this new natural law Hobbes conceived a political philosophy of absolute monarchy.

John Locke accepted the basic premisses of Hobbes's assessment of human nature but believed that his fear of civil war led him to do violence to his principles and so Locke set out to correct Hobbes's conclusions especially as they related to the structure and workings of governments. Locke's civil society is governed by a more benign sovereign (one person or several) but it is far from being an open democratic regime. In the final analysis Locke's regime is almost as tough, almost as rigidly ruled as is Hobbes's.

Despite their differences as to the degree of autocracy the regime could sustain and still honor the right to self-preservation, both Hobbes and Locke conceive of man as by nature a hedonistic individual. The only way one can get a community of men who are radically individualistic (i.e., pursuing their own goods understood as pleasures) to cooperate is by consent; but the consent could only be given on the understanding that it would provide the conditions in which they could pursue their ambitions in peace. According to Locke, the competition of the market economy is entirely appropriate to man's natural individualistic hedonism; it is not an arbitrary superimposition but flows from his competitive nature.

It is instructive to dwell on Hobbes's and Locke's refinement of Epicureanism. Epicurus apparently counseled that his disciples flee politics because it was a source of pain (anxiety). It had been widely believed that it was impossible to construct a political philosophy on such apolitical premises. But Hobbes and Locke did precisely that by showing that the continuation of the prepolitical condition was undesirable because it would perpetuate the condition of outright hostility. The positive side of their argument was that political union or civil society constitutionally constructed and maintained in recognition of the basic individualism would redound to the good of all better than the continuation of the state of nature. Indeed one can say that, according to Hobbes, nature properly understood requires that men unite into civil society without which no man could enjoy even a minimum of pleasure.

In asserting that *the* fundamental desire for self-preservation was a right of nature Hobbes and Locke went an important step beyond Epicurus; they constructed a natural-law doctrine on the foundations of this natural right. In other words, they not only acknowledged the fact of man's basic hedonism, they elevated its pursuit to the level of an "unalienable" right. The duty of the sovereign is, according to Hobbes, no longer "to make the citizens good and doers of noble things" but to "study as much as by laws can be effected, to furnish the citizens abundantly with all good things . . . which are conducive to delectation."[136]

And so with Hobbes and Locke—the two great founders of modern political philosophy—we see the principles of hedonism become the foundations of Western political life. Where Gassendi and Bernier and Charleton failed, Hobbes and Locke succeeded. But those proponents of Epicureanism failed because they did not do what Hobbes and Locke saw as necessary: the need to effect the replacement of the Socratic tradition on a foundation that would meet every major teaching of that tradition. The new concept of nature replaced the old—as the new organon replaced the old; the new natural law replaced the old natural law; and the new polity replaced the old—as the *New Atlantis* replaced in theory the old theoretical formulation of the *Republic*. By lowering their sights and by identifying a principle in all men which no man could deny (i.e., the desire for self-preservation), Hobbes and Locke succeeded where others had failed.

But our understanding of the unfolding of this great philosophic drama remains incomplete until we understand how Jean-Jacques Rousseau reacted against the new philosophies of Hobbes and Locke. We must accordingly see how Rousseau modified the basic premisses of his predecessors without abandoning the central commitment to hedonism.

NOTES

1. C. B. Macpherson, *The Political Theory of Possessive Individualism* (Oxford: Clarendon Press, 1962).

2. Leo Strauss, *Natural Right and History* (Chicago: The University of Chicago Press, 1953), p. 169. See M. Guyau, *La Morale d'Epicure et ses rapports avec les doctrines contemporaines* (Paris, 1878).

3. "Dr. Strauss on Hobbes," *Politica* 2 (1937), 379.

4. For a good but brief discussion of Hobbes and Epicureanism, see James H. Nichols, Jr., *Epicurean Political Philosophy*.

5. Strauss, *op. cit.*, p. 169.

6. *The Prince*, Chapter XV.

7. See Howard White, *Peace Among the Willows* (The Hague: Nijhoff, 1968).

8. For an account of this controversy, see Thomas A. Spragens, *The Politics of Motion: The World of Thomas Hobbes* (London: Croom Helm, 1973), and Leo Strauss, *The Political Philosophy of Hobbes* (Oxford: Clarendon Press, 1936).

9. *De Corpore, English Works of Thomas Hobbes*, ed. Sir William Molesworth, 11 Vols. (London, 1839), I, ix.

10. Spragens, *op. cit.*, p. 167.

11. Ibid. He calls it "eviscerated Aristotelian cosmology," p. 176.

12. Ibid., p. 194.

13. *Leviathan*, Ch. VI, pp. 32–33; *Elements of Law*, Ch. VII, pp. 28–29 (Tönnies ed.).

14. See Strauss, *op. cit.*, pp. 169–70.

15. As Nichols says: "Hobbes seems to regard the Epicurean aim of fully expelling the fear of death (and therewith all other fears) as impossible; certainly, his political teaching requires what Lucretius seems to admit, that most men will always remain fearful of death." *Op. cit.*, p. 187.

16. See *Leviathan*, Part II, Ch. XX, pp. 129–36.

17. *Leviathan*, Pt. I, Ch. XI, edited with an introduction by Michael Oakeshott (Oxford: Blackwell, 1960), p. 63.

18. Ibid., pp. 63–64.

19. Ibid., p. 32. On the right to the end implying the right to the means, see *Elements*, p. 72, "Reaction."

20. *Elements*, p. 71.

21. *De Cive*, I, 2, 5, 7; XII, 4–6; *Leviathan*, XI, pp. 63–64; and XIII end; *De Corpore*, I, 6.

22. *Leviathan*, Pt. IV, Ch. 46, p. 446.

23. *Leviathan*, Pt. IV, Ch. 46, p. 446. Italics added.

24. *Elements*, p. 75.

25. Ibid., p. 72.

26. Ibid., p. 71.

27. Ibid., p. 72.

28. Ibid., p. 30.

29. Ibid.

30. *Leviathan*, Pt. I, Ch. X, p. 56.

31. *Elements*, p. 94.

32. Ibid.

33. Ibid.

34. Ibid.

35. Ibid., p. 104.

36. *Leviathan*, Pt. III, Ch. XXXII, p. 242.

37. C. B. Macpherson, "The Deceptive Task of Political Theory," *Cambridge Journal*, 7 (1954), 560–68.

38. Ibid., p. 564. See also *The Political Theory of Possessive Individualism*.

39. Macpherson, *Political Theory of Possessive Individualism*, p. 272.

40. Macpherson speaks of the "penetrating analysis of human nature which had been produced by the society they [Hobbes and Locke] knew." "The Deceptive Task of Political Theory," *loc. cit.*, p. 567. He also speaks of the liberal tradition "from Hobbes through Locke, Hume, Burke and Bentham" as being "based on postulates of human nature which, within the limits of the then bourgeois vision, were profound." Ibid., p. 563.

41. Ibid.

42. Macpherson informs me that although he did not use the term, he believes the modern liberal tradition to be hedonistic. Letter to the author, 6 April 1978.

43. Richard Cox, *Locke on War and Peace* (London: Oxford University Press, 1964).

44. *Essays Concerning Human Understanding* Bk. II, Ch. 20, "Of the Modes of Pleasure and Pain" 2nd ed. (London, 1694), p. 121. See also "Pleasure and Pain: The Passions," Lovelace MS, Locke fol. 1.

45. Ibid. See Edward A. Driscoll, "The Influence of Gassendi on Locke's Hedonism," *International Philosophical Quarterly*, 12 (1972), 87–110.

46. Lovelace MS, Locke c.28. The first two have been published: *Locke Newsletter*, 5 (Summer 1974).

47. See the Christian view in Matthew 5:46–48.

48. Lovelace MS, Locke c.28, fol. 149. The manuscript contains as an alternative for "Appointment of an Intelligent Being," etc., the following expression: "intervention of the will of an intelligent free agent."

49. Ibid., fol. 152.

50. See *The Reasonableness of Christianity*, pp. 139, 142–43, 149. *Works of John Locke in Nine Volumes* (1924), Vol. VI.

51. John Locke, *Essays on the Law of Nature*, edited with a translation by W.

von Leyden (Oxford: Clarendon Press, 1954), pp. 3, 135. On many occasions I have departed from von Leyden's translation of the Latin text in the interest of a more literal rendering.

52. Ibid., p. 189. See also earlier in *Essay* VI.

53. *Reasonableness of Christianity*, p. 143. See also Strauss, *op. cit.*, pp. 109ff.

54. *Essays on the Law of Nature, Essay* VI, p. 182.

55. Leyden, *op. cit.*, II, p. 123.

56. Ibid., pp. 130–31.

57. Ibid.; italics added.

58. See Leo Strauss, *Natural Right and History*, pp. 204–205; see also, for a good discussion of Aquinas' natural law, Harry V. Jaffa, *Thomism and Aristotelianism* (Chicago: The University of Chicago Press, 1952), p. 175.

59. The epistemological doctrine contained in these two essays is clearly compatible with Locke's major philosophical work, *The Essay Concerning Human Understanding.*

60. *Essays on the Law of Nature*, p. 132.

61. Ibid., pp. 134–35.

62. Ibid.

63. Ibid., p. 149.

64. Ibid.

65. Ibid., p. 151.

66. Ibid., p. 153.

67. Ibid., pp. 154–55.

68. Ibid.

69. Ibid., p. 157.

70. Ibid., p. 151.

71. Ibid., p. 154.

72. Ibid., p. 157.

73. Ibid.

74. *Summa theologica*, Ia–IIae, qu. 94, art. 2; *Basic Works*, ed. Anton Pegis (New York: Random House, 1945).

75. Ibid., see also D. J. O'Connor, *Aquinas and Natural Law* (London: Macmillan, 1967).

76. *Essay* II, p. 157.

77. Ibid.

78. *Essay* I, p. 119.

79. See W. von Leyden, "John Locke and Natural Law," *Philosophy*, 31 (1956), 26.

80. See *Second Treatise*, Ch. II, sec. 12 end; and Ch. V, sec. 31, *Two Treatises of Government*, with introduction and notes by Peter Laslett (Toronto: New American Library of Canada, 1965).

81. *Essay* VIII, pp. 206–207; italics added.

82. Ibid., pp. 204–205.

83. Ibid., p. 207.

84. *Second Treatise*, Ch. III, No. 19.

85. *Essay* VIII p. 207.

86. Ibid., No. 12 and No. 124.

87. *Essay* VIII, pp. 206–207.

88. Ibid., pp. 210–11.

89. Ibid., pp. 212–13.

90. Ibid.

91. Ibid., p. 215.

92. Ibid.; "Impunitas" is not found in MS A but is written above the line in MS B; see also *Second Treatise*, Chs. II and VI.

93. *Second Treatise*, Ch. II, No. 6.

94. *Essay* VIII, p. 215.

95. *Essay Concerning Human Understanding*, 2nd ed. (London, 1694), Bk. II, Ch. XX, p. 144.

96. Ibid., p. 122.

97. Ibid., Ch. XXIX.9, p. 202.

98. Ibid., Bk. IV, Ch. III.18, p. 277.

99. Ibid., Bk. II, Ch. XXVIII.11, p. 203.

100. Ibid., Bk. II, Ch. XX, p. 122.

101. Ibid.

102. *Second Treatise*, Ch. IV, No. 22. This is Filmer's definition of freedom.

103. Ibid.

104. Ibid.

105. *Essay Concerning Human Understanding*, Bk. II, Ch. XX, p. 122.

106. *Leviathan*, Pt. II, Ch. XXVIII, p. 209.

107. Ibid., Ch. XVIII, p. 113.

108. Ibid., Ch. XXVIII, p. 209.

109. Ibid., Ch. XVIII, p. 113.

110. Ibid.

111. Ibid., pp. 113–18.

112. Ibid., Ch. XXX, p. 219.

113. Ibid.

114. Ibid., Ch. XXIX, p. 210.

115. *Second Treatise*, No. 13.

116. Ibid., No. 124.

117. Ibid., No. 87.

118. Ibid., No. 137.

119. Ibid.

120. Ibid., No. 131.

121. Ibid., No. 149.

122. Ibid., No. 134.

123. Ibid., No. 121.

124. Ibid., No. 96.

125. See Willmore Kendall, *John Locke and the Doctrine of Majority Rule,* 2nd ed. (Urbana: University of Illinois Press, 1959).

126. *Second Treatise,* No. 135.

127. Ibid., Ch. X, No. 132. "The Majority, having . . . upon Mens first uniting into Society, the whole power of the Community, naturally in them, may imploy all that power in making Laws for the Community from time to time, and Executing those Laws by Officers of their own appointing; and then the Form of the Government is a perfect Democracy."

128. See Ch. VIII, No. 95, No. 96, No. 97.

129. Ibid., Ch. XIII, No. 149.

130. Ibid., No. 134.

131. Ibid., No. 239.

132. Ibid., No. 230.

133. Ibid., No. 143.

134. Ibid., No. 160.

133. Ibid., No. 143.

136. *De Cive,* I, 2, 5, 7; XIII, 4–6; *Leviathan,* Ch. XI; Ch. XIII; *De Corpore,* I, 6.

4

Jean-Jacques Rousseau: The Sublime Hedonist of Modernity

ROUSSEAU CONSCIOUSLY SET OUT to redirect modern political philosophy away from the course it was beginning to assume under the guidance of Hobbes and Locke. He saw them as the chief proponents of economic hedonism or the "selfish system" which did nothing to liberate men from the enslaving consequences of their own Enlightenment. He began by attempting to re-establish the direction of modern political philosophy by beginning at the foundation of modernity, i.e., by a reassessment of man in the state of nature. Furthermore, he wished to re-establish the place of virtue in political life by a re-examination of the premises of modernity. "The ancient politicians spoke unceasingly of manners and virtue; ours speak of nothing but trade and money," he lamented.[1] He saw that the root of the problem was in a fundamental error committed by Hobbes. However wisely Hobbes began with man in the state of nature, he believed that Rousseau did not go back far enough. His portrayal of man in the state of nature as bestial was correct, Rousseau asserted, but only of man in the final or late stage of the state of nature. In the "pure state of nature" man was not hostile or selfish; it is this earlier stage which must be accepted as the starting point, this point from which all else follows.

Those who fail to understand the paradoxical character of Rousseau's thought and the paradoxical manner in which he expresses it will have difficulty extracting his complete message. Rousseau alludes to the paradoxical character of his writing on several occasions, and in one place writes of the need "to reconcile these apparent contradictions."[2] One such apparent contradiction was his claim that in the state of nature men are "good" but not "virtuous"; another is his claim that savage man is more natural than civilized man—i.e., that the sub-human is more human than the civilized. And again, that man must be forced to be free in civil society. The final paradox could be said to be his claim that while man in the *pure* state of nature sets the norm and is the means by which life in civil society can be legitimated, man must never return to the state of nature. Put another way: civil society (politics) is not natural to man and brings those luxuries (wants and aspirations) which lead to his weakening and decline, yet man must never leave the civil state. In short, Rousseau's philosophy is an enlightened attack upon the Enlightenment in the interest of rescuing men from its consequences.

But Rousseau did not choose the paradoxical expression merely as a literary device. For him it reflected reality—the human condition is itself paradoxical—man and the citizen could not be easily reconciled for Rousseau because man is by nature apolitical; man has become politicized and hence is in need of equipment which will help him survive in civil society. In other words, Rousseau began by acknowledging the *de facto* paradox of the human condition and attempted to find a practical solution. He appears to have believed that philosophically the paradoxical condition was insoluble. But he attempted to show how the paradox could be reconciled in the practical political order with as little violence as possible to man's true nature; in this he parts company with Epicurus.

Rousseau's thought is cast in the context of nature *versus* convention, and he argues for nature as the norm by which the legitimate conventional (or artificial) order must be maintained. And since modern political philosophy was founded on the doctrine of natural right derived from man's natural prepolitical condition—called the state of nature—Rousseau focused his attention on that point. His fullest account of this subject appears in his *Discourse on the Origin and Foundations of Inequality Among Men.*[3] In this treatise Rousseau ponders "the real foundations of human society."[4] Leaving aside all scientific books and "meditating on the first and simplest operations of the human soul," he says, "I believe I perceive in it two principles anterior to reason."[5] Those two principles are individual *self-preservation* and *compassion* for our species. In opposition to Hobbes and Locke he claims that there is no need to introduce a notion of sociability in order to explain how men came to live in civil society. "It is from the conjunction and combination that our mind is able to make of these two principles, without sociability, that all the rules of natural right appear to me to flow; rules which reason is later forced to re-establish upon other foundations when, by its successive developments, it has succeeded in stifling nature."[6]

His major criticism of Hobbes's portrayal of the state of nature is that Hobbes mistook the advanced condition of men in that state—where they had developed their passions and already acquired some property and possessiveness—as the true state of nature. He is especially critical of Hobbes's suggestion that men in the state of nature decided to join forces and leave the state of nature. Such a proposition, he contends, "means precisely that men must have used, for the establishment of society, enlightenment which only develops with great difficulty and in very few people in the midst of society itself."[7] Hobbes and Locke would make men philosophers before they became truly men, Rousseau contends. Furthermore, he claims that despite the efforts of those philosophers who have had recourse to man's prepolitical condition "none of them has reached it."[8] It is clear that Rousseau believed that he was the first to arrive at a correct view of man in that state.

Not surprisingly, Rousseau also rejects the natural law doctrine of Hobbes and Locke with the claim that "for it to be law, not only must the will of him who is bound by it be able to submit to it with knowledge, but also, for it to be natural, it must speak directly by nature's voice."[9] Since man in the state of nature is incapable of willing with understanding, and since nature does not speak by way of reason but by passion, there cannot have been a natural law as suggested by Hobbes and Locke.

When one goes back to the earliest time, to man in the "pure state of nature,"[10] one finds "savage man" whose "self-preservation is almost his only care."[11] Rousseau comes close to concluding, as did Hobbes, that man's earliest preoccupation or passion was for self-preservation. But he says explicitly that it is "almost" his only concern. Despite the importance of self-preservation, says Rousseau, what distinguishes man from other animals is his *freedom*.

> In every animal I see only an ingenious machine to which nature has given sense in order to revitalize itself and guarantee itself, to a certain point, from all that tends to destroy or upset it. I perceive precisely the same things in the human machine with the difference that nature alone does everything in the operations of a beast, whereas man contributes to his operations by being a free agent. The former chooses or rejects by instinct and the latter by an act of freedom, so that a beast cannot deviate from the rule that is prescribed to it even when it would be advantageous for it to do so, and a man deviates from it often to his detriment.[12]

Man's natural freedom is thus a mixed blessing from the very beginning. It is the metaphysical basis of the paradox of the human condition. As Rousseau says: "Thus dissolute men abandon themselves to excesses which cause them fever and death, because the mind depraves the senses and because the will still speaks when nature is silent."[13] This summation is close to the picture of the natural man painted by Hobbes; it shows how close Rousseau was to Hobbes's views—at least in the late state of nature.

But one begins to see from this picture that man is his own worst enemy; he contains within himself the seeds of his own degeneration. Paradoxically, his highest and most prized possession—his freedom—is the source of his eventual decline or enslavement which leads to the permanent enslavement of the human species. His freedom—i.e., his ability to will—stifles the passions. In time, man's will leads his passsions into greater and greater trouble. As Rousseau says: "To will and not to will, to desire and fear will be the first and almost the only operation of his soul until the new circumstances cause new developments in it."[14] It is those "new circumstances" which cause man in the state of nature to move further away from his original condition toward civil society. As Rousseau says,

> this period of the development of human faculties, maintaining a golden mean between the indolence of the primitive state and the petulant activity of our vanity, must have been the happiest and most

durable epoch. The more one thinks about it, the more one finds that this state was the least subject to revolutions, the best for man, and that he must have come out of it only by some fatal accident, which for the common good ought never to have happened. . . . all subsequent progress has been in appearance so many steps toward the perfection of the individual, and in fact toward the decrepitude of the species.[15]

"Accidental necessity" or "fatal necessity" brought man out of the pure state of nature—the increase in population[16] and the subsequent scarcity of resources prompted man to look around for means to protect himself and his possessions. The newly established groups of families eventually acquired "many kinds of commodities unknown to their fathers; and that was the first yoke they imposed on themselves without thinking about it, and the first source of evils they prepared for their descendants."[17] The route from the pure state of nature where man enjoyed the sweet sentiment of his own existence and the rise of civil society was one on which man accumulated habits and passions which were destined to play a part in his eventual enslavement. The quality which made one "most highly considered" in the eyes of others was "the first step towards inequality and, at the same time, vice."[18] This vanity led to the savage hostility which Hobbes misunderstood as the state of nature. Contrary to Hobbes, Rousseau says that "nothing is so gentle as man in his primitive state when placed by nature at equal distances from the stupidity of brutes and the fatal enlightenment of civil man."[19]

Gradually man began to require the assistance of other men, and this led to the introduction of property among men. "The first person who, having fenced off a plot of ground, took it into his head to say *this is mine* and found people simple enough to believe him, was the true founder of civil society."[20] The intense rivalry which followed the acquisition of property made civil society inevitable *and* desirable. Rousseau depicts the state of affairs just prior to man's entry into civil society in the following terms: "Thus the usurpations of the rich, the brigandage of the poor, the unbridled passions of all, stifling natural pity and the as yet weak voice of justice, made man avaricious, ambitious and evil. . . . Nascent society gave way to the most horrible state of war; the human race, debased and desolated, no longer able to turn back or renounce the unhappy acquisitions it had made, and working only toward its shame by abusing the faculties that honor it, brought itself to the brink of its ruin."[21] In short, man reached the point of no return; he developed passions which render laws necessary and hence civil society desirable. The tension in the human condition is therefore between natural man and the life in the political community; it is a tension between *nature* and *convention*. For Rousseau saw that man could not long survive in this last stage of the state of nature: man had indeed become a wolf to other men. When the condition of the state of nature becomes intolerable men enter into a social contract to form a civil society. And, as Rousseau relates,

> the establishment of the body politic as a true contract between the people and the chiefs it chooses for itself: a contract by which the two parties obligate themselves to observe laws that are stipulated in it and that form the bonds of their union. The people having, on the subject of social relations, united all their wills into a single one [i.e., will], all the articles on which this will is explicit become so many fundamental laws obligating all members of the state without exception, and one of these laws regulates the choice and power of magistrates charged with watching over the execution of the others. This power extends to everything that can maintain the constitution, without going so far as to change it.[22]

Here in outline we find all the ingredients of the political state detailed later in the *Social Contract*.

We observe first that, like Hobbes, Rousseau believed that the contract was based on the unanimous consent of the people. But since man cannot give away his inalienable right to life and freedom he cannot give supreme or sovereign power to anyone—the people always retain the sovereign power. Above all they unite all their wills into a single one—the general will. And since the state is a person (as it is in Hobbes), it cannot have more than one will; therefore sovereignty is indivisible. And as the people give the basic law to themselves, they obey themselves in obeying the general will.

In thus depicting man's relation to one another in the civil state Rousseau remains more faithful to the basic individualism than does Hobbes. He explicitly rejects Hobbes's claim that men may appeal to the natural right of self-preservation within civil society.

But since Rousseau believed that most men were incapable of recognizing what is in their best interests, he suggests that a legislator be appointed. As Rousseau says: "The discovery of the best rules of society suited to nations would require a superior intelligence, who saw all of men's passions yet experienced none of them; who had no relationship at all to our nature yet knew it thoroughly; whose happiness was independent of us, yet who was nevertheless willing to attend to ours; finally, one who, preparing for himself a future glory with the passage of time, could work in one century and enjoy the reward in another."[23]

In addition to the extraordinary difficulties of finding such a person, there are even greater difficulties in finding a people with the right qualities of character. "What makes the work of legislation difficult is not so much what must be established as what must be destroyed. And what makes success so rare is the impossibility of finding the simplicity of nature together with the needs of society."[24] Rousseau concludes, however, that all "these conditions . . . are hard to find together." As a result "one sees few well-constituted states."[25] Rousseau thus clearly believed that not many genuinely free states would ever exist on earth.

But what is intriguing about this matter is that Rousseau appears to place less difficulty in finding a legislator, that "extraordinary man," that person who "can win over without violence and persuade without convincing,"[26] than he does in finding a suitable people. The reason would appear to be that Rousseau himself through the power of his writings is such a legislator. Those wise men of capacity who understand him can make use of his "superior intelligence" and establish a genuine free government, given the right condition of the people.

Rousseau's new political community is ruled over by magistrates who oblige themselves to maintain according to the will of the constituents "each one in the peaceable enjoyment of what belongs to him, and to prefer on all occasions the public utility to his own interest."[27] This is what Rousseau set out to do—i.e., *legitimize* life within civil society—and to legitimize is to place property and the relations of citizens within the context of a legal order; that legal order specifies the terms and conditions of the transfer and accumulation of possessions. It is the basis of justice and one is just if one lives by that order.

Rousseau is at pains to discredit the power of reason to maintain public or civil order. Mankind would not have survived as well as it has, he says, had it been abandoned to the control of reason. Above all, it was not reason which led men to form civil society— it was the unfortunate accumulation of needs which he acquired en route from the pure state of nature. It must be clearly understood, however, that by the accumulation of needs Rousseau means the expansion of man's passionate nature into new and unnecessary directions. This expansion or development of his passionate nature led man to become the warlike beast that Hobbes mistook as man in the state of nature. But Rousseau makes it clear that it is this selfish beast who enters into civil society. The major political problem becomes therefore how to establish the legitimate relations of these men once they enter civil society. In other words, despite the fact that man in his purely natural condition is a mild and harmless fellow, by the time he enters civil society he is a dangerous warlike animal—this is the material with which the founders of states have to work. And since man in his pure condition is ruled by nature, nature must be the source of his relationships in the degenerate and artificial (or conventional) condition known as civil society. To make matters worse, in one sense, man cannot ever recapture his pure natural condition; the best he can hope for is a civil order which approximates the order nature would justify. But Rousseau makes it clear that civil society is intended to serve only the ends of protection of life and possessions. Despite his efforts to reestablish virtue, Rousseau does not say that nature implants a specific human end. Man has no final end or perfection; he is infinitely perfectible, he can become whatever he wishes to become. This flows from his fundamental freedom. Unlike Aristotle who taught that man was by nature destined for the life of moral virtue— magnanimity and justice—for Rousseau the highest virtue was the virtue of patriotism—i.e., obedience to the laws one has given to oneself in the democratic state. There are no avenues of trans- political appeal, neither theological nor philosophical. He is even more emphatic on this matter than was Hobbes. There is not even a right to revolution in Rousseau as there is in Locke.

There is one major exception to Rousseau's rule that all men in civil society are circumscribed by the horizon of the state. That exception is reserved for men like Rousseau himself; those pas- sionate souls who live on the periphery of civil society: in it but not of it; those who, like Rousseau, can appreciate through their re- fined passionate natures the sweet sentiment of existence; those who have the sensitivity to seek the repose or revery of the solitary dreamer, to drift in a boat in mid-lake, savoring the sweetness of the experience of simple existence. These men, these artists or poets—extremely few in number—are invited to seek solace in solitary retreat and appear to occupy a place of supreme importance in Rousseau's scheme of things. For "les hommes vulgaires" are consigned to a life-long struggle to extricate themselves from the tyranny of the passions. But it is only through the passions that this tyranny can be subjugated. The desire for pleasure under the guidance of reason is the passion which nature places at all men's disposal. As Rousseau says in the *Second Discourse*, "human un- derstanding owes much to the passions, which by common agree- ment also owe much to it. It is by their activity that our reason is perfected; we seek to know only because we desire to have pleas- ure; and it is impossible to conceive why one who had neither desires nor fears would go to the trouble of reasoning. The pas- sions in turn derive their origin from our needs, and their progress from our knowledge."[28]

Rousseau's most explicit thoughts on hedonism appear at the end of Book IV of *Emile*, after, that is, the Savoyard Vicar has presented his unorthodox theology. What is peculiar to these con-

cluding pages of Book IV is the fact that Rousseau speaks directly
in his own name and to the reader, not to Emile.[29] He begins by
showing that a rich man in order to acquire his wealth would in
the process have acquired insolence and unnatural needs. Rousseau
claims that were he a rich man he would use his wealth to purchase
leisure, freedom, and health: "but health can only be bought by
temperance, and as there is no real pleasure in life without health,
I should be temperate out of sensuality."[30]

Rousseau proceeds to propose to the reader a refined hedonism
rooted in nature. "I should also keep as close as possible to nature,
to gratify the senses given me by nature, being convinced that, the
greater her share in my pleasure, the more real I shall find them."[31]
He says that he would seek (if a rich man) a variety of pleasures
but "always in nature."[32] Indeed he would be "so busy with pleasure that [he would] have no time to waste."[33]

In short, Rousseau counsels that one should accommodate one's
quest for pleasure to one's social status as well as to one's age.[34]
But while some pleasures are unnatural, others are natural.[35] The
unnatural pleasures are those which men are prompted to seek
(such as debauchery) as a consequence of the dominance of *amour-
propre* (selfishness) and the unnatural wants acquired in civil society. The unnatural or "fancied" pleasures "rest on popular opinion, and popular opinion at its worst."[36] To seek popular approval
is to live outside of oneself. The natural or "true pleasures" are
those such as love and honor, which arise out of the genuine natural needs prompted by *amour de soi* (love of self).

The determination to exclude other people from the enjoyment
of natural pleasures is, claims Rousseau, a consequence of "demon
property."[37] "True amusements are those which we share with
the people."[38] These true pleasures are available at every level of
the social scale and at all times. "Pleasure is ours when we want it;
it is opinion alone which makes everything difficult and drives
happiness before us. . . . Whoever enjoys health and does not lack
the [basic] necessities is rich enough, if he will but get rid of his
opinions."[39]

Rousseau concludes his reflections on hedonism with the claim that "Emile does not know this better than I, but his heart is purer and more healthy, so he will feel it more strongly, and all that he has observed in the world will only serve to confirm his knowledge."[40] One such as Emile will not require the need to purge his inclinations or pursuit of pleasure as much as those who have been influenced by civil society and unnatural needs.

In a passage in the fifth promenade Rousseau relates his experience of living on St. Peter's Island in Lake Bienne:

> I count these two months as the happiest time of my life, and so happy, that it would have sufficed me throughout life, without for a single moment allowing in my soul the desire for a different state. What then was this happiness, and in what did its enjoyment consist? I shall let it be guessed at by all the men of this century, from the description of the life which I led there. A delicious idleness was the first and the principal enjoyment that I wished to taste in all its sweetness; and all that I did during my stay was nothing but the charming and necessary occupation of a man who is vowed to idleness.[41]

And again, he relates:

> I rowed into the midst of the lake, when the water was calm; and there, stretching myself out at full length in the boat, my eyes turned towards heaven, I let myself go and wander about slowly at the will of the water, sometimes during many hours, plunged into a thousand confused but delicious reveries, which, without having any will-determined object, nor constancy, did not fail to be in my opinion a hundred times preferable to all that I have found sweetest in what are called the pleasures of life.[42]

And later he recalls how this experience permitted him to feel his "existence with pleasure, without taking the trouble to think."[43]

The richness of the sentiment of one's own existence is a prominent theme throughout the writings of Rousseau; it appears in his earlier as well as his later writings such as the *Reveries*. In the *Second Discourse* he wrote that "the sentiment of existence is man's first feeling. It is more fundamental than the desire for preservation of his existence because existence, mere existence, is by nature pleasant."[44] This sublime hedonism is the supreme and highest

experience open to men; it is the theme with which he ends his
latest writings.

If we have emphasized the teaching of the *Second Discourse*, it
was because in this work Rousseau shows his greatest affinity with
Lucretius' *De rerum natura*. It remains to identify basic similarities and differences between Rousseau and Lucretius without in-
tending to reduce Rousseau's thought simply to the affinity it has
with the great disciple of Epicurus. But it would be a major oversight to ignore that affinity.

THE INFLUENCE OF LUCRETIUS

Most modern Rousseau scholars tend to emphasize his originality
and minimize those who influenced or, at least, inspired him. And
while that is a perfectly defensible approach, to exclude an account of those who inspired him is to exclude a major part of his
achievement. A more complete understanding of Rousseau requires an understanding of those ancient authors to whom he
turned for guidance. The major ancient inspiration for Rousseau
appears to have been the *De rerum natura* of Lucretius. The similarities between Rousseau's "Discourse on the Origins of Inequality" and the famous poem of Lucretius can hardly be said to be
coincidental; or, for that matter, incidental to his thought.[45]

There can be no denying in the *Second Discourse* Rousseau presents an account of man's origin which is clearly materialistic and
reminiscent of Book V of *De rerum natura*.[46] It is important to observe at the outset, however, that unlike Lucretius Rousseau was
concerned with tracing the account of man's origins in order to
find the basis of that political order which is in accordance with
man's nature. Lucretius had no such concern. The similarity, therefore, between the *Second Discourse* and *De rerum natura* should
not obscure the fact that Rousseau was a modern concerned with
the establishment of that political order which is best by nature. In
this respect he shares more with Plato and Aristotle than with
Lucretius; but unlike Plato and Aristotle, for whom nature was
teleological,[47] for Rousseau—under the inspiration of both Des-

cartes and modern natural science—nature is not teleological. Nature has no end in which consists the perfection of the species; human nature is infinitely perfectible; man is free to become whatever he wills to become. One finds no similar doctrine in Lucretius. Indeed, natural man in Lucretius is not complete as he is in Rousseau. The pure state of nature (Lucretius never uses the term "state of nature") is complete in Rousseau; whereas in Lucretius it is not complete, however much it may be a condition of friendship. In short, Lucretius sees defects in natural man while Rousseau sees perfection, a source of guidance for civil man.

Rousseau also saw the harshness of nature but placed some degree of hope for men living under a democratic regime rightly constituted,[48] whereas Lucretius saw no such hope for men: life was harsh and the human condition was barely endurable. The best men could hope for in Lucretius' mind was a peaceful civil condition where one could pursue the Epicurean philosophic life: a prospect open, in fact, to very few. (In this respect Lucretius and Rousseau were in agreement; for Rousseau's sublime hedonists are few and live at the fringes of civil society, as we have seen.)

One of the most important differences between Rousseau and Lucretius is on the matter of religion; both acknowledge the impact of religion on the rise of civil society. But, unlike Lucretius, Rousseau considers religion to be an important support of civil society. He makes this clear in the *Second Discourse* when he writes of the right of the people to renounce the authority of their masters:

> But the frightful dissensions, the infinite disorders that this dangerous power would necessarily entail demonstrate more than anything else how much human governments needed a basis more solid than reason alone, and how necessary it was for public repose that divine will should have intervened to give sovereign authority a sacred and inviolable character which took from the subjects the fatal right of disposing of it.[49]

His more fully developed thoughts on the subject of the role of religion in both the *Social Contract* and *Emile* remove the ambiguity as to Rousseau's thought on the question of the role of divine power in instituting and sustaining civil society. Despite the

implications of the above quotation, Rousseau's final teachings on
religion—as to both content and form—are far from orthodox. He
does, however, insist on an important role for religion—the official
natural religion—for the majority of citizens; it helps them endure the harshness of life.

Another important difference between Rousseau and Lucretius
is the understanding of the human mind. In Lucretius man's mind
places him apart and somewhat above the other creatures. Rousseau
rejects this and presents all animals as machines; he places man
above the general mechanism of the animal world by claiming that
man, unlike the brutes, is perfectible.[50] He is at pains to reject the
proposition that man is by nature a rational animal. Man's faculties became perfected fortuitously and only after a long period of
time.[51] Rousseau also makes it clear that by perfectibility of the
faculties he means that man in "progressing" retreats further from
nature; his perfectibility is not prompted by an inherent natural
design, but brought about by accident. This is perfectly consistent
with the doctrine presented by Lucretius. The development of
man as presented in the *Second Discourse* is closely akin to that
presented by Lucretius in Book V of *De rerum natura*.

Rousseau's conclusion as to the possibility of human happiness
is basically at odds with Lucretius' view. For Lucretius human
happiness consists of the acquiescence in the harsh realities of the
natural condition—i.e., life without vain aspirations and with a
minimum of fear. In Rousseau happiness consists of the active
pursuit of those pleasures which are most natural to man.

One of the most important aspects of Rousseau's achievement,
which he shares with Lucretius and which places him at odds with
his modern contemporaries, is his rejection of civil society as having been beneficial to men. In his *Discourse on the Sciences and
Arts*, Rousseau argues at length the thoroughly Lucretian proposition that man's unfortunate and accidental transition from the pure
state of nature to civil society has not resulted in genuine benefits
for men. He specifically rejects the modern project of establishing
a new political order upon the basis of a subjugation of nature by
proud men. Rousseau viewed this as a mistaken attempt to make a

virtue out of the passion of *amour-propre*, the source of pride and ambition. For Rousseau, no amount of effort could turn the new and unnatural passions of political men into a peaceful or happy condition; private vices—the gratification of selfish passions—could never have public benefits. Thus he stood as a severe critic of the proponents of possessive individualism who formally encouraged the accumulation of capital and property—i.e., the life of selfishness and unnatural pleasures. Lucretius had called those who lived this way "Blind wretched men!" and Rousseau echoed that condemnation in his *Discourse on the Sciences and Arts*. The natural man would never seek power and reputation, says Rousseau; "the savage lives in himself; the sociable man, always outside of himself, can only live in the opinion of others, and it is, so to speak, only from their judgment that he draws the sentiment of his own existence."[52]

CONCLUSION

Finally, as we saw at the beginning of this discussion, Rousseau is a disciple of modern philosophy; but we also saw that he was a critic of the major implications of modern political philosophy. Rousseau accordingly stands off from the main course of modern political philosophy, with one foot, as it were, in the main course but the other foot outside it. That is, while he accepts many of the premises of Hobbes, he does not join forces with Bacon and his disciples and counsel the conquest or subjugation of nature; nor does he place faith in the "progress" of technology, as we see from his *Discourse on the Sciences and Arts*. In these matters he was at one with Lucretius and therefore closer than other modern disciples to their common master Epicurus. This is why Rousseau occupies a unique position in the development of modern political philosophy. Rousseau attempted to establish compassion as the principle of sociability by which the dangerous and devisive force of individualism could be moderated. The principle had to flow from man's natural condition, hence his reflections on man in the state of nature. Rousseau's conclusion was that by far more important than self-preservation is the element of *freedom* which man in his natural condition experiences along with *compassion*. He understands self-preservation as *amour de soi*—i.e., as the legitimate recognition of one's natural freedom. This legitimate love becomes debased in time due to the indulgence of the passions; *amour de soi* is transformed into *amour-propre*. This kind of self-love is the root of possessiveness and has its roots in man's brutish condition (the third epoch), before he enters civil society. By the third stage of his odyssey from his bare animal existence to fully constituted civil society, man has acquired property and possessions in unequal portion. Thus the distinction between rich and poor precedes civil society. But rather than give rein to this inequality, as Adam Smith proposed, Rousseau suggests that every effort must be made to ensure that it does not increase to an intolerable or disruptive degree. Rousseau appears therefore to have foreseen the prospects of the emergence of a proprietor class and a working class. But then, so did Adam Smith and John Locke. But where the latter looked upon it as inevitable and desirable, Rousseau looked upon it with misgivings and attempted to level out the enjoyment of the fruits of the earth. To this extent he was far more egalitarian than Locke.

We must turn our attention in the following two chapters to the other important controversy—the theological–political—which arose hand-in-glove with the effort to replace the old philosophy with the new one. It should come as no surprise to learn that the modern disciples of Epicureanism took issue with the dominant theological authority. Before proceeding to an account of that theological–political controversy, we must pause and describe the religious or theological background of the issues against which the founders of modernity joined forces with so much success.

NOTES

1. All references to the Discourses are to Jean-Jacques Rousseau, *The First and Second Discourses,* edited and translated by Roger D. Masters (New York: St. Martin's Press, 1964). "First Discourse," p. 51; see also *Social Contract,* IV. 4.

2. *First Discourse*, p. 47; see also *Émile, Oeuvres complètes*, Tome III, p. 194, "contradictions apparentes." For an instructive account of this issue, see Charles E. Butterworth, "Jean Jacques Rousseau and the Great Political Paradox," paper presented at the Northeastern Political Science Association meeting, New Brunswick, New Jersey, November 13–15, 1975. As Butterworth says: "the truly paradoxical aspect of Rousseau's thought is that while criticizing the false foundation of actual society, he is unable to offer a sound alternative foundation for society in anything other than theory and yet he refuses to counsel men to abandon society," p. 8. See also Roger Masters, "Rousseau's Paradoxes," in Introduction to Rousseau's *First and Second Discourses* (New York: St. Martin's Press, 1964), pp. 24–26.

3. Hereafter referred to as the *Second Discourse*.

4. Ibid., p. 93.

5. Ibid., p. 95.

6. Ibid., pp. 95–96.

7. Ibid., p. 94.

8. Ibid., p. 102.

9. Ibid., p. 95.

10. Ibid., p. 112.

11. Ibid.

12. Ibid., p. 113.

13. Ibid., p. 114.

14. Ibid., p. 115.

15. Ibid., p. 151.

16. Ibid., p. 118.

17. Ibid., p. 147.

18. Ibid., p. 149.

19. Ibid., p. 150.

20. Ibid., p. 142.

21. Ibid., p. 157.

22. Ibid., p. 169.

23. *Social Contract* II.7. All references to the *Social Contract* are to *On the Social Contract*, ed. Roger D. Masters, trans. Judith R. Masters (New York: St. Martin's Press, 1978), pp. 67–68.

24. Ibid., p. 74.

25. Ibid., p. 75.

26. Ibid. That is to say, through rhetoric.

27. On what people are suitable, see *Social Contract*, Bk. II, Ch. X.

28. *Second Discourse*, pp. 115–16.

29. *Emile*, IV, p. 235.

30. Ibid., p. 236.

31. Ibid.

32. Ibid.

33. Ibid., p. 237.

34. Ibid., p. 239.

35. Ibid.

36. Ibid.

37. Ibid., p. 241.

38. Ibid.

39. Ibid.

40. Ibid.

41. J. J. Rousseau, *The Reveries of a Solitary*, trans. John G. Fletcher (London: Routledge, 1927), pp. 105–106.

42. Ibid., p. 109.

43. Ibid., p. 111.

44. *Second Discourse*, pp. 118, 151, 165.

45. I am especially indebted to James H. Nichols, Jr. of The New School for Social Research for assistance in understanding the relationship of Lucretius and Rousseau. His paper entitled "Rousseau and Lucretius," delivered at the American Political Science Association Meetings in New Orleans, September 1973, was very helpful. Nichols has since published a summary version of that paper in his *Epicurean Political Philosophy*.

46. On the relation of the *Second Discourse* to the *De rerum natura*, see Jean Morel, "Recherches sur les sources du Discours sur l'inégalité," *Annales de la Société J. J. Rousseau*, 5 (1909), 163–64.

47. See Aristotle, *Politics*, I, 1252B–1253A1; *Physics* II, 194A27;33.

48. See Nichols, *op. cit.*, p. 207 for a fuller discussion of this point.

49. *Second Discourse*, p. 170.

50. Ibid., p. 115; see also Leo Strauss, *Natural Right and History*, pp. 264–66.

51. Ibid., p. 140.

52. Ibid., p. 179.

5

The Seventeenth-Century
Political Theology

THE OFFICIAL SOURCE of the theological dogmatism which infused the reformed religious orthodoxy of seventeenth-century England was the *Articles of Religion*[1]—ten in number when first promulgated by Royal decree in 1536, and thirty-nine by 1571. A review of these Articles provides a glimpse of the doctrines against which the theological writings of the modern political philosophers were directed. The theological and scriptural writings of the founders of modern political philosophy become intelligible only when viewed against the background of the prevailing orthodox theology.

The primary purpose of the *Articles of Religion* was to enunciate the fundamental dogmas of Christian orthodoxy and to put a check on the impulse of inquiry unleashed by the Reformation and by the new natural philosophy. Protestantism in Britain thus assumed from the very beginning an "extremely dogmatic character."[2]

The focal point of the controversy between philosophy and theology in the seventeenth century involved the limits of natural reason, the role of revelation, and the subsequent need of divine assistance for man to overcome his sinfulness. Edward Stillingfleet drew attention to the dilemma confronting reform theologians in his *Rational Account of the Grounds of Protestant Religion* (1665).[3] Two of the great benefits of Protestantism, he claimed, were the return to Scripture and the use of reason, both of which he claimed had been denied by the Roman Church. Yet, as Stillingfleet knew, the new Protestant dogmatism was as suspicious of reason in religious matters as was the old Roman dogmatism. Article Nine of the *Articles of Religion*, entitled "Of Original or

Birth Sin," made it clear that man was by nature incapable of rising above his sinful condition.

> Original sin standeth not in the following of Adam—as the Pelagians do vainly talk—but it is the fault and corruption of the *nature* of every man, that naturally is engendered of the offspring of Adam; whereby man is very far gone from original righteousness, and is of *his own nature* inclined to evil, so that the Flesh lusteth always contrary to the Spirit; and therefore in every person born into this world, it deserveth God's wrath and damnation. And this infection of nature doth remain, yea, in them that are regenerated.[4]

The human condition was presented as a hopeless condition of misery from which man was unable to rescue himself by the use of reason. Article Ten elaborated on this condition: "The condition of man after the fall of Adam is such, that he cannot turn and prepare himself, by his own natural strength and good works, to faith and calling upon God: wherefore we have no power to do good works, pleasant and acceptable to God, without the grace of God by Christ preventing us, that we may have a good will, and working with us, when we have that good will."[5]

It would be difficult to conceive of a more hopeless predicament; man cannot do anything "by his own natural strength" to lift himself out of such a depressing condition. Even hope would appear to be beyond his own natural means. Gloom and despondency pervaded the religious atmosphere, as Godfrey Goodman wrote in *The Fall of Man, or the Corruption of Nature proved by the Light of our Natural Reason* (1616). Goodman argued that man could not rescue himself with the aid of natural reason. Human reason, Goodman claimed, was capable only of telling men how hopeless things were and how useless it was to seek refuge in reason or philosophy. Goodman was not the only one to write as he did. John Donne wrote graphically in *An Anatomie of the World* about the frailty and decay of this world. In short, the hopelessness of the human condition and the futility of the reason were common theological themes throughout the period.[6]

Such a theological doctrine placed men in a position analogous to that in which they found themselves at the time of Epicurus, whose contemporaries stood in terror before the angry gods who spoke through thunder and lightning without prospect of appeasement or relief—dumb victims of fear and superstition. There was, of course, one important difference for seventeenth-century Christians. Christian doctrine presented man with an avenue of access to God's grace—i.e., to the Scriptures through the Church. But rather than alleviate the problem for the political philosophers of the seventeenth century, this solution only aggravated it. The important role played by the Church armed with the Scriptures clearly implied that the Church had authority over men in the highest or most important matters. As a result, not only theology claimed a priority over philosophy, but the Church claimed a certain priority over the State. For man must surely pay more attention to those who can condemn him to everlasting torment in the next world than to those who can only punish him in this world, as Machiavelli acknowledged.[7]

This view of the human condition was highly unacceptable to the philosophers of the seventeenth century because it presented an uncompromising claim for the superiority of theology (i.e., scriptural theology) over philosophy. For philosophers to accept such a view would be to concede the radical inadequacy of human reason and the primacy of revelation, which was to them unreasonable.

Given such a climate of theological determination it is small wonder that the Church became involved in political matters and that political philosophers became preoccupied with the claims of Christian theology. A conflict between Church and State became inevitable, especially since the leading political philosophers—such as Hobbes—were propounding a doctrine of sovereignty which was incompatible with the political theology of the reformed Church.

II

When it came, the conflict between the theologians and the philosophers raged on two levels. On the first it involved the question of the extent to which the Church could command the civil authority on behalf of religious orthodoxy. This well-known controversy engaged the penetrating attention of the likes of John Milton, whose *Treatise of Civil Power in Ecclesiastical Causes* (1659)[8] became the clarion call for the free exercise of conscience. Speaking as a devotee of the Protestant cause, Milton wrote: "what I argue shall be drawn from the Scripture only."[9] He then proceeded to present a strong case for individual conscience in matters of religious belief free of any coercive pressures from either Church or State. He declared that "for *belief* or *practise* in religion according to his conscientious perswasion no man ought to be punished or molested by any outward force on earth whatsoever."[10] Milton was addressing the claim of the Protestant Church to enforce its authority in religious matters by means of the civil power. He argued that there was no infallible external judge and that each man had at his disposal the Scriptures and his own conscience. "If then we count it so ignorant and irreligious in the papist to think himself discharged in God's account, believing only as the church believes, how much greater condemnation will it be the protestant his condemner, to think himself justified, believing only as the state believes?"[11]

Milton argued that no *Protestant* of whatever sect ought to be molested for his religious beliefs or practices. "But," he insisted, "as for poperie and idolatrie . . . they may not plead to be tolerated."[12] His reason for denying Roman Catholics freedom of religious doctrine and practice was that "their religion the more considered, the less can be acknowledged a religion; but a Roman principalitie rather, endeavouring to keep up her old universal dominion under a new name and meer shadow of a catholic religion."[13] The Church of Rome had become, said Milton, a pretender to civil power supported by hostile foreign governments.[14] The civil authority could, therefore, use its arms to subdue Roman Catholics and idolators as it could against any other alien force.[15]

Bishop Jeremy Taylor wrote in a similar vein and reached similar conclusions. Although he was prepared to acknowledge that the "foundations of the Roman faith stand secure enough for all their vain and unhandsome superstructures,"[16] he had reservations about "their doctrines as they relate to good life, or are consistent or inconsistent with civil government."[17] When one takes many of the Roman doctrines to "the utmost issue," he cautioned, they would destroy the commonwealth. The fact that the pope can "absolve subjects from their allegiance to their natural prince" is incompatible with civil stability and cannot be tolerated.[18] "Now these opinions," he concluded, "are a direct overthrow to all human society, and mutual commerce, a destruction of government, and of the laws and duty of subordination which we own to princes."[19]

Taylor also wrote a strong attack on the insidious influence of Epicureanism, which he said was beginning to take hold of the public mind. In *A Course of Sermons for All the Sundays of the Year* (1655),[20] Taylor pressed the point that the one central purpose of this life is to prepare for the next. And after presenting Epicureanism as base hedonism, he urged upon his Christian hearers a life of frugality, a life with "the fewest desires and the most quiet passions,"[21] as the best preparation for the next life.

And Samuel Parker in *A Discourse of Ecclesiastical Politie* (1670)[22] argued the case for the authority of the civil magistrate over the consciences of subjects in all religious matters. Although it is openly directed against Thomas Hobbes, it could more appropriately be said to be a reply to Milton's *Treatise of Civil Power*, which was written eleven years before and was widely read. Parker stressed here the unsettling political implications of atheism:

So that though Atheism reigns and prevails more in the present Age, than in some that went immediately before it, yet there have been seasons, when it was mounted up to a greater height of Power and Reputation, than 'tis yet advanced to: but then those have always been black and fatal times, and have certainly brought on Changes and Dissolutions of States. For the Principles of Irreligion unjoyned the sinews, and blow up the very Foundations of Government: This turns all sense of Loyalty into Folly; this sets men at liberty from all the effectual Obligations to Obedience, and makes Rebellion as virtuous, whenever it either is, or is thought as advantageous.[23]

Parker argued that the state authority must assume the obligations of ensuring the hegemony of Christian orthodoxy because religion has always been a powerful force for stability and peace in commonwealths. He reasoned that "if the Sovereign Power cannot order and manage it, it would be but a very incompetent Instrument of publique happiness, it would want the better half of it self, and be utterly weak and ineffectual for the ends of Government."[24]

Above all, he continued, governments and princes ought not to be misled by the specious arguments advanced on behalf of the freedom of conscience. "If Princes would but consider, how liable mankind are to abuse themselves with serious and conscientious Villanies, they would quickly see it to be absolutely necessary to the Peace and Happiness of their Kingdoms, that there be set up a more severe Government over mens Consciences and Religious perswasions, than over their Vices and Immoralities."[25]

To view the conflict as one of Church versus State is to oversimplify the issues and to obscure the depth of the underlying struggle. The second level of the conflict reveals that it was nothing short of a battle between political theology and political philosophy; the former attempted to explain and construct a political order upon the foundations of theology and within the limits imposed by religious orthodoxy. The latter relied exclusively upon the use of reason and called in question the basic premisses of political theology. The participants in the conflict insisted that no superficial amalgam would satisfy either side. This is why the conflict was so fierce and ran so deep. One had to triumph over the other; no eclectic combination, such as that proposed by Gassendi or Robert Boyle, could resolve the issues for very long. The practical political problem could be and was more easily solved by accommodation, but the philosophical and theological problems could never be solved short of a triumph of political philosophy over political theology or vice versa. No one in England saw this more clearly than Thomas Hobbes and John Locke. On the Continent, Baruch Spinoza understood the problem and offered a solution in his famous *Theological–Political Treatise*, which constitutes the most explicit seventeenth-century case for the supremacy of philosophy over theology. We shall return to this matter in the next chapter in our discussion of the political philosophies of Hobbes, Locke, and Rousseau.

III

The new natural philosophy drew the critical attention of Church theologians because it was viewed as the vehicle for atheism. Were not its ancient proponents, Democritus and Epicurus, atheists? But not all of the new scientists were atheists or wished to be accused of aiding the cause of atheism. Robert Boyle, for one, took steps to show how the new natural philosophy could be rendered compatible with Christian orthodoxy.

Before he died in 1691 Boyle left an endowment for a series of annual lectures "to prove the truth of the Christian religion against, viz., Atheists, Theists and Pagans."[26] From the very beginning it became clear that the target of polemics from this platform provided by Boyle would be the devotees of Epicurus, Hobbes, and others (such as Spinoza) who taught an atheistical doctrine. The first Boyle series of eight lectures was delivered by Richard Bentley, who later became a Cambridge scholar and Master of Trinity College. With the aid of Isaac Newton's *Principia* Bentley attempted to refute the atheism of those modern atomists who drew their inspiration from Epicurus but who also forgot to purge their thinking of atheistical conclusions or the influence of his moral philosophy. Whether Newton cleansed himself of these as clearly as did Boyle has remained a controversial question to this day.[27] Many of Newton's Christian disciples appeared satisfied that the "Scholium" which Newton appended to the *Principia* was sufficient to confirm him as an orthodox Christian. More recent scholarship tends to cast doubt on this conclusion. Perry Miller claims, for example, that Newton "was holding something in reserve, not giving himself entirely to his own discoveries, stupendous as he realized them to be. As for ultimate causes, he knew how to say that he did not know."[28]

There can be no doubt, however, that Newton put his *Principia* at Bentley's disposal; and apparently he concurred in the use to which Bentley put his major work. It is also clear, as Robert E. Schofield affirms, that "the success of Bentley's lectures was immense. Published within a year of their delivery (in 1692), they were adopted as a text in moral philosophy and metaphysics in the colleges; by 1735 six editions had appeared."[29] The popularity of the Bentley lectures attests the widespread concern with atheism and the new natural philosophy at the time. Small wonder that Newton permitted Bentley the opportunity of using his *Principia* on behalf of orthodox religion. By so doing, Bentley was assisting the natural philosophers to slip out from under the sweeping condemnation of the likes of Samuel Parker. Parker, by this time Archdeacon of Canterbury, drew attention to the problem of atheism in England a decade before Bentley delivered his Boyle lectures. In the preface to his *A Demonstration of the Divine Authority of the Law of Nature and of the Christian Religion* (1681), Parker claimed that "Atheism and Irreligion are at length become as common as Vice and Debauchery, and the Vulgar (by which I intend both sorts, as Seneca expresses it, the Man of Title as well as the clowted shoe, if equally unlearned and barbarous) declare that they would not be so wicked as they are, if they thought that they lay under any obligations to be good."[30] And Parker pointed an accusing finger directly at the new natural philosophy as the source of the problem. He was explicit in his claim that "the Plebeans and Mechanicks have philosophised themselves into Principles of Impiety, and read their Lectures of Atheism in the Streets and Highways."[31] After blaming Hobbes and his *Leviathan* for teaching that there is neither God nor Providence, Parker cast his net farther and placed the blame on all those who taught that "there are no Principles of Good and Evil but onely every Man's Self-interest, nor any Self-interest but onely of this present life: that Humane Nature is a meer Machine, and that all the contrivances of the minds of Men are nothing but the mechanical Results of Matter and Motion."[32]

Parker took special pains to identify Hobbes as the villain. He charged that the foundation of natural religion as proposed by Hobbes was "nothing else but an open declaration of atheism and impiety."[33]

Parker at length presented one of the most inflexible cases on behalf of the Church of England written during this period. He wrote three major works in an attempt to arrest the heretical influence of philosophers such as Hobbes. In his earlier work, *A Discourse of Ecclesiastical Politie* (1670), Parker argued that nothing was more dangerous to both the civil and ecclesiastical powers than the appeal to conscience and the "inconveniences of toleration." "Most men's minds or consciences are weak, silly and ignorant things, acted by fond and absurd principles and imposed upon by their vices and their passions."[34] The only way that this dangerous internal enemy could be kept in check was "By proving it to be absolutely necessary to the peace and government of the world that the supreme magistrate of every Commonwealth should be vested with a power to govern and conduct the consciences of subjects in affairs of religion."[35] Parker emphasized that he was referring to those magistrates who dwelt in genuine Christian countries such as England; for Christian kings get their claim to sovereignty from God, he claimed. "All supreme power both in civil and ecclesiastical affairs issues from the same original and is founded upon the same reason of things, namely, the indisputable necessity of society to the preservation of human nature and of government to the preservation of human society, a supreme power being absolutely necessary to the decision of all those quarrels and controversies."[36] Parker insisted that the Christian Church was an indispensable aid to civil peace and authority. He wrote that Jesus

came not to unsettle the foundations of government or to diminish the natural rights of princes and settle the conduct of humane affairs upon new principles, but left the government of the world in the same condition he found it. . . . no where he takes upon him to settle, much less to limit the prerogatives of Princes; and therefore the government of religion being vested in them by an antecedent and natural right, must without all controversie belong to them, till it is derogated from them by some superior authority; so that unless our Saviour had ex-

pressly disrobed the Royal power of its ecclesiastical jurisdiction, nothing else can alienate it from their prerogative.[37]

The basis of all civil power in Parker's view was natural divine
right. But this divine right as transmitted through the Bible de-
manded that the sovereign enforce the teachings of the Christian
religion by the "sword of the civil power."[38] It is clear from Parker's treatise on ecclesiastical power that the civil sovereign is obliged
to keep a keen eye open for any potential heretics—i.e., religious
disrupters who could cause civil problems. No one fitted into this
category more firmly than Thomas Hobbes. In his discourse on the
Church of England Parker warns of the danger of Hobbes's teaching. After a review of the *Leviathan*, Parker concluded that as
Hobbes destroys the basis for the existence of God, he "takes away
the obligation of all His laws of justice and honesty, by supposing
such a state of nature in which mankind being exempt from all
government may do whatever they please without violation of any
law. Which to suppose is to suppose no Deity, for if there be a
deity, there can be no supposition of any such state of nature in
which mankind can be exempted from his government."[39]

The battle between the proponents of the new natural philosophy and the defenders of Christian orthodoxy raged for a long
time. In 1694 James Lowde wrote *A Discourse Concerning the
Nature of Man*, which consisted of a severe attack by name on
Hobbes, Spinoza, Descartes, Epicurus, Machiavelli, Locke, and
several of their disciples. Striking at the root of the new philosophy,
Lowde rejected with scorn the thesis that atoms constituted the
most basic elements of matter. "Nor is it any ways conceivable," he
scoffed, "how senseless Atoms should grow into greater Wits, only
by jumping and running their heads against one another."[40] And
Lowde identified the impious Epicurus as the source of this doctrine. The modern disciples of Epicurus, he claimed, acknowledged
the existence of God in words but in fact denied "the Common
Principles of all Religion, the immortality of the Soul, and a future State, and seem perfectly to entertain the Doctrine of Epicurus."[41]

In his *Discourse*, Lowde claimed that Hobbes was especially dangerous to the Christian religion. He argued that Hobbes mistakenly concluded that since a few men are vicious all men must be vicious. Lowde acknowledged man's disposition to evil but argued that it is not due to his nature (because that would imply a malicious God) but stemmed from the fall of Adam.[42] Lowde observed that "Now Mr. Hobbes his principles in general seem to be the suiting or fitting of the vicious practices of mankind to an hypothesis thereby endeavouring to enact wickedness by a law, and to prove the lawfulness of all possible violence and injustice, by the Magna Carta of self-preservation."[43]

Lowde wisely drew attention to the fact that Machiavelli lurks in the background of Hobbes's thought. Both Machiavelli and Hobbes should have seen, he claimed, that "it was one thing to act wickedly, and another to teach men that they might do so."[44] And while he could perhaps excuse Machiavelli, for he counseled only one man, Lowde insisted that Hobbes cannot be exonerated so easily "because his bad principles are of a more universal influence and reach not only to Princes but people too."[45]

IV

There were other Churchmen, however, who were more tolerant of the new philosophy and less fearful of its influence. Richard Cumberland, Bishop of Peterborough, wrote a *Treatise of the Laws of Nature* (*De legibus naturae*; 1672)[46] which was addressed to Hobbes. Cumberland began his book with the statement that he would prefer not to have to write it but that Hobbes has influenced "too, too many amongst us." He accordingly set out to refute the teachings of both *De Cive* and *Leviathan*, which teachings he viewed as "directly opposite, not only to all religion, but also to all the true principles of civil society and to all right discipline of rational, wise civil government."[47]

Cumberland proceeded early in the *Treatise* to define the law of nature and in so doing set the basis for his refutation of Hobbes.

He defined the law of nature—contrary to Hobbes, who roots it in the fundamental right of self-preservation—as

> some propositions of unchangeable truth and certainty which are to direct and govern the voluntary motions of rational free agents, in the election of good and in the avoiding of evil: which laws by obligations upon all outward acts of behaviour even in the state of nature, prior and antecedent to all laws of human imposition whatsoever: And are clearly distinct from every consideration of all such compacts and agreements as constitute civil government.[48]

This definition does not contain any of the ingredients of the law of nature as defined by Thomas Aquinas—the author of the orthodox Christian formulation[49]—or as defined by Richard Hooker. Cumberland's definition mentions neither God nor right reason as the source of natural law. There is also no mention of the Bible. And yet he tends to concede the existence of a prepolitical state of nature. For Thomas Aquinas the natural law was "the law of God in rational creatures";[50] there is no doubt as to its source or content. Hooker's conception depends heavily on Aristotle and the Bible. The law of nature is, according to Hooker, discernible by right reason but aided by the fact that "God hath himself by Scripture made known such laws as serve for the direction of men."[51]

The solution to Cumberland's apparent oversight is found in the fact that he was not prepared to reject the modern trends entirely. He appeared prepared to accept some but not all aspects of the new learning. He let it be known that he was hopeful for the future because "the material and corporeal parts of nature now begin to open themselves, and shine under a more excellent philosophy; a philosophy established upon mathematical principles."[52] Cumberland believed, in short, that the new philosophy could aid theological orthodoxy by bringing it to bear upon "the nature of our immortal souls . . . and from thence, by a regular subordination of natural causes (as comprehended under the same philosophy) we infer the being and attributes of God; we understand Him to be the original author and prime mover of all; And from hence we acknowledge Him the sole original cause of all necessary effect."[53]

Hobbes erred, he said, in not realizing that God was the first mover.[54]

Cumberland confirmed his faith in the new philosophy with the claim that he and Hobbes agreed in the "general principles of mathematical philosophy."[55] But what he did not see was that Hobbes understood those general principles better than he did. For Hobbes knew that a proponent of the new philosophy could not know that the first cause of motion was God. It is an inference which goes beyond the evidence. What Cumberland did not seem to realize was that by subscribing to the new philosophy—however much he wished to redirect it to the ends of orthodoxy—he was aiding its respectability and hence its general acceptability. He certainly had no way of assuring that future generations would be as prepared as he was to make the fundamental inference as to the existence of God as the first mover so indispensable to Christian orthodoxy.

But Cumberland was not the only one among the Church hierarchy who adopted the new philosophy and attempted to make it serve orthodox ends. Bishop Seth Ward, one of the original members of a group which met at Wadham College, Oxford, and which later formed the nucleus of the Royal Society, was an early and eager proponent of the new philosophy. But he was also emphatically opposed to Hobbes. In a book entitled *In Thomae Hobbii philosophiam exercitatio* (1656)[56] Ward wrote a systematic attack on Hobbes similar to that written by Cumberland. But he also wrote a treatise entitled *A Philosophical Essay Towards an Eviction of the Being and Attributes of God* (1652),[57] in which he attempted to establish that the new philosophy could be turned to the service of orthodox religion.

We must remember that Hobbes was beginning to acquire a following by this time even though it was dangerous to espouse his cause openly. It was possible to defend Hobbes in public only under the guise of refuting him. And that is precisely the course adopted by John Eachard, who wrote a dialogue entitled *Mr. Hobbes's State of Nature Considered* (1672).[58] This dialogue is a clever account of a fictitious discussion between Philautus, who

presents Hobbes's views as stated in *De Cive* and *Leviathan*, and
a youthful Timothy who attempts to refute them. Philautus presents in this dialogue a brilliant summary of the major teachings
of Hobbes in such a way as to make them appealing to common
sense, while Timothy at no time even comes close to getting the
better of the argument; his questions and answers are simply silly.
There is no doubt that by the end of the dialogue Philautus has
presented all Hobbes's views clearly and that Timothy has not refuted a single point. Eachard shows that in the person of Timothy
the opponents of Hobbes are young and silly and have neither the
patience nor the capacity to learn from the master.

It is not difficult to see why Eachard chose to write a dialogue—
he would not have been able to dissemble as easily in a narrative
account. The dialogue concludes with Timothy saying that he is
tired of the discussion. "I'm hungry," he says; "Let's eat." To
which Philautus, who utters the last word in the dialogue, replies:
"In that, Tim, I agree with thee, but in nothing else. And I am
even sorry that I have stayed thus long: for thou hast been so
perverse, that I am afraid I have done thee but little good. And so
farewell."[59]

In 1697 Thomas Burnet subjected John Locke's *Essay Concerning Human Understanding* to a critical review in a book entitled *Remarks Upon an Essay Concerning Humane Understanding*. Without any doubt, says Burnet, Locke's doctrine contained
in the *Essay* is incompatible with Christian morality, "Revealed
Religion, and the Immortality of the Soul of Man."[60] This was
the opening salvo in the war which erupted around Locke following the publication of his *Essay*.

Burnet observed in his *Remarks Upon an Essay* that the modern disciples of Epicurus were responsible for the prevailing decay
of morality and of religious practices. He observed more shrewdly
than Parker and other contemporaries that "the Epicurean Philosophers are not Atheists but rather a sort of Deists."[61] And, more
pointedly still, Burnet observed that "the Epicurean Philosophers
have given us a Method of Science, without any other Principles
than what are collected from Sense and Experience."[62] Burnet was

prepared to acknowledge that the emphasis on sense data and experience might conceivably be necessary to ferret out the persistent influence of the schoolmen. But, he warned, a reliance on sense and experience "can carry us no higher than Epicurus's Ethicks, still within the compass of a Temporal Felicity, and provision for it."[63] No one knew this better than the modern disciples of Epicurus' moral philosophy, and they were therefore obliged to write and teach with considerable caution. It was no easy matter to espouse openly in those times the cause of Epicurean moral philosophy, or, indeed, to be accused of doing so.[64] No one was unmindful of the fate of Thomas Hariot, who had been renounced as an Epicurean by Robert Parsons as early as 1591, and, despite the lack of evidence to substantiate these charges, imprisoned. He eventually gained his release but was thereafter "loath to give full expression to views which would mark him as politically or theologically Unorthodox."[65] Indeed, to be theologically unorthodox was the surest way of being politically unorthodox at this time.[66] It is not surprising to learn, therefore, that Locke first published his *Reasonableness of Christianity* anonymously. It would appear that he was prepared to acknowledge it publicly only when it was received favorably by those who were disposed to see in it a defense of the Christian religion.

v

Despite the efforts of the new philosophers to undermine the old moral philosophy and political theology, their success was blunted temporarily by the presence and enormous influence of Richard Hooker, who provided a political theology compatible with Christian orthodoxy and yet sympathetic to the cause of theological reform. The "judicious Hooker," as John Locke called him, wrote the *Laws of Ecclesiastical Polity*[67] and gave the new Church of England a document which was orthodox in every respect—a complete political theology. The first four books appeared in 1593, during the early years of the Reformation, and were sympathetic to the cause of the English Reformers. For a long time it stood as a superlative example of English Protestant thought. The *Laws of Ecclesiastical Polity* presented an account of natural law and showed how the Christian Church and state must be one. Hooker defended natural law and showed how it is expressed in the Bible, and how the Christian state must be governed by the laws of God as announced in the Bible.

Of natural law he wrote: "The Law of Reason or Human Nature is that which men by discourse of natural Reason have rightly found out themselves to be all for ever bound unto in all their actions."[68] He refers to it also as "the universal law of mankind" which men carry in their hearts.[69] Hooker went on to show that the laws of England were consistent with the divine law and the law of nature. He also argued that in England Church and State were identical and hence the laws of religion duly passed by the sovereign in Parliament were as binding on the citizens of England as any other law of the realm. He added further that the ends of the state cannot be divorced from man's highest eternal end, and that commonwealths ought to provide for the spiritual ends of man.

But even Hooker was viewed with suspicion by many Reform Church divines because he attempted to establish religion and the state in a rational account of human nature and man's relation to God. He attempted, in short, to offer a rational basis for both the orthodox religion and the relation of Church and State. In this respect he was in the tradition of Thomas Aquinas and his disciples. But this "rationalistic" approach to the Christian faith was being questioned by some among the religious reformers, such as John Calvin. The Calvinists taught that man must rely wholly upon the Scriptures and retreat from intellectual efforts of the likes of Aquinas and Hooker. Man in this conception was powerless without God; his reason was, above all, powerless to drag him up from his degrading position. Only God's grace could elevate men from the depths of the human condition. Hence there was no place for philosophy—even that kind which purported to explain and justify Christian Orthodoxy. There was no place even for speculative or natural theology. The Scriptures alone and faith based on the Scriptures were sufficient.

It is easy to see that this non-rational or anti-philosophical strain of reform thinking aided or contributed to the confusion of the times. We must remember that the entire religious, moral, and political basis of society had suddenly come unhinged and that men were actively groping for new moorings in these matters.

CONCLUSION

The heart of the new natural philosophy was the mechanical conception of nature which under the influence of Francis Bacon and Robert Boyle began to command the attention of the entire intellectual world of the seventeenth century; some looked upon it with horror while most welcomed it as the basis for a successful departure from the philosophical bondage of the Aristotelian schoolmen. As Marie Boas has written: "Fundamentally the mechanical philosophy implied the explanation of properties of bodies in terms not of Aristotelian physics but of the newly developed and developing science of mechanics which were replacing it."[70] The new science of mechanics or the new natural philosophy was rooted in the rediscovery of the Democritean metaphysics which taught that the foundations of all matter are atoms and that the task of science or philosophy was to observe the motion of these atoms and thus uncover nature's great secrets or laws. The center of the controversy was the fact that the new natural science or philosophy was anti-teleological, thereby rendering questionable the old understanding of an ordered universe in which all things— human and non-human—sought their proper ends by nature. One of the first things this new anti-teleological conception of nature called in question was the orthodox Christian doctrine of general providence. According to the Christian teachings, God actively ruled the course of things by a general and special providence.

But the new conception of nature not only threatened the orthodox Christian views of providence and miracles; it implied the irrelevance of such doctrines. No one made this more clear than Baruch Spinoza, who wrote in the *Theological–Political Treatise*[71] that the new natural philosophy applied to the Bible (Old Testament) rendered questionable the prophetic claim to miracles and the fundamental Judaeo-Christian conception of providence.[72] The alleged miracles could be explained by natural events, and what was thought to be providence could be explained as "natural necessity."[73]

The threat thus posed by the new mechanical philosophy was first and foremost confronted by the clergy as well as those new scientists—such as Boyle—who did not want to have their efforts aid the cause of atheism. Nevertheless, it proved to be a major task for the new scientists to show that their discoveries did not lead to doubt of orthodox religion. Some divines attempted to close off scientific investigation with the claim that the Biblical accounts must be taken as scientifically sound. This occasioned a heated controversy with clergy on both sides. John Wilkins argued in *A Discourse Concerning a New Planet* (1640)[74] that while the Bible is unquestionably supreme in spiritual matters it cannot be said to contain scientific wisdom. "There is not any particular by which philosophy has been more endangered than the ignorant superstition of some men who in stating the controversies of it, do so closely adhere unto the mere words of scripture."[75] Thus, says Wilkins, the new philosophy will serve the true religion by helping to drive out superstition. Alexander Ross arose as the defender of the strict theological orthodoxy and attacked Wilkin's views in a book entitled *The New Planet No Planet: or the Earth No Wandering Star; except in the Wandering Heads of Galileans* (1646).[76] Ross's condemnation of Copernican astronomy was in fact a condemnation of all scientific investigation. Addressing Wilkins, Ross began: "You say it's but a novelty in philosophy but I say it trenches upon divinity, for divinity tells us that the standing of the sun and moving of the earth are the miraculous works of God's supernatural power; your new philosophy tells us that they are the ordinary works of nature."[77] Ross was indeed striking at the core of the problem when he drew attention to the fact that the new philosophy was offering a comprehensive view of all nature which at least on its face stood in contradiction to the Bible.

Richard Baxter wrote *The Arrogancy of Reason Against Divine Revelations Repressed* (1655),[78] in which he claimed that the new philosophy was permanently inimical to the orthodox theology because it sought the knowledge of causes. And since the knowledge of divine causes was clearly outside the realm of this new natural (or empirical) philosophy, one could not achieve a knowledge of God.

In another work entitled *The Reason of the Christian Religion* (1667),[79] Baxter drew attention to the fact that the new natural philosophy was necessarily importing the old atheistic natural philosophy of Epicurus. He claimed that it was impossible merely to adopt a part of Epicurean doctrine of matter and motion and not absorb the attending doctrine of atheism. And Meric Casaubon, in like manner, after charging Epicurus with teaching that the universe came to be what it is "by a casual jumbling of atomes"[80] and not by providence, pointed an accusing finger at his modern disciple "Gassendus his friend, the great reviver and abettor of Epicureanism in this unhappy age."[81]

There can be no doubt that there were many disciples of Epicurus in the seventeenth century who not only taught his atomistic theories but who were more concerned with propounding his hedonism. The writings and sermons of divines proliferated in an effort to demonstrate the perverseness of Epicureanism and its danger to Christian orthodoxy. Bishop Jeremy Taylor spoke against the excesses of Epicureanism in a sermon entitled "The House of Feastings or the Epicures Measures,"[82] in which he denounced the doctrine of "eat and drink, for tomorrow we dye"[83] as unworthy of any true Christian. At the same time he admired and recommended as not un-Christian the peaceful repose of those who fled from the cares of this world.

Robert Boyle was a leader of the new scientists and yet wished, as we have seen, no part of atheism. The fact that Boyle considered the matter important should serve as testimony of the degree to which this problem permeated the intellectual life of the period.

In one sense, it also tends to reveal that Boyle was himself in some doubt, or at least that he had not answered the problem of science and atheism to his own satisfaction. He tried on several occasions to demonstrate the compatibility of the new science and revealed orthodox religion. We must recall that it was Boyle, a convinced atomist, who invoked the image of the universe as a large clock. It is one thing to postulate that observation and experiment confirm this mechanical conception, but it is quite another matter to claim that God designed it so. Deism or agnosticism would appear to be the more likely conclusions. If one cannot demonstrate by sense perception and confirm by observation then one has no basis in the new philosophy for making a conclusion which does not stem from the principles of that philosophy. Boyle was fully aware of that dilemma, and he was also obviously worried that agnosticism was too close to atheism.

The most important result of the clash between orthodox theology and the new philosophy was the identification of spheres of inquiry appropriate to each, one appropriate to divine matters, the other appropriate to natural and civil matters. At first sight this dichotomy appears as an appropriate division of labor, but we shall see that it resulted in the undoing of theology and the civil doctrines associated with it. John Wilkins was one of the earliest to propound this division of labor in the name of science and to write in defense of providence.[84]

Wilkins attempted to demonstrate the rational basis of "natural religion" upon the premisses provided by the new natural philosophy. He claimed in his *Principles and Duties of Natural Religion* (1675)[85] that all natural bodies are moved by necessary laws. He realized that this restricted or even eliminated the possibility of special or individual providence. But this was not incompatible, he claimed, with the maturity of Christian times; direct intervention in the form of miracles was necessary in the early ages of the Church but not now, "it being not reasonable to think that the universal laws of nature, by which things are to be regularly guided in their natural courses, should frequently or upon every little occasion be violated or disordered."[86]

But for some scientists, such as Edmund Halley, this posed a problem; for if what are called miracles today can be explained in terms of natural causes, miracles that took place fifteen hundred years earlier could also be so explained. He accordingly attempted to show before the Royal Society that the universal flood could be explained by natural causes.[87]

The purpose of the foregoing discussion is to show how the new natural philosophy was necessarily caught in a battle with the Church—the Reformed Church—and that the leading men of science—Bacon, Boyle, Newton—were obliged to respond to the religious or theological problems posed by the new natural philosophy. It is also the reason why the leading political philosophers—Hobbes and Locke—were likewise obliged to write so much on religion. As we shall see presently, in their case the attempt at compatibility was not as wholly taken up as it was by the scientists. There was no doubt in some minds—such as Bacon's—that the theological disputes ("immoderate zeal for religion," he called it) had been a major reason why it took so long for the new natural philosophy to take hold.

We shall now turn to Hobbes, Locke, and Rousseau to see how they confronted and solved the theological–political problems presented in their day.

NOTES

1. *Sermon or Homilies Appointed to be Read in Churches in the Time of Queen Elizabeth, to which are Added the Articles of Religion. And the Constitution and Canons Ecclesiastical, first published by His Majesty's Authority, 1604* (London, 1815). See also Gilbert Burnet, *An Exposition of the Thirty-nine Articles of the Church of England* (London, 1699).

2. John Tulloch, *Rational Theology and Christian Philosophy in England in the Seventeenth Century*, I (Edinburgh, 1872), 5.

3. (London, 1665).

4. *Sermons or Homilies*, p. 421; italics added.

5. Ibid.; see also John Owen, *A Discourse Concerning the Holy Spirit*, especially pp. 367ff. where he discusses the need for divine grace in restoring fallen men.

6. See, for an example of those who opposed this view, George Hakewill, *An*

Apologie or Declaration of the Power and Providence of God in the Government of the World (London, 1630).

7. Machiavelli, *Discourses*, III, i.

8. John Milton, *Treatise of Civil Power in Ecclesiastical Causes* (London, 1659).

9. Ibid., p. 2.

10. Ibid., p. 5; italics added.

11. Ibid., p. 7.

12. Ibid., p. 35.

13. Ibid.

14. Ibid. Milton also makes it clear that the Roman Church does not meet the test of Scriptural orthodoxy; he calls it a "catholic heresie against the Scripture."

15. See also Milton's *De Doctrina Christiana* (London, 1661).

16. Jeremy Taylor, *A Discourse on Freedom of Thinking in Matters of Religion*, 2nd ed. (London, 1763), p. 329.

17. Ibid.

18. Ibid., p. 332. See also Shakespeare, *King John*, III, i. Cardinal Pandulph says to King John:

> "Then, by the lawful power that I have,
> Thou shalt stand curs'd and excommunicate;
> And blessed shall he be that doth revolt
> From his allegiance to a heretic;
> And meritorious shall that hand be call'd
> Canonized and worshipped as a saint,
> That takes away by shy secret course
> Thy hateful life."

See also Grotius, *De Jure belli ac pacis*, Bk. I, ch. 4, no. 3.

19. Jeremy Taylor, *op cit.*, p. 332.

20. Jeremy Taylor, *A Course of Sermons for all the Sundays of the Year* (London, 1655).

21. Ibid., p. 195.

22. Samuel Parker, *A Discourse of Ecclesiastical Politie* (London, 1670).

23. Ibid., pp. xxi–xxii.

24. Ibid., pp. 11–12.

25. Ibid., p. liii. Parker is emphatic on this point: "To exempt Religion and the Consciences of men from the Authority of the Supreme Power is but to expose the peace of Kingdoms to every wild and fanatique Pretender, who may when ever he pleases, under pretense of Reformation thwart and unsettle Government without controul; seeing no one can have any power to restrain the perswasion of his Conscience"; pp. 14–15.

26. John F. Fulton, *A Bibliography of the Honourable Robert Boyle*, 2nd ed. (London: Oxford University Press, 1961), p. 197.

27. See Harold Fisch, "The Scientist as Priest: A Note on Robert Boyle's Natural Theology," *Isis* 44 (1953). For a good discussion of the Bentley–Newton correspondence, see Alexandre Koyré, *Newtonian Studies* (London: Chapman and Hall, 1965), Ch. IV.

28. I. Bernard Cohen, *Isaac Newton's Papers and Letters on Natural Philosophy and Related Documents* (Cambridge: Cambridge University Press, 1958); Miller's comments on p. 277.

29. Robert E. Schofield, *Mechanism and Materialism in British Natural Philosophy* (Princeton: Princeton University Press, 1970), p. 21.

30. Samuel Parker, *A Demonstration of the Divine Authority of the Law of Nature and of the Christian Religion* (London, 1681), preface.

31. Ibid., p. iii.

32. Ibid.

33. Samuel Parker, *The Case for the Church of England* (London, 1681), p. 8. See Samuel I. Mintz, *The Hunting of Leviathan* (Cambridge: Cambridge University Press, 1962) where he says that the first full-scale polemic against Hobbes as an atheist was Alexander Ross's *Leviathan Drawn out with a Hook* (London, 1653); see also John Bramhall, *The Catching of Leviathan or the Great Whale* (London, 1658).

34. Parker, *A Discourse of Ecclesiastical Politie*, p. 7.

35. Ibid., p. 10.

36. Ibid., p. 28.

37. Ibid., pp. 33 and 34.

38. Ibid., p. 48.

39. Parker, *The Case for the Church of England*, p. 12.

40. James Lowde, *Discourse Concerning the Nature of Man* (London, 1694), Chapter I, "Of the Knowledge of a Man's Self," p. 12.

41. Ibid., p. 230.

42. Ibid., p. 60.

43. Ibid., p. 166.

44. Ibid., p. 167.

45. Ibid., p. 168.

46. Richard Cumberland, *A Treatise of the Laws of Nature* (London, 1751).

47. Ibid., "Prolegomena," p. lxxv.

48. Ibid., pp. 2–3.

49. Thomas Aquinas, *Summa theologica*, Ia–IIae, qu. 94.

50. Ibid.

51. Richard Hooker, *Laws of Ecclesiastical Polity*, Bk. I, p. 33.

52. Ibid., p. 6.

53. Ibid., pp. 7–8.

54. Ibid., p. 32.

55. Ibid., p. 169.

56. Seth Ward, *In Thomae Hobbii philosophiam exercitatio* (London, 1656).

57. Seth Ward, *A Philosophical Essay towards an Eviction of the Being and Attributes of God* (London, 1652).

58. John Eachard, *Mr. Hobbes's State of Nature Considered* (London, 1672).

59. Ibid., p. 165. See also Eachard, *Some Opinions of Mr. Hobbes Considered in a Second Dialogue between Philautus and Timothy* (London, 1672).

60. Thomas Burnet, *Remarks Upon an Essay Concerning Humane Understanding* (London, 1697), p. 4.

61. Ibid., p. 26.

62. Ibid.

63. Ibid.

64. For a good recent account of this matter see John Redwood, *Reason, Ridicule and Religion* (London: Thames and Hudson, 1977).

65. Robert Kargon, "Thomas Hariot, the Northumberland Circle and Early Atomism in England," *Journal of the History of Ideas*, 27 (1966), 133.

66. Even the Earl of Clarendon thought that Hobbes ought to have been punished "with the most severe penalties," for his *Leviathan* and *De Cive. A Brief View and Survey*, p. 8.

67. *Laws of Ecclesiastical Polity* (London, 1593); Books VI–VIII in 1648; Book VII in 1661. All references are to the Everyman's Library ed. (London: Dent, 1958).

68. Ibid., I, viii, p. 182.

69. Ibid., I, xvi, p. 228.

70. Marie Boas, "The Establishment of the Mechanical Philosophy," *Osiris*, 10 (1952), 414.

71. *Baruch Spinoza, Theological–Political Treatise*, trans. R. H. M. Elwes, (New York: Dover, 1951).

72. Since a miracle is "a result which cannot be explained by its cause, a phenomenon which surpasses human understanding" (Ch. VI), only the natural philosopher can say what is beyond nature. See also Locke, "Discourse on Miracles," *Works*, IX, 256ff.

73. *Op. cit.*, p. 189.

74. John Wilkins, *A Discourse Concerning a New Planet* (London, 1640).

75. Ibid., p. 48.

76. Alexander Ross, *The New Planet No Planet: or The Earth No Wandering Star; except in the Wandering Heads of Galileans* (London, 1646).

77. Ibid., p. 2.

78. Richard Baxter, *The Arrogancy of Reason Against Divine Revelations Repressed* (London, 1655).

79. Richard Baxter, *The Reason of the Christian Religion* (London, 1667).

80. Meric Casaubon, *Of Credulity and Incredulity in Things Natural, Civil and Divine* (London, 1668), p. 203.

81. Ibid., p. 206.

82. Jeremy Taylor, *Sermons for all Sundays of the Year* (London, 1653).

83. Ibid., p. 191.

84. John Wilkins, *A Discourse Concerning the Beauty of Providence* (London, 1649), and *The Principles and Duties of Natural Religion* (London, 1675).

85. John Wilkins, *The Principles and Duties of Natural Religion* (London, 1675).

86. Ibid., p. 402.

87. Edmund Halley, "Some Considerations about the Cause of the Universal Deluge," *Philosophical Transactions of the Royal Society*, 33 (1690) 118; reprinted in *Philosophical Transactions Abridged*, 11 vols. (London, 1731–1756), VI, Pt. II, p. 3.

6

The Divine Politics of Modernity

THE FOUNDERS OF THE NEW POLITICAL PHILOSOPHY in the seventeenth century were not merely concerned with destroying the prevailing Aristotelian tradition; they were more concerned with replacing it with a new one. It therefore became an essential part of the modern project to strike at the very roots of philosophy and to establish a new foundation entirely different from that upon which the older philosophy was based. The distrust of the power of reason provided in the first instance, as we have seen, the basis of the modern project of replacement. This, along with the rejection of the classical conception of nature, which taught that men were by nature ordered to moral virtue, became the focus of considerable controversy. The first important consequence of the new modern conception of nature was that it placed man outside and above nature; it placed him in a posture of hostility toward nature, bent upon conquering nature in the name of progress. In the Socratic tradition man's proper place was in nature and his perfection was determined by nature. The new conception of nature "liberated" man from her restraints and permitted him to become whatever he wished to become.

But it is also important to note that, as philosophy under the Aristotelian schoolmen had become inextricably associated with theology, the moderns not only had the difficult task of uprooting the old philosophy,[1] they also had to undermine the philosophical basis of the official and very much established theology. We need only to recall the fate of Galileo to recollect the closeness of science and philosophy to theology at the early modern period.[2] This theological or religious aspect of the modern project rendered it especially dangerous to engage in. One could easily be imprisoned or exiled before as well as after the Reformation for heretical philosophical views which tended to call in question the established religious orthodoxy. It became necessary, therefore, for the modern writers, especially in England, to write with considerable caution. John Toland, a young contemporary of John Locke's, wrote in 1720 about the "exoteric and esoteric philosophy," by which he meant the deliberate or conscious attempt of an author to conceal his real intention from the casual reader. After showing how this manner of writing prevailed in ancient times, Toland says that it was still practiced in his time. The reason for employing this literary device in his day was, he says, the same as in ancient times: the fear of religious reprisal. As Toland relates:

> the philosophers therefore and other well-wishers to mankind in most nations, were constrained by this holy tyranny to make use of a two-fold doctrine; the one popular accommodated to the prejudices of the vulgar, and the received customs or religion; the other philosophical conformable to the nature of things and consequently to truth which with doors fast shut and under all other precautions, they communicated only to friends of known probity, prudence and capacity.[3]

No one was more fully aware than Samuel Parker that the writings of Hobbes constituted a danger to the established theological orthodoxy. In his *Case for the Church of England* (1681) Parker disparages "the absurdity of Mr. Hobbes's principle that the sovereign power is the only founder of all religion in every commonwealth."[4] Parker revealed that he understood Hobbes's comments on religion when he writes that Hobbes taught that "neither himself nor any wise man ought to regard the tales of religion and that they are only designed to abuse the ignorant and the silly."[5] In short, Parker concludes, "The Hobbesian religion . . . is nothing else but an open declaration of atheism and impiety."[6]

With regard to Hobbes's state of nature Parker observed: "And in the same manner that he has destroyed the evidence of a Deity, has he taken away the obligation of all His laws of justice and honesty, by supposing such a state of nature in which mankind being exempt from all government may do whatever they please without the violation of any law. Which to suppose is to suppose no Deity."[7] For, concluded Parker, if one acknowledges the existence of God then there can have been no such state of nature in which God had no jurisdiction from the beginning of the world.

In like manner, Bishop Edward Stillingfleet became Locke's chief adversary, charging him with laying the foundation of heresy.[8] He was quick to say that he did not charge Locke himself with heresy, but that his doctrine gave rise to it. In confirmation of this Stillingfleet identified John Toland's book *Christianity Not Mysterious*, which drew its major strength from Locke's Essay on *Human Understanding*. He even went so far as to concede the possibility that others would use Locke's thoughts "to other purposes than you intended them."[9] Nevertheless, he said it was necessary to inquire whether what Locke says regarding the foundation of certainty in fact contradicts the belief in the major canons of the Christian religion. Accordingly, the first part of his discourse is directed against the philosophical propositions regarding certainty, which Locke claimed stems from the agreement or disagreement of our ideas. Stillingfleet responded: "But for you to talk so much of certainty by ideas, and yet to allow obscurity and imperfection in those ideas [as though] . . . one would undertake to show with certainty the agreement or disagreement of two men at a distance from him, in their habit, features, and stature and yet at the same time confess that he could not clearly distinguish one from the other."[10]

Stillingfleet's argument was that Locke's doctrine contains implicit contradictions; that the terms "agreement" and "disagreement" themselves have no basis of uncertainty. But his main objective was to show that Locke's *Essay* was dangerous to theological orthodoxy. If, said Stillingfleet, our certainty depends solely upon the agreement or disagreement of our ideas regardless of the source of those ideas, "we can be no more certain than we have clear perception of the agreement or disagreement of ideas contained in it."[11] This clearly lays the foundation for doubt in those theological matters touching testimony and mysteries, said Stillingfleet, as John Toland was quick to perceive in *Christianity Not Mysterious*. Furthermore, Stillingfleet agreed with Toland that there was reasonable basis for believing that Locke's doctrine led to the conclusions which the author was proposing in his treatise on Christian mysteries.[12] Stillingfleet also claimed that Locke "cannot clear [himself] from the foundation which the author of *Christianity not Mysterious* built upon."[13] A careful reading of Locke's *Essay* will lead a discerning reader to conclude that the doctrine set forth there can in no way be compatible with Christian orthodoxy; the *Essay* leads at least to skepticism or agnosticism, as Stillingfleet suggested.[14]

Stillingfleet's conclusion was that Locke's method concerning the certainty of ideas shakes the foundation of belief in revelation and casts doubts upon particular key articles of the Christian faith.[15]

In their attempt to wrest philosophy from the schoolmen, the moderns were attempting to do exactly what the ancient philosophers had done, i.e., to place reason alone as the sole guide to human life. Philosophy thus became the test of the reasonableness of Christian dogma.

Paradoxically, the moderns began their assault on theology by accepting the theological invitation to acknowledge two distinct spheres, one theological, the other temporal. As Francis Bacon said: "this likewise I humbly pray, that things human may not interfere with things divine, . . . that the understanding . . . may give to faith that which is faith's."[16] This apparent concession tells us nothing about what one should take on faith. But Bacon scolds those who attempt to "deduce the truth of the Christian religion from the principles of philosophers";[17] this leads to "desparaging things divine by mingling them with things human."[18] Rather than settle the issue, this merely helps philosophers to ignore theological claims and to get on with their work.

Francis Bacon was not only the first to see the necessity of undermining the foundations of Christian orthodoxy; he was also the one to set the direction others, such as Hobbes, were later to follow. The rationalistic character of Bacon's attack on Biblical religion emerges with clarity in the *De Augmentis*. "Sacred theology," he wrote, "must be drawn from the word and oracles of God, not from the light of nature, or the dictates of reason."[19] We are even obliged to believe the word of God, said Bacon, "though our reason be shocked at it."[20] Indeed, he said: "the more absurd

and incredible any divine mystery is, the greater honour we do to
God in believing it; and so much the more noble the victory of
faith."[21] Superficially these statements would appear to confirm
the theological view that the mysteries of sacred theology defy rational explanation; that they are matters to be taken on faith and
beyond the capacity of mere human understanding. A more reflec-
tive consideration reveals, however, that Bacon is laying the foundation for judging the claims of the Bible and hence the claims of
orthodox Christianity. We saw in Chapter 1 that Bacon makes a
laconic remark about a little natural philosophy leading to atheism.
He does not say there, or elsewhere, that a great deal leads to
Christian orthodoxy. We will also recall that Bacon claimed that
the inquiring into the divine mysteries led to man's fall from divine
favor.[22] By urging men to concentrate their attention on this world
and by placing theology beyond human capacity, Bacon effectively
established the foundations for natural philosophy without the
interference of theology.[23] Knowledge derived from theological
speculation he called secondary reason.

> So in human laws, there by many grounds and maxims which are
> *placita juris*, positive authority [such as "in games of wit, and chess"],
> and not upon reason, and therefore not to be disputed: but what is
> most just, not absolutely but relatively, and according to those max-
> ims, that affordeth a long field of disputation. Such therefore is that
> secondary reason, which hath place in divinity, which is grounded
> upon the placets of God.[24]

He restricts natural theology or "divine Philosophy" to the contemplation of God in His creatures. Thus understood, natural theology not only is compatible with natural philosophy (since it remains in the realm of secondary causes) but is also governed by the
limits and methodology of natural philosophy. All doctrines of
religion are the produce of "inspiration and revelation from
God."[25]

But Bacon appears to have taught that most religions are the
product of fears; fears which spring from an awareness of the unknown. He notes that only knowledge, i.e., natural philosophy,
can take away or mitigate these fears.[26] Quoting Virgil's lines in

praise of Epicurus, Bacon affirms that man will become much more peaceful, i.e., happier, once he removes the causes of his religious fears. He reasons in his commentary on the Book of Job in a manner similar to that of Epicurus and Lucretius that men cannot offend God; nor can they appease Him by good works: "I believe that God is so holy, pure and zealous, as it is impossible for him to be pleased in any creature, through the work of his own hands."[27]

Bacon's Biblical commentaries tend to give the impression that they were addressed to two audiences. On the one hand, he gives the vulgar, the larger audience, the basis for dispelling their fears by deflating the traditional orthodox claims regarding punishment in the next life. He does this by placing God beyond their reach. On the other, he appears to be speaking to philosophers, or those who read Scripture "with diligence."[28] Bacon invites this smaller audience to pursue natural philosophy and to subject the claims of revealed religion to the test of reason. Indeed, he even suggests that the Bible is "pregnant and swelling with natural philosophy."[29]

Bacon wrote on two levels because he had a sense of responsibility. He counseled philosophers to be prudent, and never once denied the need for religious practices for the common people. On the contrary, he affirmed that atheism leads to civil unrest.[30] In counseling philosophers or potential philosophers, Bacon reminded them that "The Scripture saith: 'The fool hath said it in his heart, there is no God'; it is not said, 'The fool hath thought in his heart'."[31] But atheism of thought must not lead to atheism of word or deed. "Among statesmen of politics, those who have been of greatest depth and compass, and of largest and most universal understanding, have not only in cunning made their profit in seeming religious to the people, but in truth have been touched with an inward sense of the knowledge of Deity, as they which you shall evermore note to have attributed much to fortune and Providence."[32] Is this what Bacon meant when he wrote that "much natural philosophy" will lead to religion?

The seventeenth-century founders of modern political philosophy were confronted with a twofold problem. On the one hand, they were obliged to refute the claims of political theology, while, on the other, they were obliged to replace the Aristotelian doctrine of natural right. We have seen how they replaced the classical natural right doctrine with a new natural right based on the right of self-preservation. We must now see how they responded to the political–theological problems.

It is important at the outset to understand how the moderns viewed the political implications of the theological claims. Hugo Grotius stated the problem earlier when he wrote in *De jure belli ac pacis* that

> Among all good men one principle at any rate is beyond controversy, that if the authorities issue any order that is contrary to the law of nature or to the command of God, the order should not be carried out. For when the Apostles said that obedience should be rendered to God rather than to men, they appealed to an infallible rule of action, which is written in the hearts of all men and which you may find in Plato expressed in about as many words.[33]

And Richard Hooker wrote in *The Laws of Ecclesiastical Polity* that "the public power of all societies is above every soul contained in the same societies. And the principal use of that power is to give laws unto all that are under it; which laws in such case we must obey, unless there be reason shewed which may necessarily enforce that the laws of Reason or of God doth enjoin the contrary."[34]

Both Grotius and Hooker thus made it clear that there were two avenues by which the citizen may (indeed, *must*) judge the commands of the civil sovereign: one was reason and another was God's will.[35] The founders of modern political philosophy were obliged to confront and refute the claim that the law of God puts at man's disposal an "infallible rule" by which to judge the civil laws. This is nothing less, as Hooker makes plain, than a premiss which could lead to civil disobedience or rebellion. Small wonder that the political philosophers felt obliged to subject the Scriptures to the test of reason; the Scriptures provided the foundation for political theology and a doctrine of political disobedience.

Thomas Hobbes, in particular, viewed the theological injunction to place the law of God above the civil law as dangerous folly; such an injunction makes believers (and especially Christians) qualified citizens, i.e., prepared on the basis of appeal to God or a transcendent natural right to disobey the law. Hobbes was pre-occupied with the problem of civil stability and saw that a concept of absolute or unqualified sovereignty was the only means by which such stability could be achieved. Christian suprapolitical allegiance to a higher authority clearly eliminates the possibility of absolute civil sovereignty. That supernatural authority which can threaten punishment "of infinite weight and duration" (as Locke expressed it) in the next life is clearly superior to the temporal authority and ought to be feared more than the civil authority.[36]

It becomes understandable, therefore, to see how much attention the founders of modernity gave to theological or scriptural matters. One third of *De Cive* and one half of *Leviathan* treat theological matters. And John Locke's *Reasonableness of Christianity* (including the *Vindications*) and his *Paraphrase and Notes on the Epistles of St. Paul* constitute two volumes.

For both Hobbes and Locke the contest was between philosophy and theology. Both philosophy and theology claim to teach the truth about all reality. But a philosophy cannot accept the claims of revealed religion which are inconsistent with the light of human reason. And theology is based on the belief in the revealed word of God and on the possibility of certain matters' being beyond human reason. From the purely philosophical point of view nothing can be beyond human reason.

In political philosophy the best regime is the just regime under-stood solely from the point of view of philosophy; from the theological view the best or just regime is that regime which subscribes to precepts of God's will. Furthermore, since God's will is revealed in the Scriptures, the theological view meant the hegemony of those who were in charge of the Scriptures—i.e., the priesthood or the Church. This placed the State below the Church. It also meant that the Church will be obeyed before the State because the Church has the threat of punishment of infinite weight and duration to back up its instructions.

In other words, the theological or Biblical claims rendered the matter of civil obedience or citizenship highly problematic. Jesus counsels in the New Testament that believers should "render to Caesar the things that are Caesar's and to God the things that are God's."[37] This implies that citizens in a Christian commonwealth must before obeying the laws pause and examine them in the light of this *higher* injunction. And since sovereignty cannot be divided in a state there can be no stability in a state which is beset with the conflicting commands, one "temporal" and the other "ghostly."[38]

HOBBES: THE THEOLOGY OF FEAR

Hobbes was unequivocal in his rejection of the divided sovereignty implied in the Christian doctrine of spheres of authority. He said in *Leviathan* that as it is impossible for the human body to be commanded by two souls,

> so also in the body politic, when the spiritual power, moveth the members of a commonwealth, by the terror of punishments, and hopes of rewards, which are the nerves of it, otherwise than by the civil power, which is the soul of the commonwealth, they ought to be moved; and by strange, and hard words suffocates their understanding, it must needs thereby distract the people, and either overwhelm the commonwealth with oppression, or cast it into the fire of a civil war.[39]

Hobbes was deeply concerned with the evils of civil war, which he calls "the worst of all possible calamities," because it is in fact a return to the vicious condition of the state of nature; and that must be avoided at all cost. He goes so far as to claim that most civil wars can be traced to the presence of the conflicting claim to sovereignty. "For what civil war was there ever in the Christian world, which did not either grow from, or was nourished by this root"[40]— i.e., the claims of the clergy to be obeyed, and of laity to withhold obedience under pretense of religion.

For Hobbes, the chief weaknesses of the Christian tradition emerged out of the power concentrated in the hands of the Church as well as the philosophy of Thomas Aquinas, which taught a dangerous doctrine regarding private conscience, or the ability to judge of right and wrong. In *Leviathan* he speaks of

> the poison of seditious doctrines, whereof one is, *that every private man is judge of good and evil actions*. This is true in the conditions of mere nature, where there are no civil laws; . . . From this false doctrine, men are disposed to debate with themselves, and dispute the commands of the commonwealth; and afterwards to obey, or disobey them as in their private judgments they shall think fit; whereby the commonwealth is distracted and weakened.[41]

There can be no peace or civil order unless the civil sovereign be the supreme and sole judge of what is good and evil.

Hobbes is here consciously addressing himself to the Socratic tradition as well as to the Thomistic or school philosophy, because Aristotle and Plato taught that the regime must be judged by the transcendent standard of natural justice. This led them not only to a conception of the best regime by nature but also to the distinction between just and unjust regimes by nature. The distinction between monarch and tyrant is based on the distinction between just and unjust rule. Hobbes rejected both the distinction and the right to appeal to a transcendent norm above the regime.[42] But he did not deny philosophy; on the contrary, he said clearly that "Reason is the pace; increase of science, the way; and the benefit of mankind, the end."[43] But it is reason guided by the new natural philosophy, i.e., based upon a new conception of nature and the new understanding of the limits of human knowledge. He scorned the "innumerable absurdities" of the schoolmen, which led to contention, sedition, and contempt. Furthermore, he wrote, "every man then and now is bound to make use of his Naturall Reason, to apply to all prophesy those rules which God hath given us, to discern the true from the false."[44]

Thomas Hobbes set out in *Leviathan* to question the claims of divine revelation and undermine the foundations of the prevailing Christian political theology, which claimed that the Church was the authoritative interpreter of God's commands. Turning to the natural philosophy for support, Hobbes applied natural reason to the Scriptural claims to sovereignty over men. This was undertaken in the conviction that the new natural philosophy provided access to a complete knowledge of all reality and that the interpretation of Scripture must be subjected to the test of the canons of reason provided by the new natural philosophy. Hobbes implied that political philosophers were obliged to make such a test. Taking Bacon—a major founder of the new natural philosophy—as his guide, Hobbes claimed that natural science alone could provide philosophy the one thing it lacked up to this time: a methodical search for the causes of things. If modern natural science provided anything, it was the methodical searching after causes. With this as his fundamental premiss, Hobbes proceeded to show that religion is *the* unmethodical searching into the causes of the belief in divinity. Hobbes's critique of religion is therefore cloaked in the appearance of impartial or objective science attempting to solve a scientific problem. But he made it clear that if the new knowledge obtained through the application of the new philosophy contradicts the old explanations provided by the former unmethodical approach (i.e., of the theologians), then the new explanations must prevail over the old. Hobbes did not blame ancient or modern men for the unmethodical seeking of explanations in religious matters; there was very little choice until modern natural science provided the method. He was sympathetic toward those who assumed and believed that the gods were the causes of good and evil fortune. The belief in the gods was the direct result of human fear, i.e., a fear which could not be eliminated without the aid of natural science.[45]

Hobbes's critique of the Bible contains two points. First, that the conflict between Church and State would not arise if the clergy kept strictly to the teachings of the Bible (a proposition which must surely have appealed to the new orthodoxy, which believed in following strictly the teachings of the Bible). Hobbes's second point is that the teachings of the Bible can be understood by the use of human reason alone. (This was less acceptable to contemporary divines, but those disposed to believe that natural reason would only affirm the theological understanding of the Bible found it acceptable.) But when Hobbes argued that the Bible cannot command that which was in conflict with natural reason, he was beginning to challenge the allegiance of his clerical friends. He lost all allegiance when he concluded that the authority of the Bible is not grounded in the Bible itself, but exclusively in the command given by the temporal power, and is dependent on the temporal power.[46] This clearly solved the conflict of Church and State by subsuming the Church within the State and under the civil authority. In *Behemoth* Hobbes wrote:

> true politics should be, such as are fit to make men know, that it is
> their duty to obey all laws whatsoever that shall by the authority of
> the King be enacted, till by the same authority they shall be repealed;
> such as are fit to make men understand, that the civil laws are God's
> laws, as they that make them are by God appointed to make them;
> and to make men know, that the people and the Church are one thing,
> and have but one head, the King; and that no man has title to govern
> under him, that has it not from him; that the King owes his crown
> to God only, and to no man, ecclesiastical or other; and that the re-
> ligion they teach there, be a quiet waiting for the coming again of our
> blessed Saviour, and in the mean time a resolution to obey the King's
> laws, which also are God's laws.[47]

Since the Christian commonwealth is founded "upon supernatural revelations of the will of God,"[48] Hobbes turned his attention to the scriptural teachings presented by the Church over the ages. But he made it clear early in *Leviathan* that he was scrutinizing not only the clergy of the Roman Church but also the clergy of "that church that hath presumed most of reformation."[49]

Hobbes accordingly analysed in Part III of *Leviathan* the scriptural foundations of "Christian politics." He began by noting that what he had established up to this point were "the rights of sovereign power, and the duty of subjects, hitherto from the principles of nature only."[50] What remained to be established were the "rights of a Christian Commonwealth" which "dependeth much upon supernatural revelations of the will of God."[51] But Hobbes's scrutiny of the "prophetical" basis of the Christian Commonwealth was undertaken under the guidance of natural reason, which he called "the undoubted word of God."[52] And however much there may be "things in God's words above reason,"[53] human reason cannot contradict the word of God. When reason appears to do so it is the fault "either in our unskilful interpretation, or erroneous ratiocination."[54]

The reader is left with the initial impression that Hobbes believed that human reason must attempt to bring its ratiocinations into line with the word of God as reported in the Scriptures. But such an impression is not supported by the evidence of the succeeding chapters. There Hobbes subjects every facet of revelation to the scrutiny of reason (to the "submission of the intellectual faculty"); this forbids, in the first place, a submission to the opinion of "any other man."[55]

This led Hobbes to examine the way in which God speaks to men. In other words, he set out to scrutinize the transmission of the word of God through the testimony of men. Since God speaks to men either immediately (directly) or "by the mediation of another man" (i.e., through the testimony of the prophets), one must first determine which form of communication one is confronted with. Hobbes denied that God speaks immediately to men in Holy Scriptures but "by mediation of the prophets, or of the apostles, or of the church, in such manner as he speaks to all other Christian men."[56] In other words, Hobbes subjects to the test of reason ("forbear contradiction") the testimony of the prophets and apostles. Reason is the "*undoubted* word of God," while the prophetical testimony is the *doubted* word; the latter must meet the test of reason. By so doing, Hobbes challenged the very foundations of Christian orthodoxy. He acknowledges that God may speak immediately to a man in dreams or visions but says that this "obliges no man to believe he hath so done to him that pretends it; who, being a man, may err, and, which is more, may lie."[57] The test by which one is to judge of the veracity of a prophet is, says Hobbes, twofold: he must be a performer of miracles and not teach "any other religion than that which is already established."[58] Miracles alone are insufficient because even the Egyptian sorcerers performed "great miracles."

What Hobbes does here is establish that, on the testimony of the Old Testament, one can conclude that God was the civil sovereign of the Jews, for God spoke immediately to Moses on Mount Sinai. The second test of a true prophet is important because the true prophet will not "stir up revolt against the king, or him that governeth by the king's authority."[59] Indeed, argued Hobbes, the words, *"revolt from the Lord your God*, are in this place equivalent to *revolt from your king."*[60] In short, in the history of the Jews from the establishment of the kingdom of God until the Captivity, the civil and religious authority were vested in the same sovereign power.

Hobbes noted that Jesus issued a similar warning against false prophets; the implication being that the testimony of miracles alone is in no way sufficient testimony of the veracity of the Christian prophet. Furthermore, Hobbes emphasizes, Jesus did not counsel disobedience of the Jewish or Roman civil laws, i.e., he did not challenge the temporal authority or claim to be king of *this* world: "My kingdom is not of this world," he said. The important implications of this disclaimer to temporal rule is crucial for Hobbes. The founder of Christianity would appear to have relinquished any title to temporal rule. This led Hobbes to say that the Scriptures have no status as law in the Christian commonwealth unless established by the authority of the civil sovereign. It is for this reason that Hobbes attempts to discover what it is that the New Testament teaches with regard to man's temporal life.

What compounds the problem is that miracles have now ceased. We are left, says Hobbes, with the Holy Scriptures, from which we must "by wise and learned interpretation, and careful ratiocination" deduce "all the rules and precepts necessary to the knowledge of our duty both to God and man."[61]

Hobbes begins by accepting the Old and New Testaments as "the true registers of those things, which were done and said by the prophets and apostles."[62] He is careful not to say that he accepts them as the word of God. Furthermore, he claims that "it is not the writer, but the authority of the church, that maketh the book canonical."

The key question for Hobbes was not "from whence the Scriptures derive their authority" but "by what authority they are made law."[63] In other words, the civil authority they carry is of more importance than any claim to supernatural authority, because for Hobbes there can be only one sovereign authority and that must be temporal.[64] What Hobbes does here is open the Scriptures to see to what extent they can contribute to the stability of the civil authority.

"As far as they [the Scriptures] differ not from the laws of nature, there is no doubt, but they are the law of God."[65] The area of doubt emerges where the teachings of the Scriptures differ from the laws of nature or claim authority over the civil authority. Hobbes says:

> Again, if it be not the legislative authority of the commonwealth, that giveth them the force of laws, it must be some other authority derived from God, either private, or public: if private, it obliges only him, to whom in particular God hath been pleased to reveal it. For if every man should be obliged, to take for God's law, what particular men, on pretence of private inspiration, or revelation, should obtrude upon him, in such a number of men, that out of pride and ignorance, take their own dreams, and extravagant fancies, and madness, for testimonies of God's spirit; or out of ambition, pretend to such divine testimonies, falsely, and contrary to their own consciences, it were impossible that any divine law should be acknowledged.[66]

In the Christian commonwealth there is an absolute union of Church and State "because it consisteth in Christian men, united in one Christian sovereign."[67] The Christian commonwealth lives completely under the Christian civil sovereign.

Hobbes attempted to understand how God is said to have spoken to the prophets. He says that the Scriptures usually say a "vision" and that one cannot say that God spoke in words since that would mean he had all the other attributes of the human body.[68] God "speaks" to men, says Hobbes, in many ways and they are "to be sought only in the Holy Scripture."[69] In the final analysis Hobbes concluded that "in what manner God spoke to those sovereign prophets of the Old Testament . . . is not intelligible. In the time of the New Testament, there was no sovereign prophet, but our Saviour; who was both that spoke, and the prophet to whom he spoke." [70] But Hobbes further claims that there were only two real prophets: Moses and Christ. God spoke directly to Moses and since Christ was God he spoke to himself. All other minor prophets (those he calls "subordinate prophets of perpetual calling") [71] have a much less certain status. Hobbes claims that God moved them "to piety, to belief, to righteousness, and to other virtues [shared by] all other Christian men." How can one distinguish between these prophets and the manner in which God spoke to them? This is the question which led Hobbes to conclude:

> Seeing then, all prophecy supposeth vision, or dream, (which two, when they are natural, are the same), or some especial gift of God so rarely observed in mankind as to be admired where observed; and seeing as well such gifts, as the most extraordinary dreams and visions, may proceed from God, not only by his supernatural and immediate, but also by his natural operation, and by mediation of second causes; there is need of reason and judgment to discern between natural and supernatural gifts, and between natural, and supernatural visions, and dreams. [72]

Natural Reason thus becomes the test by which man can be sure that those who speak in God's name and promise happiness through obedience are indeed genuine prophets. [73] The warning is placed in the context of the scriptural testimony of the large number of false prophets. [74]

According to Hobbes, the rules God gave to men in the time of the Old Testament (i.e., those rules arrived at by natural reason) were two in number: first, that the prophet taught a doctrine conformable to that which Moses taught; and, second, that they possessed the miraculous power of foretelling what God would bring to pass. But the New Testament requires only that one believe *"that Jesus is the Christ."* [75] The Christian citizen must accordingly consider who is the true sovereign prophet or God's viceregent on earth with the authority of governing men. This leads Hobbes to consider "The Office of Our Blessed Saviour," but only after he applies natural reason to key theological concepts such as miracles, salvation, the world to come, and redemption. With regard to miracles, Hobbes contends that one must attempt to discover the natural cause; if such can be discerned then it cannot be called a miracle. One simply cannot assume that some event is a miracle simply because it is beyond our comprehension; one must know the total range of the natural possibilities or the limits of nature before ascribing an event to God or have it on the explicit testimony of God.

Since the Christian doctrine which placed a priority on allegiance to the commands of God was a challenge to the civil power, Hobbes paid careful attention to the foundations of the Christian commonwealth. The key role played by Jesus in the establishment of this commonwealth meant that his claims had to be properly understood. Hobbes set out to prove from Scripture that Jesus did not come to uproot the civil sovereign but to establish a new kingdom in the next life. He not only acknowledged Caesar's authority over subjects but counseled them to pay tribute to him as their lawful sovereign.[76] Jesus made no pretense to rule on this earth as king or as "his Father's lieutenant"; that he would do at his second coming.[77] In short, "our Saviour, and his apostles, left not new laws to oblige us in this world, but new doctrine to prepare us for the next."[78] This doctrine acquires authority in this world where the Christian monarch appropriates the New Testament and commands his subjects to obey the doctrine contained therein. As Hobbes says, "the Scripture of the New Testament is there only law, where the lawful civil power hath made it so."[79]

In this manner Hobbes effectively subsumes the religious claims within the civil power. The civil sovereign is clearly head of the Church. As Hobbes states:

> From this consolidation of the right politic and ecclesiastic in Christian sovereigns, it is evident, they have all manner of power over their subjects, that can be given to man, for the government of men's *external actions*, both in policy and religion; and may make such laws as themselves shall judge fittest, for the government or their own subjects, both as they are the commonwealth, and as they are the Church; for both State and Church are the same men.[80]

It is not without significance that Hobbes specified that the civil sovereign can command "external actions" and not internal actions. This is because Hobbes believed that the civil sovereign cannot command belief but can command public compliance: "For internal faith is in its own nature invisible, and consequently exempted from it, as breaches of our civil obedience, are injustice both before God and man."[81]

This teaching did not simply solve the practical problems for the non-Christian or non-believing Christians; it raised questions as to Hobbes's real thoughts about the claims of Biblical religion— especially the Christian religion. It is beyond our present purposes to inquire whether Hobbes was an atheist or a deist. But it is to our purpose to see how he casts doubts upon fundamental aspects of Christian orthodoxy. For example, Hobbes took a special interest in comparing Jesus with Moses;[82] in doing so he carefully acknowledged the orthodox claim that Jesus was the Son of God, but the clear implication of the contrasts with Moses and the work Moses did is the conclusion that Jesus was a man—however extraordinary—much like Moses. Indeed, since Jesus did not alter the Mosaic law but built upon it, one can conclude that Jesus was less great than Moses, who led the Israelites out of captivity and gave them the tablets of the law of God and established a kingdom on this earth. This implication is enforced by the doubts Hobbes raises about the reception Jesus received at the hands of the Jews who were expecting a Messiah on the authority of the Scriptures. Jesus clearly failed in one major part of his mission: to persuade the Jews to return to the kingdom of his Father. Hobbes asks pointedly: "If then Christ, whilst he was on earth, had no kingdom in this world, to what end was his first coming?"[83] It was certainly of no benefit to the Jews, the very ones who believed that they had been promised an earthly kingdom.

Hobbes's reply to this question was: "It was to restore unto God, by a new covenant, the kingdom, which being his by the Old covenant, had been cut off by the rebellion of the Israelites in the election of Saul." But Jesus failed in this mission; the Jews refused to acknowledge him as the Messiah promised by the prophets. Hobbes asks why all the Jews did not believe the testimony of St. Paul. "What was the reason, when they all believed the Scripture, that they did not all believe alike; but that some approved, others disapproved the interpretations of St. Paul that cited them; and every one interpreted them to himself?"[84] The answer, said Hobbes, lies in the fact that Paul came without any legal command and hence had to rely on the principles of reasoning contained in Scripture. But, said Hobbes, this "maketh him to whom he [St. Paul] speaketh judge, both of the meaning of those principles, and also of the force of his influences upon them."[85] The Jews of Thessalonica refused to be persuaded; those with the closest contact with the Scriptures, those who jealously preserved them and longed for their fulfillment, were not convinced by the testimony of Paul or the other apostles. Paul accordingly turned his attention to the Gentiles who, being without the Old Testament, were more easily persuaded and hence converted.[86]

The political importance of Hobbes's theological views can be seen from his remarks on the priority of statute law over the common law in his posthumously published *Dialogue Between a Philosopher and a Student of the Common-Laws of England*.[87] In this work Hobbes asserts that even the laws governing heresy are subject to the positive law of the state, a view consistent with *Leviathan*. Anyone familiar with the life of Hobbes knows how close he came to being formally denounced as an atheist. His famous dispute with Bishop Bramhall was followed closely by contemporaries. Even Hobbes (whom Spinoza considered bold in expressing his unorthodox views) apparently knew the limits of indiscretion. A select committee of the House of Commons cited Hobbes's *Leviathan* as a source of atheism and profaneness. And John Aubrey relates that a number of Bishops in the House of Lords "made a motion to have the good old gentleman burn't for a heretique."[88] Even Edward Hyde, the Earl of Clarendon (who knew Hobbes and counted him among his friends), wrote from exile in France *A Brief View and Survey of the Dangerous and Pernicious Errors to Church and State in Mr. Hobbes's Book entitled Leviathan* (1676), in which he claimed that Hobbes ought to have been punished "with the most severe penalties"[89] for his doctrines. Most of Hobbes's writings on heresy, in which he claims that no man could be punished for heresy, were published posthumously since he was under a royal injunction not to publish anything relating to Church or State for the rest of his life. Hobbes was contending against the claims of certain Bishops that Parliament ought to re-enact the law against heresy which had been repealed during the reign of Elizabeth I. The law declaring heresy a capital crime was first passed during the reign of Richard II and reaffirmed by and remained in force under Henry VIII; it was repealed under Edward VI but reinstated under Mary. This is why Hobbes said that Bishop Bramhall "and others of this opinion had been in their Element, if they had been Bishops in Queen Maries time."[90]

One cannot escape the conclusion that for Hobbes all religion was rooted in fear and constituted varying degrees of superstition. In *Leviathan* he writes reminiscent of Lucretius that this "perpetual fear, always accompanying mankind and the ignorance of causes, as it were in the dark, must needs have for object something. And therefore when there is nothing to be seen, there is nothing to accuse, either of their good or evil fortune, but some power or agent invisible in which sense perhaps it was that some of the old poets said that the gods were created by human fear."[91] Hobbes made it clear that religious belief can distract men from their civic duties. "If this superstitious fear of Spirits were taken away and with it, Prognostiques from Dreams, false Prophecies, and many other things depending thereon, by which crafty ambitious persons abuse the simple people, men would be much more fitted than they are for civil obedience."[92]

Hobbes did not say, however, that there is no need for religion in civil society; but his conception of religion is radically different from that of orthodox Christian theology. In *Leviathan* he defined religion as "the fear of things invisible."[93] The origin of religious belief is fear, which he believed arises out of the peculiarly human propensity "to be inquisitive into the causes of the events they see."[94] This fear of "innumerable variety of fancy" has resulted in the creation in the world of "innumerable sorts of gods."[95] And this "fear of things invisible, is the natural seed of that which every one in himself calleth religion; and in them that worship, or fear that power otherwise than they do, superstition."[96] And since it cannot be obliterated from the minds of the vast majority of men, the sovereign is to take care to turn this weakness of human nature to the benefit of the state as the founders of ancient commonwealths.

> And therefore the first founders and legislators of commonwealths among the Gentiles, whose ends were only to keep the people in obedience, and peace, have in all places taken care; first, to imprint in their minds a belief, that those precepts which they gave concerning religion, might not be thought to proceed from their own device, but from the dictates of some god, or other spirit; or else that they themselves were of a higher nature than mere mortals, that their laws might the more easily be received.[97]

LOCKE: THE UNREASONABLENESS OF CHRISTIANITY

John Locke's response to the teachings of Christian political theology is contained in *The Reasonableness of Christianity*,[98] which he wrote in 1695 at the age of sixty-three. Locke says in the "Preface" to this work that he undertook to explore the reasonableness of the Christian religion as presented in the Scriptures because of "the little satisfaction and consistency that is to be found in most of the systems of divinity" he had encountered throughout his life; this dissatisfaction must be understood to include the works of his contemporary reform theologians as well as the traditional writings of the Roman theologians. In other words, Locke's writing on the Scriptures is intended as a challenge to the reform doctrine as well as the older orthodox theology.

In the "Preface to the Reader" of his *A Second Vindication of the Reasonableness of Christianity*, Locke writes that the doctrinal disagreement among his contemporaries prompted him to "a stricter and more thorough inquiry into the question about justification."[99] He indicates here that he was principally concerned with identifying what faith it was that leads to justification—i.e., what it is that men are to believe before they can be called righteous. It is important to observe, however, that Locke undertook to study the Scriptures (the New Testament almost exclusively) in the interest of a better understanding of the truth; his object is to increase knowledge, or understanding, not faith. One of the first things that emerges from a careful reading of *The Reasonableness of Christianity* is that Locke nowhere promises an increase in faith as a result of his efforts. This is a radical departure from the traditional Christian approach to Scripture, and Locke must surely have known it. Indeed the main clue to Locke's major theological writing is found in the title: his chief concern is to discover how much the basic tenets of the Christian religion, as presented in Scripture, conform with reason. Locke was a rationalist who delineated clearly the boundaries of faith and reason. In his major philosophical work, *An Essay of Human Understanding*,[100] He wrote that "Reason is natural revelation whereby the eternal Father of light and fountain of all knowledge communicates to mankind that portion of truth which He has laid within the reach of their natural faculties; revelation is natural reason enlarged by a new set of discoveries communicated by God immediately, which reason vouches the truth of by the testimony and proofs it gives that they come from God."[101] This is why Locke went directly to the New Testament, i.e., because "My Christianity, I confess, is contained in the written word of God."[102] And later in the same work he says that "All that is contained in the inspired writings, is all of divine authority, must be allowed as much, and received for divine and infallible truth by every subject of Christ's kingdom, i.e., every Christian."[103] Thus did Locke identify not only the subject matter of his inquiry but how he would approach it. He accordingly set about to subject the New Testament (i.e., the document in which the complete Christian doctrine is contained) to "a diligent and unbiassed search."[104]

What has misled many people in reading *The Reasonableness of Christianity* is the failure to grasp the important distinction Locke makes between believing what God has revealed and believing something to have been revealed by God. In other words, Locke says clearly that we are under an obligation to obey the commands of God but only after we have certain knowledge that what we are told is commanded by God can be proved to have been *in fact* commanded by God.

The second important thing which emerges from a careful reading of *The Reasonableness of Christianity* follows from what Locke says about Jesus' concealing himself and his refusal to speak in plain and clear terms. What Locke says here about Jesus must be applied to Locke himself. It will prove instructive in this connection to reflect upon what Locke says about how one must read the Epistles of St. Paul. In *An Essay for the Understanding of St. Paul's Epistles*,[105] Locke writes that a "careful reader" should be particularly concerned to note that Paul

> often breaks off in the middle of an argument, to let in some new thought suggested by his own words; which having pursued and explained, as far as conduced to his present purpose, he re-assumes again the thread of his discourse, and goes on with it, without taking any notice that he returns again to what he had been before saying; though sometimes it be so far off, that it may well have slipped out of his mind, and requires a very attentive reader to observe, and so bring the disjointed members together, as to make up the connexion, and see how the scattered parts of the discourse hang together in a coherent, well-agreeing sense, that makes it all of a piece.[106]

The main issues Locke explored in *The Reasonableness of Christianity* can be summarized in the following questions: "What is the connection between the law of works, the law of faith, and the law of reason?" "What is *the* essential ingredient of righteousness?" "Did Jesus ever say explicitly that he was the Messiah?" "What was the intellectual capacity of his apostles and disciples?" "Can reasonable men place faith in their testimony?" "What code of morality did Jesus establish?" "Is that code attainable by the light of natural reason?" "What has been the advantage to mankind of Jesus' moral code?"

The major portion of *The Reasonableness of Christianity* is a tedious account of the New Testament references by the apostles that Jesus was the Messiah. But before approaching this part of his task, Locke asks whether it was fair (i.e., reasonable) that the descendents of Adam should be punished for Adam's transgression. There can be no doubt, he says, that the descendents of Adam lost bliss and immortality, "that death came on all men by Adam's sin."[107] But, he says, there is considerable disagreement as to what constituted death in this context. He says that

> some will have it to be a state of guilt, wherein not only he, but all his posterity was so involved, that every one descended of him deserved endless torment, in hell-fire. I shall say nothing more here, how far, in the apprehensions of men, this consists with the justice of goodness of God, having mentioned it above; but it seems a strange way of understanding a law, which required the plainest and directest words, that by death should be meant eternal life in misery. Could any one be supposed, by a law, that says, "For felony thou shalt die," not that he should lose his life; but be kept alive in perpetual exquisite torments? And would any one think himself fairly dealt with, that was so used? [108]

The essential unfairness of such a doctrine was repulsive to Locke and must be viewed in the context of the later discussion of superstition. "Before our Saviour's time," ha says later, "the doctrine of a future state though it were not wholly hid, yet it was not clearly known in the world. It was an imperfect view of reason, or, perhaps, the decayed remains of an ancient tradition, which seemed rather to float on men's fancies, than sink deep into their hearts."[109]

From here Locke proceeds to discuss the old law of works, i.e., "that law which requires perfect obedience without any remission or abatement; so that, by that law, a man cannot be just, or justified, without an exact performance of every title."[110] This law was the Mosaic law and is to be understood in contrast with the law of faith, the new law brought by Jesus. But before turning to the law of faith, Locke disposes of the law of works by showing on the authority of St. Paul that there is in fact no difference between the law of conscience which Gentiles followed and the law of God. St. Paul said that "Not the hearers of the law are just before God, but the doers of the law are justified."[111] It is needless to quote any more of Paul in this connection, says Locke, since "his Epistles are full of it."[112] He then continues at length to cite further passages from St. Paul. It is instructive to note that he has St. Paul ask the following question: "But the law given by Moses, being not given to all mankind, how are all men sinners; since without a law, there is no transgression?" The answer St. Paul gives to Locke's question is: "For when the Gentiles which have not the law, do [i.e., find it reasonable to do][113] by nature the things contained in the law; these having not the law, are a law unto themselves: which show the work of the law written in their hearts; their consciences also bearing witness, and amongst themselves their thoughts accusing or excusing one another."[114] Locke concludes by saying that St. Paul's authority makes it clear "that under the law of works, is comprehended also the law of nature, knowable by reason, as well as the law given by Moses."[115] This point is confirmed later in the treatise where Locke attempts with considerable caution to bring the "scattered parts of the discourse" to a single conclusion.

The next step in Locke's argument is to relate the Mosaic law to the Christian law. He does so in the following manner: "Thus then, as to the law, in short: the civil and ritual part of the law, delivered by Moses, obliges not Christians, though to the Jews, it were a part of the law of works. . . . But the moral part of Moses's law, or the moral law, (which is everywhere the same, the eternal rule of right) obliges Christians, and all men, everywhere, and is to all men the standing law of works."[116] But in addition to this Christians "have the privileges to be under the law of faith too."[117] This law, which Locke says is peculiar only to Christians and is a privilege, is "that law whereby God justifies a man for believing, though by his works he be not just or righteous, i.e., though he came short of perfect obedience to the law of works."[118] In other words, Christians are under a much more fair law of works than the followers of Moses; the compassion of God is a result of that faith which is essential to the Christian dispensation. Locke accordingly sets out to establish what it is that men are required to believe before they can be incorporated into the Christian faith.

There follows a systematic search through the New Testament for what that faith was. Locke's conclusion—stated many times throughout—is that "it is plain, that believing on the Son is the believing that Jesus was the Messiah; giving credit to the miracles he did, and the profession he made of himself."[119] This statement contains the three parts of Locke's inquiry. In the first, he traces the fact that the apostles believed that Jesus was the Messiah and that this was the sole condition for admission to the Christian dispensation. Second, the proofs which confirm that Jesus was the Messiah were the miracles he performed and to which his disciples gave testimony. Finally, Locke undertakes to inquire whether Jesus himself ever claimed to be the Messiah.

On the matter of Jesus as the Messiah, Locke says that "'salvation or perdition depends upon believing or rejecting this one proposition."[120] But he adds immediately that despite the fact that this is the only required article of faith "there is something more required to salvation, besides believing."[121] At the end of *The Reasonableness of Christianity* where Locke returns to this theme we discover that Jesus taught a complete morality which all Christians are obliged to follow. We shall leave to a later point a discussion of what that morality contained. Suffice it for the moment to observe that for Locke *doing* replaces *believing*. This says Locke is particularly clear from the words of Jesus himself. And he makes it clear that the testimony of Jesus ought to be preferred to that of his disciples. In the final analysis the transition from believing to doing is crucial.[122]

Locke begins to undermine the essential dogma of belief in Jesus as the Messiah by declaring that one must make the distinction between "historical faith" and "saving faith."[123] Locke says that he can allow

to the makers of systems and their followers to invent and use what distinctions they please, and to call things by what names they think fit. But I cannot allow them, *or to any man*, an authority to make a religion for me, or to alter that which God hath revealed. And if they please to call the believing that which our Saviour and his apostles preached, and proposed alone to be believed, an historical faith; they have their liberty. But they must have a care, how they deny it to be a justifying or saving faith, when our Saviour and his apostles have declared it so to be.[124]

Locke cleverly disguises his own preference here; one must surely note that he advises care or caution in denying the belief in Jesus as the Messiah as a saving faith. For when one considers this statement in the context of his searches into what Jesus himself said about this matter we find that Jesus himself never once claims to be the Messiah. His disciples make the claim repeatedly, but Jesus skillfully and persistently—in private as well as in public—refuses to claim to be the Messiah. Furthermore, Locke raises serious doubts about the possibility of the belief in Jesus as the Messiah being a saving faith from the fact that devils proclaimed Jesus to be the Messiah. Surely, he implies, *they* are beyond salvation.

One must observe in reading *The Reasonableness of Christianity* that Locke skillfully separates the testimony of the apostles from that provided by the words of Jesus himself. The early implication that the apostles were not intelligent men is made explicit later in the work.[125] And since they are the only source of testimony on the miracles Jesus performed, Locke implies that it must be taken with considerable skepticism. On the other hand, he is clearly impressed with the responsibility of Jesus and the morality he taught. He is particularly impressed at the end of *The Reasonableness of Christianity* because he judges Christian morality to be compatible with reason. But Locke at no time concedes belief in Jesus as the Messiah; he was especially impressed with the fact that Jesus never once stirred up the people to rebellion; he implies that he not only had many occasions to do so, but that he had at his disposal a doctrine which could have been very effective as a revolutionary doctrine.

Locke's attitude toward Jesus emerges only obliquely throughout *The Reasonableness of Christianity*. He is clearly puzzled by Jesus' words, especially since it appears to him that Jesus had doubts himself about being the Messiah. If he had not, Locke says, he would certainly have declared himself in plain words; God had promised to send a Messiah to the Jews and they were in clear expectation of the Messiah. The best Locke appears to concede as to the person of Jesus himself is that he was an extraordinary man; but he had at least as much doubt as to the Messianic role as he seems to think that Jesus himself did. Locke appears to ponder how Jesus' fate could have been any different had he explicitly claimed to be the Messiah. This leads him to ask toward the end of the discourse: "What advantage have we by Jesus Christ?"[126] One thing is clear to Locke: Jesus' coming has been of no value to the Jews. It has the appearance of a cruel hoax, for God had chosen them to be his people and promised them a Messiah. Yet they above all reaped no benefit by his coming.

The last twenty-five pages of *The Reasonableness of Christianity* contain Locke's reflection on the advantage to mankind of Jesus' coming. His answer is that to "the greatest part of mankind"[127] it was of considerable value because he taught them their duties.[128] The morality Jesus taught was especially suited to the mean capacities of the bulk of mankind and it was imposed as a duty with the full force of a sovereign law-maker.[129] Says Locke:

> And it is at least a surer and shorter way to the apprehensions of the vulgar, and mass of mankind, that one manifestly sent from God, and coming with visible authority from him, should, as a king and law-maker, tell them their duties, and require their obedience, than leave it to the long and sometimes intricate deductions of reason, to be made out to them. Such trains of reasonings the greatest part of mankind have neither leisure to weigh nor, for the want of education and use, skill to judge of.[130]

Locke clearly distinguishes between "the few"[131] (i.e., the thinking part of mankind) and the "greatest part of mankind." He proceeds to demonstrate in the last pages of *The Reasonableness of Christianity* that "the knowledge of morality by mere natural light . . . makes slow progress"[132] among men because they lack both leisure and capacity to discover it and because without the command of a supreme power who can threaten punishments and promise rewards it remains unobserved. One might as well attempt to make all men "perfect mathematicians" as to have them comply with the morality of reason. Clearly the morality taught by Jesus is suited to "the lowest capacities of reasonable creatures."[133] In short, says Locke, reason needs religion's assistance in establishing morality and the morality taught by Jesus is especially conducive.

Finally, despite Locke's apparent praise for the morality taught by Jesus he does not appear to condone the embellishments of that morality imposed by the Church divines. His message is that the simple morality of Jesus as presented in the Sermon on the Mount is all that is required for Christians to obtain happiness on this earth.[134] He is emphatically silent about happiness in another world after death. The good Christian will be a dutiful person living honestly and responsibly with his fellows in peace. It is for this reason that Locke concludes that Jesus' doctrine "tends to the good of mankind."[135]

ROUSSEAU: THE CIVIL RELIGION

The last topic Rousseau treats in his most political writing, the *Social Contract*, is "The Civil Religion." He left to the last his most explicit account of the nature and function of religion in civil society. Few writers are more concise or unambiguous in this matter than Rousseau; and if there is any doubt as to the danger of orthodox religion in some writers, or its place in the state, there is no such doubt in Rousseau's opinion on these matters.

Early in Chapter 8 of Book IV of the *Social Contract* Rousseau claims emphatically that the religion founded by Jesus, the Christian religion, has been a divisive force in the state; he claims that the kingdom Jesus came to establish "by separating the theological system from the political system . . . brought about the end of the unity of the State, and caused the internal divisions that have never ceased to stir up Christian peoples."[136] The division of realms— spiritual and temporal—has not eliminated the possibility of conflict, it has increased it because in such circumstances "no people has ever been able to figure out when it was obliged to obey the master or the priest."[137] And since Rousseau, following Hobbes, asserts that sovereignty is inalienable and indivisible, there can be no place for a doctrine of divided sovereignty.

Rousseau explicitly acknowledged Hobbes as the only one "who correctly saw the evil and the remedy, who dared to propose the reunification of the two heads of the eagle, and the complete return of political unity, without which no State or government will ever be well constituted."[138] The reason Rousseau objected to orthodox religion—especially of the Roman Church—is that it gives men two homelands, two rulers, and as a result places them under contradictory obligations and prevents them from being both good Christians and good citizens.[139] But just as one is led to believe that Rousseau dismissed Christianity altogether from the state he says that the genuine Christianity, "not that of today, but of the Gospel, ... is totally different."[140] He concludes this turn in his argument with the laconic remark: "Through this saintly, true religion, men, children of the same God, all acknowledge one another as brothers, and the society which unites them is not even dissolved by death."[141] The supreme virtue of the early faith, as opposed to the institutionalized Church, was that it taught and practiced a communal fellowship of all men. But despite his praise for the primitive Church, Rousseau nowhere implies that it is possible to recapture its strength.

In the *Social Contract*, Rousseau claimed that the Christian can be *at best* a lukewarm citizen. "After all, what does it matter whether one is free or a serf in this vale of tears? The essential thing is to go to heaven, and resignation is but an additional means of doing so."[142]

But Rousseau is not content to let the matter rest there. He completes the matter by relating it to the sovereign power—the most fundamental civil power—and to the content of that religion which is allowable. In this respect he is almost assuredly following Hobbes, who describes religion as that which is publicly allowed and specified by the sovereign. He begins by stating that "subjects have no duty to account to the sovereign for their beliefs"; he then adds the important qualification "except insofar as these opinions matter to the community."[143] The sovereign has no concern for the religion of his subjects, he insists, "as long as they are good citizens in this [life]."[144] The implication is that as long as one keeps one's religious thoughts to oneself, one will not incur the sovereign's wrath. But the matter does not end here, for Rousseau believed that the private thoughts of citizens have consequences for the public order. In this respect it becomes almost impossible to conceive of religious beliefs which cannot have some impact on the public realm. Rousseau appears to reject the radical distinction between private and public morality.

One thing is clearly within the realm of the sovereign and that is the profession or practice of religion. And since the state cannot survive without some form of religion, it becomes a matter of sovereign concern to ensure that there is a public or state religion. Indeed it is the sovereign function to determine the articles of religion, "not exactly as religious dogmas, but as sentiments of sociability without which it is impossible to be a good citizen or a faithful subject."[145] Thus the purpose of religion is sociability—i.e., its end is clearly *this-worldly*.

Despite the right of the sovereign to determine the articles of religion and the public rites that accompany them, Rousseau says that the sovereign cannot oblige anyone to believe the articles, although "the sovereign can banish from the State anyone who does not believe them."[146] The implication is clear: if you cannot believe them, keep it to yourself. Rousseau attempted to soften the matter somewhat by adding that in such circumstances one would be banished not for impiety but for an anti-social disposition: "for being incapable of sincerely loving the laws, and justice, and giving his life if need be, for his duty."[147]

In addition to the danger of expressing disbelief in the official articles of the state, Rousseau adds that if "someone who has publicly acknowledged these same dogmas *behaves* as though he does not believe them, he should be punished with death. He has committed the greatest crime: he lied before the laws."[148] This is the only time in the *Social Contract* when Rousseau counsels capital punishment. It confirms the point made earlier about Rousseau's state being as rigidly governed as Hobbes's.

Rousseau's concluding remarks on religion in the *Social Contract* are directed to the topic of religious tolerance. Two issues emerge. First, that, by implication, there may be religions in the state other than the official religion, "provided only that their dogmas contain

nothing contrary to the duties of the citizen."¹⁴⁹ And all those religions which tolerate other religions must be tolerated. But those
religions which decree that "there is no salvation outside the
church" (i.e., the Roman religion) are not to be tolerated.

The Vicar's Profession of Disbelief

The only other major statement on the subject of the role of the
orthodox Christian religion in civil society is found in *Emile* where
the Savoyard Vicar reveals that he has lost faith in Roman theology.

The first problem one encounters in reading the Vicar's profession of faith is the extent to which the doctrine contained there re-
flects Rousseau's thoughts. We cannot simply assume that Rousseau shared the theological doctrine presented by the Vicar. One
must never forget that Rousseau identified by name two actual
priests who served as his models. In the *Confessions* he recalls: "I
made of these two worthy priests [Messrs. Gâtier and Gaime] the
original of the Savoyard Vicar."¹⁵⁰ Rousseau adds that he hopes
that "the imitation has not dishonored its originals."¹⁵¹ And the
fact that Rousseau identified his lot with the lot of the Vicar in no
way indicates that he shared his doctrine.¹⁵² Furthermore, the Vicar
is presented as a reasonably intelligent man and no more;¹⁵³ he
was no philosopher, as he says himself.¹⁵⁴ He was a man who was
confused and bewildered by all the systems of philosophers; he
rejected them all and chose instead another guide: "the inner
light."¹⁵⁵ Feeling was his guide because "it is never untrue that I
feel what I feel."¹⁵⁶ But at the same time there can be no doubt that
Rousseau has the Vicar instruct Emile in theological matters.

The theological doctrine the Vicar presents to Emile, an "ordinary man" ("*homme vulgaire*")—i.e., not a philosopher—is in
stark contrast to orthodox Roman Catholicism; it is in fact a doctrine of natural religion which conflicts at every major point with
Christian orthodoxy. The Vicar's religion is based on nature and is
elicited through consultation with his feelings and conscience.
Rousseau considered this natural religion preferable to the old contentious religion because it led men to greater tolerance; the old

dogmatic religion led to "bloody intolerance and [is] the cause of all the futile teaching which strikes a deadly blow at human reason by training it to cheat itself with mere words."[157]

What is crucial to an understanding of the Vicar as the theological teacher of Emile is the fact that he never once mentions political matters; he presents a theological doctrine which is close to the Christian heresy of Manicheanism: matter is the principle of evil. The solution to the problem of human evil is for the Vicar in the next world.[158] The solution to the human problems is clearly in this world for Rousseau because for Rousseau the source of human problems is man's pride ("*amour-propre*"), which under the direction of reason has invented debasing wants. The solution for Rousseau is accordingly political reform in this world. But religion —the consoling religion of the Vicar—is essential in order to make men citizens, Rousseau teaches. And it is to vary from place to place;[159] Rousseau's own theological teaching appears to be skepticism or agnosticism.[160] A knowledge of the divinity is clearly beyond human capacity, but the citizen must be instructed in that understanding of divinity which teaches him his divine duties and leads him to tolerance of the religions of other peoples. Above all, the Vicar's natural theology will inculcate into the likes of Emile a natural morality of the utmost simplicity—the morality of conscience, which is the voice of the soul; this voice will help to keep passion in check, which is "the voice of the body."[161] As the Vicar says: "There is therefore at the bottom of our souls an innate principle of justice and virtue, by which, in spite of our maxims, we judge our own actions or those of others to be good or bad; and it is to this principle that I give the name of conscience."[162] The Vicar emphasizes, though, that the "decrees of conscience are not judgments but feeling."[163] "To exist is to feel; our feeling is undoubtedly earlier than our intelligence, and we had feelings before we had ideas."[164]

The Vicar's theological doctrine is one of natural religion, and hence available to all men in all countries. It leads men to preserve themselves because the innate principle of conscience renders men capable of living in harmony. It also leads men to abandon prayer because they understand that it is futile to pray. "Has he [God] not given me conscience that I may love the right, reason that I may perceive it, and freedom that I may choose it?"[165]

And finally, when Rousseau asks the Vicar to explain the place of revelation, the Vicar replies that what he has taught is "nothing but natural religion"[166] and that there is no need for revelation, which has brought fire and the sword upon earth and not peace. The Vicar categorically rejects the Scriptures in favour of natural religion: "There is one book which is open to every one—the book of nature," he affirms.[167]

CONCLUSION

It should come as no surprise that the theological doctrines of the leading modern political philosophers have much in common with the doctrines of Epicurus and Lucretius. For both Epicurus and Lucretius religion is the consequence of the fear of the awesome forces of nature; it is the result of ignorance of the causes of the natural phenomena, such as thunder and earthquakes. As Hobbes relates in *Leviathan*, echoing Lucretius, primitive men believed that "ill success in war, great contagions of sickness, earthquakes, and each man's private misery, came from the anger of the gods, and their anger from the neglect of their worship, or the forgetting, or mistaking some point of the ceremonies required."[168]

Epicurus and Lucretius did not deny the existence of the gods; they merely argued that the gods were removed from men and not vengeful. Above all, the fearful phenomena of nature can be explained by an understanding of the physical causes of those phenomena; they were not the expressions of the angry gods.

In addition, as Strodach correctly notes,[169] Epicurus and Lucretius do not counsel the abandonment of religion; rather do they transform it into contemplation as opposed to worship. As understood, religion has a consoling character and can be a valuable social benefit.

This means, however, that there is no such thing as divine providence, "no theological order in the world, since all apparent design is the result of the chance union of atoms."[170]

Armed with this kind of theological ammunition, Hobbes, Locke, and Rousseau had little difficulty undermining the main tenets of Christian orthodoxy.

NOTES

1. See Hobbes, *Leviathan*, Pt. IV, Ch. 46, "And for the study of philosophy, it hath no otherwise place, than as a handmaid to the Roman religion."

2. See Giorgio De Santillana, *The Crime of Galileo* (Chicago: The University of Chicago Press, 1955).

3. John Toland, *Tetradymus* (London, 1720), p. 66.

4. Samuel Parker, *The Case for the Church of England* (London, 1681).

5. Ibid., p. 7.

6. Ibid., p. 8.

7. Ibid., p. 12.

8. Edward Stillingfleet, *Answer to Mr. Locke's Second Letter* (London, 1698), p. 5. See also Stillingfleet, *Answer to Mr. Locke's Letter Concerning Some Passages Relating to his Essay of Humane Understanding* (London, 1697).

9. Ibid., p. 6.

10. Ibid., p. 14.

11. Ibid., p. 21.

12. Ibid.

13. Ibid., p. 20.

14. Ibid., p. 30.

15. Ibid., p. 65.

16. Francis Bacon, Preface to *Great Instauration*, *Works*, I, 208. See also Howard White, *Peace Among the Willows* (The Hague: Nijhoff, 1968), pp. 67–75.

17. *Novum Organum*, I, No. 89.

18. Ibid.

19. *De Augmentis*, Bk. IX, pp. 368ff.

20. Ibid.

21. Ibid.

22. This warning is repeated in Bacon's Commentary on John 3:9. See J. G. Hall, *Thoughts on Holy Scripture by Francis Bacon* (London, 1862), pp. 256–57.

23. Ibid., Bacon's commentary on Psalm 137, pp. 130–31; also pp. 278–79.

24. Ibid., p. 257.

25. Ibid., p. 281.

26. Ibid., commentary on Job, pp. 83–84.

27. Ibid., p. 85.

28. Ibid.

29. Ibid. See also Hobbes's comment on this same matter in *Leviathan*, Pt. I, Ch. XV, p. 95.

30. Bacon's commentary on Job, p. 108.

31. Ibid., p. 96; also pp. 105–106.

32. Ibid., p. 109.

33. *De jure belli ac pacis*, Bk. I, Ch. 4, No. 3, p. 138.

34. *The Laws of Ecclesiastical Polity*, Bk. I, p. 228.

35. See van Limborch, *A Compleat System or Body of Divinity*, ed. Wm. Jones (London, 1713), where he counsels Christians to take up arms against a tyrant, Vol. II, 713–14.

36. See Joseph Cropsey, *Ancients and Moderns* (New York: Basic Books, 1964), "Hobbes and the Transition to Modernity," p. 213.

37. Matthew 22:21; see also Paul, Romans 13:7.

38. *Leviathan*, Pt. II, Ch. XXIX, p. 215 (Oakeshott).

39. Ibid., pp. 215–16.

40. *De Cive*, Ch. VI, sec. 11, p. 79, *English Works*, Vol. II (Molesworth ed. 1941; repr. Aalen: Scientia, 1962).

41. *Leviathan*, XXIX, p. 211.

42. Ibid., pp. 214–15; see also XLVI, p. 447.

43. Ibid., V, p. 30. This is remarkably close to the Biblical "I am the Way, the Truth and the Light."

44. Ibid., XXXVI, p. 284.

45. See *Leviathan*, XI, pp. 68–69.

46. Ibid., Chs. XL–XLIII.

47. *Behemoth, English Works*, VI, 236–37. Italics added.

48. *Leviathan*, Pt. II, Ch. XXXII, p. 242.

49. Ibid., Ch. XII, p. 80.

50. Ibid., Ch. XXXII, p. 242.

51. Ibid.

52. Ibid.; see also p. 244.

53. Ibid.

54. Ibid.

55. Ibid., p. 243.

56. Ibid.

57. Ibid., p. 244.

58. Ibid.

59. Ibid.

60. Ibid.

61. Ibid., p. 246.

62. Ibid., Ch. XXXIII, pp. 252–53.

63. Ibid., p. 254.

64. Ibid.

65. Ibid.

66. Ibid., pp. 254–55.

67. Ibid.

68. Ibid., Ch. XXXVI, pp. 277–78.

69. Ibid.

70. Ibid., p. 281.

71. Ibid.

72. Ibid., p. 283.

73. Ibid., p. 284. "Every man then was, and now is bound to make use of his natural reason, to apply to all prophesy those rules which God hath given us, to discern the true from the false."

74. Ibid., p. 283. "And first, that there were many more false prophets than true prophets, appears by this, that when Ahab (I Kings XXII) consulted four hundred prophets, they were all false imposters, but only one Micaiah."

75. Ibid., Ch. XXXVI, p. 284; also Ch. XLII, p. 338.

76. Ibid., XLI, p. 319.

77. Ibid., XLII, p. 325.

78. Ibid., p. 343.

79. Ibid., p. 344. Later in the same chapter Hobbes says that "the Books of the New Testament, though most perfect rules of Christian doctrine, could not be made laws by any other authority than that of kings or sovereign assemblies."

80. Ibid., p. 360. Italics added.

81. Ibid., p. 343.

82. Ibid., p. 344; Ch. XLI, p. 320; Ibid., p. 322: "Our Saviour . . . representing as Moses did, the person of God."

83. Ibid., Ch. XLI, p. 318.

84. Ibid., Ch. XLII, p. 337.

85. Ibid., pp. 337–38.

86. Ibid.

87. Thomas Hobbes, *A Dialogue Between a Philosopher and a Student of the Common Laws of England*, ed. with intro. by Joseph Cropsey (Chicago: The University of Chicago Press, 1971).

88. John Aubrey, *Brief Lives*, ed. Andrew Clark (Oxford, 1898), I, 339.

89. *A Brief View and Survey*, p. 8.

90. *An Answer to a Book by Dr. Bramhall called the Catching of Leviathan* (London, 1682), p. 45.

91. *Leviathan*, Ch. XII, *Works*, III, 95; see also Lucretius, *De rerum natura*, 2.11.55–61.

92. Ibid., Ch. XI. See F. C. Hood, *The Divine Politics of Hobbes* (London: Oxford University Press, 1964).

93. *Leviathan*, XI, end.

94. Ibid., Ch. XII, p. 69.

95. Ibid.

96. Ibid.

97. Ibid., Ch. XII, pp. 75–76.

98. *The Reasonableness of Christianity, Works*, VIII. See Ellis Sandoz, "The Civil Theology of Liberal Democracy: Locke and His Predecessors," *The Journal of Politics*, 34 (1972), 2–36.

99. *The Reasonableness of Christianity, Works*, VIII, 186–87.

100. *Works*, III.

101. Ibid., p. 149.

102. Ibid., VII, 289.

103. Ibid., p. 35.

104. Ibid., p. 4.

105. Ibid., Vol. VIII.

106. Ibid., pp. 5–6. Compare this with what Locke says about Filmer's manner of writing in the *First Treatise of Government*, Ch. 11.7.

107. Ibid., Vol. VII, p. 6.

108. Ibid.

109. Ibid., p. 149.

110. Ibid., p. 12.

111. Ibid., Vol. VIII, Romans 11:13.

112. Ibid., Vol. VII, p. 13.

113. This clause is added by Locke.

114. *Works*, VII, 13.

115. Ibid. Locke used the 1611 edition of the King James version of the Bible. See paraphrase of St. Paul's Epistles, *Works*, VIII. Locke frequently alters Biblical quotations in *The Reasonableness of Christianity*; see, for example, his use of Romans 3:9 and 23. In the text of the *Reasonableness* he reduces the two texts so as to appear as a single citation.

116. Ibid., Vol. VII, 15.

117. Ibid.

118. Ibid.

119. Ibid., p. 17.

120. Ibid., p. 26.

121. Ibid.

122. Ibid., p. 127.

123. Ibid., pp. 101–102.

124. Ibid. Italics added.

125. Locke later refers to them as "ignorant but inspired fishermen." Vol. VII, 140.

126. Ibid., Vol. VII, 134.

127. Ibid., p. 146.

128. Ibid., p. 139.

129. Ibid., p. 143.

130. Ibid., p. 139.

131. Ibid., p. 146.

132. Ibid., p. 140.

133. Ibid., p. 147.

134. Ibid.

135. See *Works*, VII, where Locke says that the Epistles do not teach "the fundamental articles of the Christian religion," p. 153; and that "many disbelieve the Epistles," p. 156.

136. J. J. Rousseau, *On the Social Contract*, ed. Roger D. Masters, trans. Judith R. Masters (New York: St. Martin's Press, 1978), p. 126.

137. Ibid.

138. Ibid., p. 127.

139. Ibid.

140. Ibid., p. 128.

141. Ibid.

142. Ibid., p. 129.

143. Ibid., p. 130.

144. Ibid.

145. Ibid.

146. Ibid., p. 131.

147. Ibid.

148. Ibid.

149. Ibid.

150. *Confessions*, Vol. II, Bk. iii, p. 107 (London: Everyman's Library, 1961; introduction by R. Niklaus). I have altered the translations occasionally in the interest of a more literal rendering. Abbé Gâtier was from Le Faucigny, in the Duchy of Savoy. See also p. 81.

151. Ibid.

152. See, for example, *Troisième promenade*: "Le résultat de mes pénibles recherches fut tel à peu pres que je l'ai consigné depuis dans la *Profession de foi du vicaire savoyard*, ouvrage indignement prostitué et profané dans la génération présent, mais qui peut faire un jour révolution parmi les hommes si jamais il y renaît du bon sens et de la bonne foi" (*Oeuvres Complètes* [Paris: Editions du Seuil, 1967], I, 512).

153. Ibid., "Il n'était ni sans ésprit ni sans lettres" (III, 182).

154. Ibid., "Je ne suis pas un grand philosophe, et je me soucie peu de l'être" (184).

155. *Emile*, trans. Barbara Foxley, intro. André Boutet de Monvel (London: Everyman's Library; 1961).

156. Ibid., p. 233.

157. Ibid., p. 220.

158. Ibid., p. 246. The Vicar implies that the union of body and soul is an unnatural state.

159. Ibid., p. 220.

160. Ibid., pp. 220–21.

161. Ibid., p. 249.

162. Ibid., p. 252.

163. Ibid., p. 253.

164. Ibid.

165. Ibid., p. 257.

166. Ibid., p. 259.

167. Ibid., p. 270.

168. *Leviathan* XII, p. 76. See Lucretius, *De rerum natura*, IV, pp. 381–82. For Lucretius religious fear also stemmed from ignorance of the nature of the soul; see ibid., I, pp. 117–19.

169. George K. Strodach, *The Philosophy of Epicurus* (Evanston: Northwestern University Press, 1963), p. 55.

170. Rist, *op. cit.*, p. 148.

7

Political Hedonism Entrenched

IN ORDER TO UNDERSTAND how successfully the principles of hedonism have penetrated into succeeding centuries, we must review the philosophies of David Hume, Jeremy Bentham, and John Stuart Mill.

DAVID HUME (1711–1776)

The philosophy of David Hume is frequently summarized in his famous statement that "reason is and ought only to be the slave of the passions and can never pretend to any other office than to serve and obey them."[1] The impression given by this oversimplified statement of his thought is that he is a crass hedonist or at least a champion of the vulgar play of passions. Despite his commitment to the supremacy of passions over reason, Hume is emphatically not a proponent of the unbridled fulfillment of the lower passions, any more than Epicurus was a base hedonist. There can be no denying that his philosophy is based on the acknowledgment of man's passionate nature; but it also posits the need for the direction and restraint of passion.

His political philosophy is peculiarly replete with tension if not contradiction. He appears initially as an avowed proponent of modernity; as one who is fully in agreement with the objectives of the modern project; yet, at the same time, as one suspicious of the nationalistic premises of modernity. His teaching regarding the state of nature is one example of those suspicions.

He begins with an explicit denial of the existence of a state of nature mainly because it is contrary to the custom and history available. It appears to him as a figment of philosophical imagination. He wrote: "This state of nature is, therefore, to be regarded as a mere fiction, not unlike that of the Golden Age which poets have invented."[2]

Yet despite this explicit rejection of a prepolitical condition out of which men were said by Hobbes and Locke to have emerged into civil society, Hume writes as if he believed it existed and warns against the dangers of lapsing back into that condition. He frequently writes of men in "their wild—uncultivated state";[3] he even says that " 'tis utterly impossible for men to remain any considerable time in that savage condition, which precedes society."[4] He attempts at times to correct this use of the state of nature by saying that since no one can reasonably concede that such a condition could prevail for very long, it must be concluded that it is a mere philosophical fiction "which never had, and never could have any reality."[5] At one point he traced the rise of civil society from the union of the two sexes in what must be considered a prepolitical condition.

> Thanks to the first and original principle of human society . . . i.e. that natural appetite between the sexes . . . this new concern, i.e. the concern for common offsprings becomes also a principle of union betwixt the parents and offspring and forms a more numerous society. . . . In a little time, custom and habit operating on the tender minds of the children, makes them sensible of the advantages, which they may reap from society, as well as fashions them by degrees for it, by rubbing off those rough corners and untouched affections, which prevent their coalition.[6]

In another place Hume sounds very much like Hobbes when he writes that the "circumstances of human nature . . . render an union necessary and . . . the passions of lust and natural affection . . . render it unavoidable."[7] But he was at pains to insist that by nature man is not a social and political animal. Experience of the advantages moved men to adopt civil forms. The philosophies of Hobbes and Locke—which affirm that men enter into a contract or compact and thereby freely leave the state of nature—concedes too much to reason for Hume. Yet he says that when men experience how unstable things are in the original condition due to the transferability of external goods they seek a means of stability: "This can be done," he says, "after no other manner than by a convention entered into by all the members of the society to bestow stability on the possession of those external goods, and leave every one in the peaceable enjoyment of what he may acquire by his fortune and industry."[8] This sounds very close to Locke and Hobbes. Yet he insisted that it is not a promise or a contract—i.e., it has no other element of reason in it than the judgment on the inconvenience of the original pre-civil condition. "This convention is not of the nature of a promise . . . it is only a general sense of common interest; which sense all the members of the society express to one another, and which induces them to regulate their conduct by certain rules. I observe that it will be for my interest to leave another in the possession of his goods, *providing* he will act in the same manner with regard to me."[9] This would seem to imply that self-interest is the sole motive for entering into the convention. He certainly talks of the "avidity of acquiring goods and possessions for ourselves and our nearest friends."[10] This passion is said to be "insatiable, perpetual, universal and directly destructive of society."[11] It would be difficult to find a statement on possessiveness which concurs more with both Hobbes and Locke than this one. Hume even says that societies or states are to be judged in terms of their ability to constrain this passion.[12]

What compounds man's avidity, i.e., his "selfishness and confined generosity," is the "scanty provision nature has made for his wants."[13] That is to say, Hume not only says that men are driven by the passion of avidity but that things capable of being possessed are scarce. This gives rise to a highly competitive and even violent condition among men. The experience of the inconvenience of this condition lead men to "enter" civil society. Once there, they contrive certain rules governing the ownership and disposability of property. " 'Twas therefore a concern for our own and the public interest, which made us establish the laws of justice."[14] If men did not do this, if they pursued their own interest without any precaution, "they would run head-long into every kind of injustice and violence."[15]

It would appear from Hume's own words that these men are driven by the passion of avarice before and after they enter civil society. Yet he disavows the proposition that men calculatedly enter civil society in order to protect their property and to increase it. When men find by experience that life outside civil society is intolerable they willingly "lay themselves under the restraint of such rules, as may render their commerce more safe and commodious."[16]

In many respects Hume's premises and conclusions are closely akin to Locke's—with one major exception. Locke said that men operate under the guidance of reason; Hume says they operate in exactly the same way as Locke but under the impulse of passion, not reason. He suggests emphatically that history and personal observation prove that men do in fact act on the basis of passion and not by reason. History teaches us that "society is absolutely necessary for the well-being of men"; and that the three fundamental laws of nature—the laws enjoining the abstinence from the property of others, its transference by consent, and the obligation to fulfill promises—are "necessary to the support of society."[17] Hume emphasizes that it is on "the strict observance of those three laws, that the peace and security of human society entirely depend."[18] The basis of Hume's natural-law doctrine is thus decidedly different from Locke's natural law which is founded in reason. For Locke the natural law is in an important sense identical with reason.[19] For Hume the natural law is an artifice of human reason prompted by the natural course of passions. It is in no sense identical with reason.

Hume affirmed that everything is done under the guidance of passion, not reason. "Nothing is more vigilant and inventive than our passions; and nothing is more obvious than the convention for the observance of these rules. Nature has, therefore, trusted this affair entirely to the conduct of men, and has not placed in the mind any peculiar original principles, to determine us to a set of actions, into which the other principles of our frame and constitution were sufficient to lead us."[20]

There is no such thing as natural virtue—justice is of human artifice;[21] it is the act of abstaining from what is not ours and the act of restoring property to the first (rightful) possessor.[22] And while insisting that the "laws of justice are universal," he claims that they are not derived from nature.[23] " 'Tis evident these laws can only be derived from human conventions, when men have perceived the disorders that result from following their natural and variable principles."[24] Experience leads men to conclude that they are in need of such laws because their natural love of self is a constant threat to stability. " 'Tis self-love which is their real origin; and as self-love of one person is naturally contrary to that of another, these several interested passions are obliged to adjust themselves after such a manner as to concur in some system of conduct and behaviour."[25] Despite the acknowledgment of self-love—which he tends to portray as more benevolent than the possessive individualism of Locke—Hume concluded that "the origin of property and obligation . . . depend on public utility."[26] Without property there can be no justice, for justice is the agreed manner of regulating the possession and transfer of property.

As to the origin of government—which he tended to distinguish from the origin of civil society (although he uses the two terms synonymously at times)—Hume affirmed that "nothing is more certain than that men are in a great measure governed by interest."[27] Furthermore, it is equally as certain that men cannot allow themselves to fall back "into that wretched and savage condition which is commonly represented as the state of nature."[28]

And since men are governed by the preference for the proximate interest over the remote—i.e., more concerned with the interest of their families and friends than with the interests of those whom they do not know—the only resolution of any conflict can come from the "consent of men."[29] "Here then," he says, "is the origin of civil government and society. Men are not able radically to cure, either in themselves or others, that narrowness of soul, which makes them prefer the present to the remote. They cannot change their natures. All they can do is to change their situation, and render the observance of justice the immediate interest of some particular persons, and its violation thus more remote."[30] Government in society appears therefore to be a desirable but not natural means by which man can direct or restrain his passions. Man does not require society or government in the sense that he needs it as a means for self-fulfillment because man is not destined by nature toward the fulfillment of more virtue. That is why Hume takes so much trouble to ensure that he is not misunderstood as to the character of civil society. But he also attempts to dissociate himself from modern philosophers such as Locke by claiming that men do not reason their way into society.[31] When they do enter civil society they do so because they *experience* the inconvenience of life without "*some* system of conduct and behaviour." "When men have once perceived i.e. experienced the necessity of government to maintain peace, and execute justice, they would naturally assemble together, would choose magistrates, determine their power, and promise them obedience."[32]

Unlike Hobbes and Locke, Hume attempted to present a political philosophy which placed the emphasis on communal duty and not on individual rights. But it was established on the acknowledgment of man's passionate self-interest, however much it is infused with "a sympathy with public interest."[33] There can be no such thing as natural right in Hume as there was for Hobbes and Locke. For them the basic passion of the fear of violent death provided the basis for *the* fundamental natural right of self-preservation. Hume rejected this formulation, with the claim that experience shows that a person can willingly throw one's life away for another.[34] He firmly denied the "selfish system of morals" but does not deny the fact of pride or sense of self; indeed, it is the key or controlling passion. Men must seek government and submit themselves to the authority or magistrates in order to "procure themselves some security against the *wickedness* and *injustice of men* who are *perpetually* carried by their *unruly passions* and by their present and immediate interest, to the violation of all the laws of society."[35] This, it must be remembered, is a portrait of men in civil society. It has all the earmarks of Hobbes's men. Little wonder that Hume concludes that there must be strong government.

Before turning to Hume's thoughts on the forms of governments and the right to revolution, we must emphasize the fact that Hume speaks of the disruptive or "unruly passions" as "imperfections inherent in human nature."[36] And they are even found in those chosen as governors. "But as this imperfection is inherent in human nature we know that it must attend men in all their states and condition; and that those whom we chuse for rulers do not immediately become of a superior nature to the rest of mankind, upon account of a superior power and authority."[37] Indeed we have reason to expect that they too will be driven by "their passions into all the excesses of cruelty and ambition."[38] This led Hume to insist on the form of government which provides for an elective body which will serve as a check on the magistrates.

And despite Hume's claims on behalf of free government and a doctrine of revolution, he does not espouse an easy revolutionary course. Indeed he makes it clear that revolution cannot be undertaken lightly or on minor pretext; one must weigh the advantages against the disadvantages. " 'Tis only in cases of grevious tyranny and oppression that the exception can take place."[39] Hume even goes so far as to counsel against probing the legitimacy of an established government. "No maxim is more conformable, both to prudence and morals, than to submit quietly to the government, which we find established in the country where we happen to live, without enquiring too curiously into its origin and first establishment."[40] Leave well enough alone; "few governments will bear being examined so rigorously."[41]

It is important to note that Hume does not call the claim to revolution a right. It is not in his view a right properly so called. For rights can be of only two kinds: the right to power, and the right to property; upon these two concepts of right and the concept of interest "are all governments founded and all authority of the few over the many."[42]

We must turn now to the concept of interest and how Hume makes that the bond or cement of civil society. After acknowledging that private interest is the reason or justification for civil society, and after noting that the private interest of everyone is different, an agreed-upon perception of the public interest of everyone becomes "the source of the different opinions of particular persons concerning it."[43] In other words, public debate inevitably attends the quest for a conception of the public interest. But a public interest must be achieved, says Hume, for "what other principle is there in human nature capable of subduing the natural ambition of men and forcing them to such a submission?"[44]

This is the key to Hume's social bond—the "public interest," which must not be understood as the sum total of private interest, although the private interest is furthered in the pursuit of the public interest. The first element of the public interest is the peaceful condition in which the private interest can be pursued without violence or interference from others. And we have seen Hume talk about ambition and possession as elements of man's private interest. Society therefore exists with a view to providing the conditions in which the private interest can be pursued. The security and protection provided by government is, in fact, the basis of allegiance to the government.[45] And it is only when the government has failed in its duty to provide those conditions that we may withdraw allegiance to it. "As the interest, therefore, is the immediate sanction of government, the one can have no longer being than the other; and whenever the civil magistrate carries his oppression so far as to render his authority perfectly intolerable, we are no longer bound to submit to it."[46]

Hume made it clear in an essay entitled "Of Commerce" that he considers life in society as one of active pursuit of "all the commodities which are necessary or ornamental to human life."[47] He traces the advantage of trade in the same place:

> If we consult history, we shall find, that, in most nations, foreign trade has preceded any refinement in home manufacturers, and given birth to domestic luxury. The temptation is stronger to make use of foreign commodities, which are ready for use, and which are entirely new to us, than to make improvements on any domestic commodity which always advance by slow degrees, and never affect us by their novelty. The profit is also very great, in exporting superfluous at home, and what bears no price, to foreign nations, whose soil or climate is not favorable to that commodity. Thus men become acquainted with the pleasures of luxury and the profits of commerce; and their delicacy and industry, being once awakened, carry them on to further improvements, in every branch of domestic as well as foreign trade.

And this perhaps is the chief advantage which arises from a commerce
with strangers. It rouses men from their indolence; and presenting the
gayer and more opulent part of the nation with objects of luxury,
which they never before dreamed of, raises in them a desire of a more
splendid way of life than what their ancestors enjoyed. And at the
same time, the few merchants who possess the secret of this importa-
tion and exportation, make great profits; and becoming rivals in
wealth to the ancient nobility, tempt other adventurers to become their
rivals in commerce.[48]

This was Hume's great hope—the Golden Age of commerce assuring "a more splendid way of life," a life of "refinement," "luxury," and "opulence" based on the "profits of commerce"; the age
of economic hedonism.

The Roots of Natural Religion

On the matter of religion—both natural and revealed—Hume
wrote at considerable length. His unambiguous rejection of the
cardinal tenets of Christian orthodoxy appeared in the closing sections of *An Enquiry Concerning Human Understanding*. In the
discussion of miracles Hume presents a derisive critique of the possibility of miracles, claiming that in these matters a "wise man . . .
proportions his belief to the evidence."[49] And the evidence of past
events transmitted through the testimony of men ought not to re-
ceive special exemption from the rigorous test applied to other
forms of evidence. In the final analysis, the testimony of the disciples of Jesus does not meet the "ultimate standard," i.e., the test
of our own experience and observation.

In his discussion of particular providence and a future state,
Hume links arms with Epicurus and rejects the basic tenets of
Christian orthodoxy as the presumptuous assertions of philosophers. Speaking through the mouth of Epicurus, Hume says that
whenever philosophers speak of a providence and such matters he
asks:

who carried them into the celestrial regions, who admitted them into
the councils of the gods, who opened to them the book of fate, that
they thus rashly affirm, that their deities have executed, or will exe-

cute, any purpose beyond what has actually appeared? If they tell me
that they have mounted on the steps or by the gradual ascent of reason,
and by drawing inferences from effects to causes, I still insist that
they have aided the ascent of reason by the wings of imagination.[50]

The argument against causality is also the basis of his rejection
of natural religion in his *Natural History of Religion* (1757) and
Dialogues Concerning Natural Religion (1779).[51] In the first of
these works, Hume demonstrates that the seeds of natural religion
are in the ignorant fears and hopes of primitive men: "the anxious
concern for happiness, the dread of future misery, the terror of
death, the thirst of revenge, the appetite for food and other necessities."[52] As Frank E. Manuel has observed, the *Natural History
of Religion* is "in the same psychological tradition that flows from
the Epicureans through Hobbes and Spinoza, through Boyle and
Fontenelle, a current swollen by tributaries from Shaftesbury and,
more recently, from Hartley."[53]

The *Dialogues Concerning Natural Religion* constitutes a
lengthy and critical rejection of the argument from design. In the
final analysis, for Hume the only reasonable position for a philosopher on the question of belief in the existence of God is one of
philosophic skepticism. The uneducated, or vulgar, will always be
disposed to religion out of fear or out of an imaginative and groundless inference from order in the universe.

Hume's final judgment against religion is that it distracts men
from their terrestrial duties. The teachers of religion cannot be
"good citizens and politicians; since they free men from one restraint upon their passions, and make the infringement of the laws
of society, in one respect, more easy and secure."[54]

Conclusion

The fact that Hume did not write extensively on political matters
means that his political philosophy must be drawn from his major
philosophical works and essays. But this is not to imply that he did
not have a political philosophy. The closest he came to a formal
political treatise is his *Essays Moral and Political*.

In concluding this discussion of Hume's political philosophy we must relate what we have seen to the rise of hedonism. Despite the fact that Hume can in no sense be called an Epicurean, there can be no denying that he is an important link in the progression of modern hedonism. For despite his efforts to dissociate himself from the "selfish system," as he called it, his philosophy is clearly and unmistakably hedonistic. Virtue and vice are defined in terms of pleasure and pain, and one can never be mistaken as to one's experiences of pleasure and pain. And since "morality had no foundation in nature, it must still be allowed that vice and virtue, either from self-interest or the prejudice of education, produce in us a real pain and pleasure."[55] Hume goes further and claims that "if all morality were founded on the pain or pleasure which arises from the prospect of any loss or advantage that may result from our own characters or from those of others, all the effects of morality must be derived from the same pain or pleasure."[56]

Hume's commitment to hedonism is beyond dispute, but he clearly did not abandon himself or counsel others to abandon themselves to the "turbulent and clamorous pleasures," to the "barbarous dissonance of Bacchus and his revellers." Those pleasures were, he taught, the cause of greater disquietude, while happiness implies "ease, contentment, repose, . . . not watchfulness, care, and fatigue."

When Hume said that reason ought to be only the slave of the passions he was expressing one of the fundamental principles of his entire philosophy. A passion cannot be false or unreasonable in itself—only our judgment can. "In short, a passion must be accompanied with some false judgment, in order to its being unreasonable; and even then 'tis not the passion, properly speaking, which is unreasonable, but the judgment."[57]

Hume's contribution to the development of modern political philosophy has been substantial.[58] He aided that part of the modern project which liberated men from reason and placed them under the control of the passions. And we must not forget that, however much Hobbes and Locke labored to present a rational system, it was one based on passion: the strongest passion (the fear of violent death) became the base of the philosophy of the state.

Hume clearly developed or advanced the cause of the passions and connected them with government and opinion. That is to say, since passion (understood as the desire for pleasure and the avoidance of pain) is now the foundation and end of government, those who control government in states based on consent must not only be careful to consider the objects of the public passions, they have their entire legitimacy in advancing the objects of public passion. It is vain for moralists or politicians to attempt "to tamper with us": "All they can pretend to is to give a new direction to those natural passions, and teach us that we can better satisfy our appetites in an oblique and artificial manner than by their headlong and impetuous motion."[59] It is no wonder that public opinion has become such a powerful force in modern governments. This is the only way a free people have of expressing to governments what they want. Government no longer exists to provide citizens the means and path to moral virtue; it now exists to further the passions of its citizens. As Hume claims unequivocally "the governors have nothing to support them but opinion. 'Tis therefore, on opinion only that government is founded."[60]

Hume's efforts to reject the "selfish system" of ethics and politics were unsuccessful. They are based on the attempt to extend Hobbes's concept of individual selfishness beyond the individual to his immediate family and friends. This in no way eliminated the quest for possessions or even luxuries for oneself and one's family and friends. In other words, however much Hume can be said to have modified Hobbes's individualism, he merely extended the possessive character to one's family and friends. This hardly refutes Hobbes's or Locke's basic arguments.

Finally, it is important to understand that at the center of the modern project was the reinterpretation of nature as the norm of morality—private and public. This is why the moderns began by deposing and replacing the classical conception of nature, which taught that nature imposes the norm for all beings, including especially human beings. All men are *by nature* oriented toward (and ought to seek) moral virtue according to the classical understanding of nature. As Hume himself put it in his great effort to recon-

stitute *human* nature in the light of the new natural philosophy:
"I found that the moral philosophy transmitted to us by Antiquity,
labored under the same inconvenience that has been found in their
natural philosophy, of being entirely hypothetical and depending
more upon invention than experience. Every one consulted his
fancy in erecting Schemes of virtue and happiness, without regarding human nature upon which every moral conclusion must depend. This, therefore, I resolved to make my principal study."[61]

By experience Hume meant the account of how men *do in fact
act* as opposed to how they *ought to act* according to a transcendent
conception of morality. We will recall that Machiavelli was the
first to urge just such a redirection. Hume redirected his attention
in this manner and in so doing helped in the redirection of modern
politics away from the Socratic understanding of human nature to
the new modern politics of passion based on a new conception of
human nature as predominantly directed by passion and not reason.

JEREMY BENTHAM (1748–1832)

No one establishes more direct contact with Epicurean hedonism
than does Jeremy Bentham. And unlike Hobbes and Locke, Bentham did not dilute his hedonism by a natural-right doctrine. For
Bentham all claim to natural right or rights was considered as
"nonsense upon stilts."[62] Bentham began with an individualistic
concept of man as motivated by *pleasure* and *pain* and transforms
that into the basis for social bond by way of the principle of utility.[63]
This principle becomes the source and standard of all laws. Let us
begin, therefore, by examining Bentham's concept of man and his
hedonistic nature.

Bentham identified as the fundamental human fact the desire
for pleasure and the aversion to pain, and judged all actions, both
private and public, by that fact. In the observations of his *A Table
of the Springs of Action* he wrote: "Among all the several species
of psychological entities[64] . . . the two which are as it were the *roots*
—the main pillars or foundations of all the rest—the matter of
which all the rest are composed—or the receptacles of the matter—

whichsoever may be the *physical* image employed to give aid, if not existence to conception—will be, it is believed, if they have not been already, seen to be, *Pleasures* and *Pains*."[65] Bentham never looked back once he enunciated this basic principle of human action; it is, he says, a matter of "universal and constant experience"; in other words, it cannot be denied by anyone since it forms the most fundamental core of all human experiences.

He extended the application of the pleasure–pain principle to the question of virtue and vice. With full confidence he affirmed that "destitute of reference to the ideas of pain and pleasure, whatever ideas are annexed to the words *virtue* and *vice* amount to nothing more than that of groundless approbation or disapprobation. All language in which these appelations are employed is no better than empty declamation."[66]

All morality—both private and public—is based on the pleasure–pain principle. There is, therefore, no such thing as moral virtue sought for its own sake, as in Aristotle. Above all there is no *summum bonum* as proposed by Plato or Aristotle. That concept, especially as proposed by Plato—"the master-manufacturer of nonsense"[67]—was, for Bentham, beneath contempt. If it signified anything it means simply happiness and can be adequately understood in terms of the principles of utilitarianism. Bentham acknowledged the concept of *summum bonum* as forming a part of that "rubbish" which must be cleared away, once for all.[68]

On the matter of "good" and "bad" motives Bentham once again resolved all difficulties by reference to the principle of pleasure/pain. He says: "As there is not any sort of pleasure, the enjoyment of which, if taken by itself, is not good . . . nor any sort of pain, from which taken in like matter by itself, the exemption is not a good . . . a necessary consequence is . . . there is not any such thing as a bad motive."[69] But despite the obvious clarity of this matter, people continue to talk about good and bad motives. "From this speculative error," Bentham claimed, "a practical error of the very first importance may be seen to have taken their rise."[70]

It is instructive to note that Bentham acknowledged nature as the source of the pleasure/pain principle. In the *Introduction to the Principles of Morals and Legislation* Bentham announced that "Nature has placed mankind under the governance of two sovereign masters, pain and pleasure. It is for them alone to point out what we ought to do, as well as to determine what we shall do."[71] All men are captives of what must be acknowledged to be the source of all moral action. It is interesting to note that Bentham acknowledges Nature as the source of the two—not *one*—sovereign masters; nature itself is somehow the source of the dual sovereignty but not itself sovereign; indeed, nature is for Bentham simply the single expression for the two sovereign masters. Furthermore, man is irrevocably tied to the divided sovereignty of these two masters. "They govern us in all we do, in all we say, in all we think; every effort we can make to throw off our subjection, will serve but to demonstrate and confirm it."[72] By placing the sovereign principles within each man, Bentham opens the prospects of radical individualism because every man becomes the judge of his pleasures and pains—i.e., the sole judge of what is good and bad for him. But Bentham believed that the human species was uniformly in subjection to nature's two sovereign masters; by pursuing the greatest good of the greatest number in legislation, the state would thereby pursue the most common—i.e., least individualistic—good of its citizens and thus moderate the force of individualism. There can be no doubt that for Bentham pleasure and pain are the only legitimate sources of action and must therefore be the sources of moral (internal) and political (external) restraint. Pleasure is to be sought in both private and public actions.

But when one asks what the end result of this pleasure will be, one is left without a reply except "happiness." The impression given by Bentham is that pleasure exists for its own sake—or men seek pleasure simply for the enjoyment of pleasure. There is no conception of happiness as a final condition of peaceful repose, as in Epicurus. Rather is there a perpetual and restless desire for pleasure after pleasure—similar to that found in Hobbes. Since for Bentham man has no end there can be no conception of ultimate end in terms of happiness; despite the social principle of the greatest happiness of the greatest number, Bentham never defines the

content of happiness. There is no conception of happiness as fulfillment (except in satiety) since that implies a limitation by nature.

One cannot say that Bentham even has a conception of ordered
pleasure or a hierarchy of pleasures which prompts the preference
for some over others.[73] His sole qualification is based on quantity—
that pleasure which gives greater (in quantum terms) pleasure is
to be preferred to that which gives lesser pleasure. Individual
motives have beginnings but not ends. Bentham says explicitly that
"Ethics at large may be defined, as the art of directing men's actions to the production of the greatest possible *quantity* of happiness, on the part of those whose interest is in view."[74] One thing is
certain: in contrast to the thought of Epicurus, there is no conception in Bentham of a higher intellectual pleasure which constitutes
the highest condition of human happiness. Bentham is pointedly
silent on the possibility of the highest pleasures corresponding to
satisfaction of the highest human faculties. He considered such
discussions to be presumptuous. The role of the moral philosopher
—the "Deontologist," as Bentham preferred—"is to act as a guide
suggesting courses of action if and when consulted."[75]

This follows logically from the individualism which resides at
the heart of Bentham's utilitarianism. No one can tell another
what his or her best interests (i.e., pleasures) are. For pleasure is
what every man judges (with the aid of memory) to be pleasurable to his feelings.[76] And each man must decide this for himself.
For, "No man can allow another to decide for him as to what is
pleasure—or what is the balance or the amount of pleasure."[77] In
the internal or moral realm, this must be decided by each individual who calls his past experiences to assist him. In the external or
political realm, the legislator (principally those like Bentham)
shall give such guidance with the aid of the general principle of
utility.

What is ironic here is that Bentham restricts such right of individual autonomy to "every man of ripe age and sound mind."[78]
This would seem to imply clearly that he was excluding the young
(since they lack experience and hence "good" judgment) and those
who are mentally deficient (meaning, one assumes, mentally ill).

But what are the foundations for eliminating both the young and the mentally deficient from determining their own pleasures? There is nothing in Bentham that would lead one to exclude these two groups. On what grounds does Bentham say that the young are not the best judges of their feelings? Surely the mentally deficient are as aware of their physical pleasures as are those of sound mind. Bentham's paternalism, however desirable and understandable it might be to those with sound minds, cannot flow from his basic principles. The only possibility is that these two groups might not be able to prefer the greater good of the community—i.e., that they are unable to understand and apply the principle of utility. But not all pleasures are public; indeed, most are private.

Bentham is also relatively silent on the matter of enjoyment and accumulation of possessions. The most explicit statement on one's rights to acquire property in civil society emerges in his *Defence of Usury* (1788). In this document Bentham says that "No man of ripe years and of sound mind, acting freely, and with his eyes open, ought to be hindered, with a view to his advantages, from making such bargain in the way of obtaining money as he thinks fit; nor (what is the necessary consequence) anybody hindered from supplying him, upon any terms he thinks proper to accede to."[79]

One sees here that the freedom to enter into this kind of business arrangement is also restricted to "men of ripe years and sound mind." But what is not readily apparent is that what he says with regard to money must surely be applicable to all other market relations, as to both seller and buyer. He explicitly noted on one occasion that "it was in the interest of all to possess, to retain, and upon occasion acquire property."[80]

It is interesting to observe that Bentham's treatise on usury is directed at the "Impolicy of the Present Legal Restraints on the terms of Pecuniary Bargains" proposed by Adam Smith.

When one turns to Bentham's political teachings regarding the origin and end of civil society one notes that he rejects emphatically the notion of a prepolitical condition known as the state of nature. And he is particularly severe in his treatment of the natural law. He calls it a dangerous doctrine: "I see no remedy but that the natural tendency of such doctrine is to impel a man by force of conscience to rise up in arms against any law whatever that he happens not to like."[81] No state could long survive, he says, with a flimsy avenue of appeal to revolution. With scorn he says he will leave it to Blackstone to demonstrate how any sort of government could survive with such a doctrine available to citizens. He claims that the state of nature is a fiction used by his predecessors in order to arrive at a basis of political legitimacy—i.e., the social contract. Bentham says that this is not only unnecessary but inadequate as a basis for affirming the duty to obey contracts. The fact that our forefathers contracted with a medieval king is no reason for us to continue to abide by the agreement. The issue can be resolved more easily—and without resorting to dubious historical material—by way of the principle of utility. It is wise to abide by contracts because they redound to our greater happiness. The key difference between a state of nature and civil society, says Bentham, is the presence of a habit of obedience. The mark which distinguishes a society in which there is a habit of obedience from one in which there is not is: "the establishment of names of office: the appearance of a certain man, or set of men with a certain name, serving to mark them out as objects of obedience: such as king. . . . This, I think, may serve tolerably well to distinguish a set of men in a state of political union among themselves from the same set of men not yet in such a state."[82] Bentham makes it clear that the habit of obedience manifests itself in "the number of points of duty incumbent on each person."[83]

By far the most important point to observe in Bentham's political philosophy is the manner in which he brings a collection of individuals motivated by nature in terms of their own pleasures and pains into a social and political unity where they seek their own happiness by and through seeking the public happiness. The means of achieving this is the principle of utility—i.e., the greatest happiness of the greatest number. This principle is not only the source of law but also the means by which its content is measured. All public right and wrong is to be measured by appeal to this principle.[84] Bentham described the principle of utility as: "The principle which furnishes us with that reason which alone depends not upon any higher reason, but which is itself the sole and all-sufficient reason for every point of practice whatsoever."[85]

Bentham resolved the conflict between the individual and the state through his doctrine of "self-regarding prudence" and "extra-regarding prudence." He tended at times to approach Rousseau's concept of natural compassion, but since he found little basis for this in his understanding of nature—he found it unnecessary— he avoided the matter or at least subsumed it under his discussion of "self-regarding" and "extra-regarding prudence."[86]

Bentham began by stating that "Nature, artless and untutored nature, engaged man in the pursuit of *immediate* pleasure and in the avoidance of *immediate* pain."[87] That is to say, nature has made man in such a way as to make him prefer his own present, short-term, pleasure. It is obvious, says Bentham, that such an attitude is not compatible with sociality. The problem is then, he continued, to show individuals how their own happiness is indispensably dependent upon others. In order to do this Bentham did not abandon his commitment to the two sovereign masters under which nature places man, for this is *the* fundamental principle. In other words, he could not abandon the principle which says that all men desire first and foremost their own pleasure. What he did therefore was to show that men are dependent upon other men for their happiness.[88] "Of man's pleasures, a great proportion is dependent on the will of others, and can only be possessed by him with their concurrence and cooperation."[89] Indeed, he continued, "there is no possibility of disregarding the happiness of others without, at the same time, risking the happiness of our own."[90] In other words, one wishes and works for the greatest happiness of all because in so doing one pursues one's own happiness. Or, as Bentham puts it, "Each individual is linked to his race by a tie, of all ties the strongest, the tie of self-regard."[91] The social bond is simply the united self-interest of all members of the community. This means of course that there is no good proper to the collective whole which is different from those of the individuals who make up the community.

Yet Bentham speaks on occasion of the "general will"[92] and the "general good."[93] At times he approaches the language of Rousseau, but the similarity goes no further than one of words.[94] In Rousseau the general will is not the sum total of particular wills as it is in Bentham.

Bentham's great contribution to government has been that he prescribed the principle of utility as the rule and standard for all laws and constitutions for those nations which call themselves liberal. In his *Codification Proposal* (1822), Bentham addresses "all nations professing liberal opinions," and claims that "in every political state, the greatest happiness of the greatest number requires, that it be provided with an all-comprehensive body of law."[95] It is not by accident that Bentham's influence has been greatest in the area of constitutionalism and law reform (including legislation). For he believed that the most effective way to ensure the liberal or enlightened character of a regime—be it British, French, Portuguese, Spanish, or American—was to insist that all laws be drafted with an eye to the principle of utility. This is why he wrote in an effort to influence the nations of the West; he had discovered, he believed, the universal and irrefutable principle of morals and legislation. All that was needed now was to put it into practice.

One of the anomalies of Bentham's constitutionalism is that he restricts the judicial power and yet does not restrict the press or the right of public discussion. Of the judiciary he says: "Give to the judges a power of annulling its [the legislature's] acts, and you transfer a portion of the supreme power from an assembly which the people have had some share, at least, in chusing, to a set of men in the choice of whom they have not the least imaginable share."[96] This stricture on the judiciary shows a great deal more than a rejection of the prospects of judicial supremacy; it begins to show that faith in the people which Bentham later championed. In *On the Liberty of the Press and Public Discussion* (1821), Bentham claimed—originally for the benefit of the Spanish—that a free press was the "only remaining check to arbitrary power."[97] He went so far as to suggest that public officials can legitimately be treated harshly in the press. He wrote that "to place on any more advantageous footing, the official reputation of a public functionary, is to destroy or proportionately to weaken, that liberty which under the name of liberty of the press operates as a check upon the conduct of the ruling few; and in that character constitutes a controlling power indispensibly necessary to the maintenance of good government."[98] Bentham claims implicitly that the judicial branch of government is more to be feared than are the owners of newspapers. Bentham appears to have viewed judge-made law as the rule of men and not of laws. His distrust of the judiciary was a consequence of his distrust of the rule of men as opposed to the rule of law through legislation or the political process.

Bentham did admire aspects of the American (or, as he preferred, the "Anglo-American United States") Declaration of Independence. But his admiration for the Declaration of Independence did not extend to the "pattern of logic of that document." Any real virtues it possessed, he claimed, could be attributed to the implicit utilitarian features or principles it contained.[99]

Bentham claimed that a good government will encourage public discussion of public affairs. As he puts it: "The characteristic then of an undespotic government—in a word of every government that has any tenable claim to the appelation of a *good government* is, the allowing and giving facility to the communication"[100] of public matters. But he made it clear that a good government ought to provide a forum not only for instruction but for excitation as a means of keeping "on foot every facility for eventual resistance."[101] Bentham added that this resistance could—"should necessity require"—lead to a change in government.[102] The implication here seems to be that the judicial power will more than likely err on the side of the executive power, while the people will err (if at all) on the side of the people. It is impossible not to conclude that in Bentham the majority will is the closest approximation to the unanimous will of the community.

On the Temporal Benefit of Religion

Bentham's major writings on religion are: *Analysis of the Influences of Natural Religion on the Temporal Happiness of Mankind*

(1822), published under the name of Philip Beauchamp; *Not Paul, But Jesus* (1823), published under the name of Gamaliel Smith; and the earlier work, *Church-of-Englandism* (1817–1818), which Bentham published under his own name.

Bentham's attitude toward the Christian religion was permanently influenced by his experience at Oxford where he, along with all undergraduates, was required to acknowledge the Thirty-nine Articles of the Church of England.[103] He found the stern application of these articles of dogma much to his distaste. He thought that the proper or intelligent approach to the articles was to examine them in order to see whether the propositions contained therein were true.[104] When he did this he found that "the examination was unfortunate. In some of them no meaning at all could I find: in others, no meaning but one which, in my eyes, was but too plainly irreconcileable either to reason or to Scripture."[105] His attitude toward Christianity remained skeptical for the rest of his life. His rejection of Paul in favor of the more simple and straightforward message of Jesus set him at odds with the theologians of his day.

But Bentham's interest in religion was as to its usefulness or benefit to mankind. Upon reflection and study, he concluded that religion had a pernicious effect on mankind. And the intolerance of religion filtered down to every Englishman through the tutorial method of instruction.

Bentham accepted religion as he found it and attempted to correct its negative social impact by means of the principle of utility. The first step in this process was, Bentham proposed, to exclude religious sanctions from the realm of politics and morals. As Mary P. Mack observes, Bentham "did not expect to purge deep-rooted ignorance, habits, and prejudices by forced draughts. The ranks behind the religious sanction were too powerful to be overthrown at once, but they could and must be driven from their illegitimate invasions of politics and morals back to more narrow boundaries of religion proper."[106]

But Bentham had no doubts about the benefits of natural religion. In his analysis of the benefits to mankind of natural religion,

Bentham challenges the common belief that religion is a "bond of union between the different members of society" and "the most efficient prop both of inward happiness and of virtuous practice in this world."[107] He shows throughout the work that these claims are far from justified; that on the contrary dissention, war, and intrigue are more frequently the fruits of religion. Above all, the promise of posthumous pleasure and pain is peculiarly perverse for the simple reason that such a future state is "unknown and impervious to human vision."[108] Fear and superstition are the source of these false expectations and hence a threat to genuine pleasures of this life. From the simple fact that "natural religion communicates to mankind no rule of guidance,"[109] Bentham concludes that it cannot be of temporal benefit to mankind. "Natural religion merely implants in a man the expectations of a posthumous existence, involving awards of enjoyment and suffering apportioned by an invisible Being."[110] Indeed the God of natural religion emerges as "a capricious tyrant."[111]

Not only does Bentham chronicle at length the complete social ineffectiveness of superhuman inducements, he also relates a catalogue of "the various modes in which Natural Religion produces temporal mischief."[112] It is not surprising to find Bentham conclude that "the influence possessed by natural religion over human conduct is, with reference to the present life, injurious to an extent incalculably greater than it is beneficial."[113]

Bentham distinguishes, of course, between natural religion and revealed religion. In so doing he gives the impression that the revealed Christian religion provides a code of human conduct, but this impression is, in the final analysis, unsupportable. For Bentham criticized both Christian asceticism and its condemnation of harmless sensual pleasures (especially sexual pleasures). Christian asceticism made it the enemy of human happiness under the utilitarian calculus. When judged by the standards of utilitarianism, as it must be judged, even Christianity was found defective as a guide to men in this life.

Bentham could never find grounds for accommodation with Cleanthes, who argues in Hume's *Dialogues Concerning Natural*

Religion that religious morals have been a benefit to mankind. For Bentham religion—in all its forms—has had the effect of distracting men's attention from their proper pursuits in this life with irrational expectations of future reward.

Conclusion

We must note in drawing this discussion to a close that Bentham's hedonism is not of the nature of Epicurus' hedonism. Bentham's is clearly of a lower order; not only does he deny the existence and priority of intellectual pleasures, he equates the pleasures of the lowest with those of the highest. As he put it: "the happiness of the worst man of the species is as much an integral part of the whole mass of human happiness as that of the best man."[114] What puzzles one in this statement is the use of such adjectives as "worst" and "best." In what precise sense is Bentham employing these terms? Worst and best in what sense? Surely he has established that judgments of merit can only be made by appeal to pleasure and pain. On this basis he has made it abundantly clear that it is impossible to call one man's pleasures bad and another's good, because all pleasures are inherently good. The more accurate conclusion from the principle would appear to be the obliteration of any distinction between good and bad men (and by implication the distinction between worst and best men).

Furthermore, Bentham's constitutionalism (or emphasis on institutions and laws) appears to follow logically upon the obliteration of the distinction between good and bad men. Since utilitarianism makes all men philosophers—i.e., calculators of their pleasures—there is no way the state can command the service of men of wisdom because wisdom as traditionally understood (knowledge plus prudence) is replaced by the principle of utility, which is accessible to all men—not to just a few wise men. As a result Bentham has not only driven wise men (or philosophers) from politics, he has driven out philosophy altogether. There is no longer any need for political philosophy once the principle of utility has been promulgated as the beginning and end of all laws.

His distrust of wisdom is carried to the logical extreme in his distrust of the judiciary and his corresponding faith in the majority of the citizens. This is why he denies to the judiciary the function of judicial review and grants to the people the right (it would appear) to a free press and unrestrained public discussion. We must never forget that it is the greatest good of the *greatest number* which is sought—hence by definition it becomes the rule of the majority.

Before turning our attention to John Stuart Mill and the final extension of utilitarianism into our time, it will be well to conclude that Bentham must be viewed as a major proponent of political hedonism—the state exists simply as a means by which a collectivity of individuals can achieve its own pleasures.

The end result of this doctrine is the politics of mass ideology where the people are called upon to pronounce on all matters of public importance (through referenda) and where the statesman's role is reduced to being a calculator of the public pleasures. Little wonder that the public-opinion poll has become such a major instrument of Western governments. The law has no object apart from securing "the greatest good of the community"[115]—understood as pleasure.

Whatever doubt there may be surrounding the role of the sovereign there is no doubt surrounding the end of those who obey the law—it is "no other than his own particular benefit or satisfaction."[116] This is not to deny to the sovereign the task of shaping public perceptions of public pleasures upon the advice of the majority.[117]

In the final analysis, no matter how hard Bentham tried to meld the multiplicity of individual desires for pleasure into a social whole, he ended in dividing the human condition into public and private spheres. And despite his efforts to the contrary, the private sphere remains prior to and hence in competition with the public sphere. The general principle of utility attempted to resolve this tension, but only by ensuring the hegemony of the most widely held conceptions of pleasure or taste.

JOHN STUART MILL (1806–1873)

J. S. Mill claimed in his comments on Bentham that utilitarianism or Epicureanism has permeated the course of history since the earliest times. He further claimed that without knowing it Bentham was in that tradition. But Mill is quick to point out that Bentham was not a philosopher or, indeed, very profound; he says: "We must not look for subtlety, or the power of recondite analysis, among his intellectual characteristics."[118] His work not only suffered from a lack of intellectual rigor but also from a narrow range of experience. In so describing Bentham, Mill wished to be understood that he was far more profound and worthy to be called— unlike Bentham—a philosopher.

There is no question that Mill's writings not only contain a great deal more of what can be properly called philosophical but also demonstrate a greater awareness of the history of philosophy than do the works of Bentham.

Before turning to Mill's utilitarianism for an examination of the character of his hedonism, it will be instructive to review his short treatise on nature. For in that work Mill addressed himself explicitly to a major theme which Robert Boyle discussed earlier. Indeed, a glance at this work leads one to suspect that Mill had read Boyle's *Vulgarly Receiv'd Notion of Nature*. There is an uncanny parallel between the two, not to say identity. Mill set out in this work to put the axe once for all to the confusing and useless concept of nature—just as Boyle had hoped someone would eventually do. Mill begins his discussion with the lament that Plato had not bequeathed to posterity a discourse on nature; this might have saved his disciples from a great number of errors, he says.[119] In reply to the question: What is the nature of a thing? Mill says that it is obvious that it is "the modes in which it acts on other things . . . and the modes in which other things act upon it; to which, in the case of a sentient being, must be added, its own capacities of feeling, or being conscious."[120] In short, nature is the aggregate of things, powers, and properties. "Nature means the sum of all phenomena, together with the causes which produce them; including not only all that happens, but all that is capable of happening; the unused capabilities of causes being as much a part of the idea of Nature as those which take effect."[121] The regularity with which these phenomena occur is what is meant by laws of nature. Having thus given the "proper" definition of the word nature, Mill set out to discredit alternative conceptions. But before doing that he paused to consider the term as used in contradistinction to the artificial and art. Art is as much nature for Mill as anything else, for it is "but the employment of the powers of Nature for an end."[122]

Mill concluded that a proper understanding of the term "nature" must begin with the recognition that there are at least two principal meanings to be attached to the word. "In one sense, it means all the powers existing in either the outer or inner world and everything which takes place by means of those powers. In another sense, it means, not everything which happens, but only what takes place without the agency, or without the voluntary and intentional agency, of man."[123]

Mill addressed himself explicitly to those moralists who taught that nature dictates the course of moral behavior for all men. "The employment of the word Nature as a term of ethics seems to disclose a third meaning, in which nature does not stand for what is, but for what ought to be."[124] He rejected the effort of those who propose an "external criterion of what we should do."[125] To expose and refute this third and dangerous understanding of nature was the prime purpose of the treatise, claimed Mill. He noted in the first place that this understanding of nature is most frequently ensconced in a "natural law" teaching. He therefore began by showing that nature does not dictate a law in any proper sense of the term. He does so by arguing that there is "no mode of acting which is not conformable to nature . . . [since] every action is the exertion of some natural power, and its effects of all sorts are so many phenomena of nature, produced by the powers and properties of some of the objects of nature, in exact obedience to law or laws of nature."[126] In other words, Mill accepts the proposition that there are physical laws of nature but rejects any suggestion that these are the basis for an ethical or moral law. In one sense, he argued, since man has no other choice but to follow the laws of nature (i.e., the physical laws), it is useless to exhort him to obey nature. Appealing to the testimony of Bacon, he says that "we can obey nature in such a manner as to command it."[127]

Mill struck at the heart of the controversy when he claimed that the natural is not superior to the artificial or that which is produced by art. "If the artificial is not better than the natural, to what end are all the arts of life? To dig, to plough, to build, to wear clothes, are direct infringements of the injunction to follow nature."[128] Indeed, continued Mill, if one looks at how nature treats man—in floods, rain, thunder, etc.—one must conclude that "her powers are often towards men in the position of enemies, from whom he must wrest, by force and ingenuity, what little he can for his own use."[129]

The remainder of the treatise is a tirade against nature and the counsel that man ought to respect and obey it. Mill explicitly disclaims the Christian notion that God's providence is manifest through the course of nature. All of these notions he calls *a priori* fallacies.[130] "For however offensive the proposition may appear to many religious persons, they should be willing to look in the face the undeniable fact, that the order of nature, in so far as unmodified by man, is such as no being, whose attributes are justice and benevolence, would have made, with the intention that his rational creatures should follow it as an example."[131]

Mill's attack on nature leaves little or nothing in the concept when he finishes. He even goes so far as to claim that nature is a murderous monster. "In sober truth, nearly all the things which men are hanged or imprisoned for doing to one another, are nature's every day performance. Killing, the most criminal act recognized by human laws, Nature does once to every being that lives; and in a large proportion of cases, after protracted tortures such as only the greatest monsters whom we read of ever purposely inflicted on their living fellow-creatures."[132] Nature murders, starves, freezes, and burns men "with the most supercilious disregard both of mercy and of justice, emptying her shafts upon the best and noblest indifferently with the meanest and worst."[133] In short, nature acts with "habitual injustice."[134]

Mill took particular delight in heaping scorn upon the idea that nature is the source and measure of human virtue. "If the creator of mankind willed that they should all be virtuous, his designs are as completely baffled as if he had willed that they should all be happy."[135] Furthermore, "if it be said that God does not take sufficient account of pleasure and pain to make them the reward and punishment of the good or the wicked, but that virtue is itself the greatest good and vice the greatest evil, then these at least ought to be dispensed to all according to what they have done to deserve them."[136] But, says Mill, we all know that we live in a different world.

Mill's major conclusion was that nature is intended to be not followed but amended.[137] This is particularly true of human nature. "The truth is that there is hardly a single point of excellence belonging to human character which is not decidedly repugnant to the untutored feelings of human nature."[138] Indeed, nature does not even counsel men to be clean; the artificial is what leads men to be clean—another proof that even in the lowest of matters nature does not provide for men. Above all, says Mill, if there is one thing we learn from a study of human nature it is that nature has made men selfish.[139] And by nature all men are liars.[140]

As for "natural justice," Mill reserved for it his most severe strictures. He began by flatly denying that it exists. "I believe . . . that the sentiment of justice is entirely of artificial origin."[141] He goes on to say that were it not for the idea of conventional justice the idea of natural justice would never have emerged. "The notion of a higher justice, to which laws themselves are amenable, and by which the conscience is bound without a positive prescription of law, is a later extension of the idea, suggested by, and following the analogy of, legal justice, to which it maintains a parallel direction through all the shades and varieties of sentiment, and from which it borrows nearly the whole of its phraseology."[142]

Mill concluded his foray into natural virtue with the claim that the conclusion is the same here as it was for the early discussion of the physical course of nature: nature appears to counsel one thing in both spheres, and that is to amend nature, *not* to follow it. He conceded only one sense in which the term "natural" can be applied to men with a degree of profit, and that is when it is used to denote the absence of affectation.[143]

He is adamant in affirming that "conformity to nature has no connection whatever with right and wrong."[144] We are led therefore in matters of morals (including justice) to the conclusion that all virtue is based on agreement among men—i.e., all virtue is conventional. History shows, he says, that the acquisition of virtue among men has always coincided with the greatest effort to conquer the greatest number of natural inclinations. This contains the paradox in Mill's position: nature does indeed give men natural drives or inclinations, but these drives or inclinations do not lead him to his happiness, except insofar as they point out the paths of pleasure and pain. By nature man appears to be fated to a life directed against his best interests.

We must contrast this understanding of nature with that of Bentham. As we saw earlier, Bentham began his major work on morals and legislation with the acknowledgment that nature was beneficent because it placed men under two sovereign masters— pleasure and pain. The former dictates his happiness; the latter, his misery. Mill appears reluctant to accord to nature this minimal benevolence in his treatise on nature.

Mill began his *Utilitarianism* by restating in capsule form what he had said in his treatise on nature—i.e., that we must avoid "recourse to the popular theory of a natural faculty, a sense or instinct, informing us of right and wrong."[145] He sets down as a test of his doctrine that "Whatever can be proved to be good, must be so by being shown to be a means to something admitted to be good without proof."[146]

He makes an initial effort to refute those who claim that utility is other than pleasure. "Those who know anything about the matter are aware that every writer, from Epicurus to Bentham, who maintained the theory of utility, meant by it, not something to be contradistinguished from pleasure—but pleasure itself, together with

exemption from pain."[147] He attempts to clear the air by a forth-
right definition of what the principle of utility means: "Utility, or
the Greatest Happiness Principle, holds that actions are right in
proportion as they tend to promote happiness, wrong as they tend
to produce the reverse of happiness."[148] He left no room for doubt
as to what constitutes happiness by adding: "By happiness is intended pleasure, and the absence of pain; by unhappiness, pain,
and the privation of pleasure."[149] Mill went on to say that the
whole of utilitarian morality is constructed upon this basic principle: "pleasure, and freedom from pain, are the only things desirable as ends."[150] But despite this lapse into teleology, Mill does not
appear to concede that these pleasurable ends are so by nature. He
never attempts to reconcile his doctrine of moral ends with his unqualified rejection of nature.

One of the most interesting aspects of Mill's account or defense
of utilitarianism is that he links it with its Epicurean roots. He is
particularly anxious to dispell the charge—frequently made in his
day—that utilitarianism leads to base hedonism such as was attributed to the disciples of Epicurus. Mill acknowledged that the
human conception of happiness is higher than the animal conception because human beings "have faculties more elevated than the
animal appetites, and when once made conscious of them, do not
regard anything as happiness which does not include their gratification."[151] But Mill does not say on what basis these "more elevated" appetites are designated as higher than the other appetites—such as the appetite for food. He simply retorts with the
claim that "there is no known Epicurean theory of life which does
not assign to the pleasures of the intellect, of the feelings and
imagination, and of the moral sentiments, a much higher value as
pleasures than to those of mere sensation."[152] He does, however,
come to grips with the problem of nature by suggesting that utilitarian writers claim as the basis of superiority of the "elevated appetites" their "greater permanency, safety, uncostliness,"[153] rather
than in their intrinsic nature. Mill here implies that they have no
greater intrinsic worth by nature than the other appetites. Yet he
writes later of the "intrinsic superiority of higher" pleasures.[154]

This leaves open the possibility that they cannot claim a priority over the other appetites. They may *not* be of greater permanence, safety, or uncostliness. It is important to note in addition to Mill's insistence that utilitarianism be connected with Epicureanism, that his is a defense of Epicureanism understood as a higher form of hedonism.

But Mill attempted to rescue utilitarianism (hedonism) from the charge that it depends simply on *quantity* and the disregard of quality. In so doing Mill was rejecting explicitly the quantum theory as proposed by Bentham. Despite his rejection of the quantity principle, Mill makes it clear that it is replaced by the weight of numbers. That is to say: "Of two pleasures, if there be one to which all or almost all who have experience of both give a decided preference, irrespective of any feeling of moral obligation to prefer it, that is the most desirable pleasure."[155] But how can the weight of preference be an indication as to the *quality* of a thing? Furthermore, Mill appears to be saying that the individual is *not* the best judge of his feelings (i.e., pleasures, and hence his happiness). This proposition strikes at the roots of hedonism and Bentham's utilitarianism, where the individual is the judge of all pleasures.

Mill attempted to justify his departure from the individualistic basis of utilitarianism and hence justify the reliance on a third-party judgment by using such phrases as "those who are competently acquainted" with the pleasure in question, or those who are "capable of appreciating and enjoying" the pleasure. One can only surmise what Bentham would do with this kind of gratuitous acknowledgment of wisdom or superior capacity for enjoyment—to say nothing of the implied right to announce their preferences as standards to be followed by others. But Mill is unequivocal in this matter. "On a question which is the best worth having of two pleasures, or which of two modes of existence is the most grateful to the feelings, apart from its moral attributes and from its consequences, the judgment of those who are qualified by knowledge [experience?] of both, or, if they differ, that of the majority among them, must be admitted as final."[156] Surprisingly enough, he says that this is the same final court of appeal as to quantity.

One of the most striking aspects of Mill's treatise on utilitarianism is his effort to uproot it from its foundation in individualism. The happiness at which utilitarians aim is "not the agent's own greatest happiness but the greatest amount of happiness altogether."[157] This reinforces his claim to the right of majority determination of both quantity and quality of pleasure.

No one could sum up the essentials of the case better than Mill. He wrote that

> According to the Greatest Happiness Principle, as above explained, the ultimate end [sic], with reference to and for the sake of which all other things are desirable (whether we are considering our own good or that of other people), is an existence exempt as far as possible from pain, and as rich as possible in enjoyments, both in point of quantity and quality; the test of quality, and the rule for measuring it against quantity, being the preference felt by those who in their opportunities of experience, to which must be added their habits of self-consciousness and self-observation, are best furnished with the means of comparison. This being, according to the utilitarian opinion, the end of human action, is necessarily also the standard of morality; which may accordingly be defined, the rules and precepts for human conduct, by the observance of which an existence such as has been described might be, to the greatest extent possible, secured to all mankind; and not to them only, but, as far as the nature of things admits, to the whole sentient creation.[158]

Mill says that the two main stumbling blocks to the attainment of happiness are "the present wretched education, and wretched social arrangement."[159] But he also warned that next to selfishness "the principle cause which makes life unsatisfactory is want of mental cultivation."[160] But he made it clear that he is not thinking of philosophers. His main concern was with instruction which would lead people to prefer the pleasures of the higher appetites. This would ensure against the spread of base hedonism. Every "rightly brought up human being" would experience a proper balance between his individual appetites and yet engender a sincere interest in the public good. Mill appears at pains to reject Bentham's contention that one ought to seek the public good because in so doing one seeks one's own. According to Mill the "utilitarian morality does recognize in human beings the power of sacrificing their own greatest good for the good of others."[161] He insists on attempting to set the record straight by stating that "what the assailants of utilitarianism seldom have the justice to acknowledge, that the happiness which forms the utilitarian standard of what is right in conduct, is not the agent's own happiness, but that of all concerned."[162] Indeed, utilitarianism requires man "to be as strictly impartial as a disinterested and benevolent spectator."[163] But how can he be when he in fact is not a spectator but the subject of the pleasures experienced?

Mill's instruction to governments was that laws and social arrangements should place the happiness or the interest of every "individual as nearly as possible in harmony with the interest of the whole."[164] Education should especially be designed to show how one's individual happiness is indissolubly associated with the happiness of the whole community—thus to inculcate a sense of social preference. It was Mill's hope that through education the preference for the social happiness will take priority over the private or selfish quest for happiness.[165]

As to the sanctions of utilitarian morality, Mill says they are as any other, internal or external. The external sanction lies in the approbation or disapprobation of the community. The internal sanction consists of a feeling in one's own mind, "a pain, more or less intense, attendant on violation of duty, which in properly cultivated moral natures rises, in the more serious cases, into shrinking from it as an impossibility."[166]

One of the most intriguing points in Mill is, despite his attack on nature and his preference for the artificial over the natural, the claim that the "social state is at once so natural, so necessary, and so habitual to man, that, except in some unusual circumstances or by an effort of voluntary abstraction, he never conceives himself otherwise than as a member of a body; and this association is riveted more and more, as mankind are further removed from the state of savage independence."[167] He says that in time we will all feel the social force of utilitarianism, but at present we live in "the

comparatively early state of human advancement."[168] Mill built
his social bond upon "the deeply rooted conception which every
individual even now has of himself as a social being."[169] This, he
says, "tends to make [man] feel it one of his *natural* wants that
there should be harmony between his feelings and aims and those of
his fellow-creatures."[170] This kind of optimism sets off Mill from
the entire tradition of modernity, which is rooted in a deep distrust
of man's willingness to assume freely social responsibilities or
duties.

Mill states that "the utilitarian doctrine is, that happiness is desirable, and the only thing desirable, as an end."[171] All else adds
to or subtracts from that end. The proof for this doctrine is in the
general acceptance in experience—everyone desires his own happiness. This is not a proposition, but a fact. "This, however, being a
fact, we have not only all the proof which the case admits of, but all
which it is possible to require, that happiness is a good: that each
person's happiness is a good to that person, and the general happiness, therefore, a good to the aggregate of all persons."[172]

On the question of the source of justice,[173] Mill says that we
must begin by looking for the common attribute in those things
called just and unjust. He concluded that it is "simply the natural
feeling of resentment,"[174] which we make moral by making it co-
extensive with the demands of social good—i.e., by making it useful. This the sentiment which leads to thoughts and judgments of
justice and injustice is subsumed within the principle of utility.
One thing is clear here, as well as in his discourse on Nature: that
there is no such thing as "natural right" or "natural justice." "The
sentiment of justice appears to me to be, the animal desire to repel
or retaliate a hurt or damage to oneself, or to those with whom one
sympathizes, widened so as to include all persons, by the human
capacity of enlarged sympathy, and the human conception of intelligent self-interest."[175] Mill stated in concluding that "I account the justice which is grounded on utility to be the chief part,
and incomparably the most sacred and binding part, of all morality."[176]

One important consequence of Mill's theory of justice is that it provides the people and their representatives with a rule of reform. And Mill made it abundantly clear that the utilitarian understanding of justice requires the gradual elimination of social inequalities. As soon as "all social inequalities have ceased to be considered expedient,"[177] they assume the character of injustice and appear tyrannical. "The entire history of social improvement has been a series of transitions, by which one custom or institution after another, from being a supposed primary necessity of social existence, has passed into the rank of a universally stigmatized injustice and tyranny."[178] But far from being simply a statement of historic fact, this comment assumes the character of an injunction addressed to all individuals and states calling themselves liberal.

And yet Mill appeared anxious to ensure that the individual not become submerged in the mass mediocrity. In *On Liberty*, he went to great lengths to distinguish the boundaries of the public and private realms in the interest of ensuring that the state did not violate the private realm. In short, Mill feared the tendency toward democracy, and approved of representative government as a check on the movement toward universal democracy. A clearly delineated private realm and the representative form of government provide the necessary conditions for the rise of individualism. As Hilail Gildin has observed: "In *On Liberty*, he tries to protect the individual against [the tendency to democracy]. His chief concern is to construct an impassable barrier between the individual and society beyond which the individual cannot be forced to conform to the collective mediocrity of others or, indeed, to anything at all."[179] Mill's individualism permeates all his writings but is explicitly acknowledged in the *System of Logic*: "Human beings in society have no properties but those which are derived from and may be resolved into the larva of the nature of the individual man."[180]

In *Representative Government* Mill acknowledged, as the first element of good government, the virtue and intelligence of citizens; political institutions are good to the extent that they tend to foster the highest moral and intellectual qualities of members of the community.[181] His conclusion is that the main criterion for judging a government is whether and to what extent its laws and institutions increase the sum of good qualities in the governed, both individually and collectively. For Mill, unlike Bentham, the entire tone of the community is not left to chance—it is to be modeled after the tastes and standards of the higher classes (to which Mill, of course, belonged).

On the question of the ideal form of government, Mill concluded that it is "that in which the sovereignty, or supreme controlling power in the last resort, is vested in the entire aggregate of the community; every citizen not only having a voice in the exercise of that ultimate sovereignty, but being, at least occasionally, called on to take an actual part in the government, by the personal discharge of some public function, local or general."[182] This definition prepares the way for Mill's preference for representative government; it is the only form of government capable of fulfilling his hope that the citizens of the better sort will be chosen to preside over the affairs of the community, thereby ensuring the likelihood of that tone and character consistent with his high-toned utilitarianism. Since it is virtually and actually impossible (and undesirable) that all citizens participate in the exercise of government, "it follows that the ideal type of a perfect government must be representative."[183]

Theism and the Utility of Religion

John Stuart Mill's essay on "Nature," which we have seen earlier, is included with two other essays—one entitled "Utility of Religion," and another entitled "Theism"—in his collected works as "Three Essays on Religion." Mill did not himself group these essays together under the general category of religion, but they do in fact fit together quite easily. Since we have already had reason to review the contents of the essay on nature, we shall restrict our attention in this brief review of his writings on religion to "Utility of Religion" and "Theism."

Mill himself claimed that Bentham's *Analysis of the Influence of Natural Religion on the Temporal Happiness of Mankind* "was one of the books which by the searching character of its analysis produced the greatest effect" on him.[184] Mill's reflections on religion led him to conclude that "the natural attitude of a thinking mind towards the supernatural, whether in natural or in revealed religion, is that of skepticism as distinguished from belief on the one hand, and from atheism on the other."[185] This conclusion would not have displeased Bentham. His judgment on Jesus as a model, however, might not have been as readily approved by Bentham. Mill says that "the most valuable part of the effect on the character which Christianity has produced by holding up in a Divine Person a standard of excellence and a model for imitation, is available even to the absolute unbeliever and can never more be lost to humanity."[186] The implication here is that the extraordinary character of Jesus could serve as a model for all men, whether Christian or not. But Mill makes no pretense to abandon his skepticism with respect to the reasonable basis of Christian theology. It is also important to observe that, according to Mill's account, Jesus is "the God incarnate, more than the God of the Jews or of Nature, who being idealized has taken so great and salutory a hold on the modern mind."[187] His explicit dissociation of Jesus from the Jews —i.e., from the God of the Old Testament—and from nature is completely incompatible with Christian orthodoxy. Indeed Jesus emerges as the "translation of the rule of virtue from the abstract into the concrete"[188] rather than as the actual son of God. Mill claims that Jesus was not God "for he never made the smallest pretension to that character and would probably have thought such a pretension as blasphemous as it seemed to the men who condemned him."[189] Nothing more need be said to conclude that Mill was not a believing orthodox Christian. He remained all his life a rational skeptic. Unlike Bentham, however, Mill foresaw a benefit to mankind of religious sentiments which arose out of Christianity —of "a religious devotion to the welfare of our fellow-creatures as an obligatory limit to every selfish aim."[190]

Mill's discussion of theism constitutes an application of science to matters of religion—an attempt to view the matter of religion "not from the point of view of reverence but from that of science."[191] His first and most fundamental conclusion is that science cannot lead one to the existence of a Deity; rather does it confirm merely that the "phenomena of Nature do take place according to general laws."[192]

The traditional theological arguments for a first cause, and from design in the universe, are subjected to careful scrutiny. His conclusions are that science cannot lead us to affirm with certainty the existence of a God: "I think it must be allowed that, in the present state of our knowledge, the adaptations in Nature afford a large balance of probability in favour of creation by intelligence."[193] Beyond this, Mill claimed, science could not take man.

The final posture prompted by science is one of "rational skepticism"; this applies to all aspects of religion, both natural and revealed. Mill thus contributed his part in the secularization of life as did his immediate predecessors, who built upon the work of their predecessors.

NOTES

1. *A Treatise of Human Nature, being an Attempt to Introduce the Experimental Method of Reasoning into Moral Subjects*, 2 Vols. (London, 1817), Vol. II, Book III, Part iii, Sect. iii, p. 106.

2. Ibid., Vol. II, Bk. III, Pt. ii, p. 200.

3. Ibid., Vol. II, p. 191. In *Essays* I, Hume also says: "As soon as men quit their savage state, where they lived chiefly by hunting and fishing, etc." (p. 289). John Stewart, *The Moral and Political Philosophy of David Hume* (New York: Columbia University Press, 1963); see n. 44.

4. Ibid., p. 199.

5. Ibid., pp. 199–200.

6. Ibid., p. 191.

7. Ibid.

8. Ibid., p. 195.

9. Ibid., p. 196.

10. Ibid., p. 198.

11. Ibid.

12. Ibid.

13. Ibid., p. 202.

14. Ibid., p. 203.

15. Ibid., p. 204.
16. Ibid., p. 207.
17. Ibid., p. 241.
18. Ibid.
19. *Second Treatise*, Ch. II, "Of the State of Nature," No. 6.
20. *A Treatise of Human Nature*, p. 241.
21. Ibid.
22. Ibid., p. 243.
23. Ibid., p. 248.
24. Ibid., p. 250.
25. Ibid., p. 245.
26. Ibid., p. 247.
27. Ibid., p. 251.
28. Ibid.
29. Ibid., p. 253.
30. Ibid., p. 255.
31. Ibid., p. 266. Yet Hume claims: "I have all along endeavoured to establish my system on pure reason."
32. Ibid., p. 260.
33. Ibid., Vol. III, Bk. III, pp. 2–5.
34. *A Treatise of Human Nature*, Vol. II, pp. 275–77.
35. Ibid., p. 272, Sect. IX, italics added.
36. Ibid.
37. Ibid., p. 273.
38. Ibid.
39. Ibid., p. 275, Sect. X.
40. Ibid., p. 280.
41. Ibid.
42. *Essays, Moral and Political, Essay* V, "Of the First Principles of Government" (Edinburgh, 1714), p. 51.
43. *Treatise of Human Nature* II, 277.
44. Ibid., p. 274.
45. Ibid., p. 271, Sect. IX.
46. Ibid.
47. *Essay* I, p. 289.
48. Ibid., pp. 295–96.
49. *An Enquiry Concerning Human Understanding* (Chicago: Regnery, 1956), p. 113.
50. Ibid.
51. The best edition of these works is *Natural History of Religion*, ed. A. Wayne Colver, *Dialogues Concerning Natural Religion*, ed. John Valdimir Price (Oxford: Clarendon Press, 1976).

52. *Natural History of Religion*, p. 32.

53. *The Eighteenth Century Confronts the Gods* (Cambridge: Harvard University Press, 1959), p. 169.

54. *Dialogues Concerning Natural Religion*, p. 153.

55. See David Furley, *Two Studies in the Greek Atomists* (Princeton: Princeton University Press, 1967), Ch. 10: "Epicurus and David Hume," pp. 136–47.

56. *Treatise of Human Nature*, Vol. I, Bk. II, Pt. I, Sect. VII, "Of Vice and Virtue."

57. Ibid., Vol. II, Pt. III, Sect. III, p. 108.

58. See Albert O. Hirschman, *The Passions and the Interest* (Princeton: Princeton University Press, 1976); see also Páll S. Árdal, *Passion and Value in Hume's Treatise* (Edinburgh: University of Edinburgh Press, 1966).

59. *Treatise of Human Nature*, Vol. III, Pt. II, Sect. V, "Of the Obligation of Promises," p. 426.

60. *Essays, Moral and Political*, Essay V, "Of the First Principles of Government," p. 49.

61. *Treatise of Human Nature*, Vol. II, p. 273.

62. *Works*, ed. J. Bowring (London, 1843), II, 501.

63. For an interesting discussion of this issue, see C. B. Macpherson, *The Life and Times of Liberal Democracy* (London: Oxford University Press, 1977), Ch. II, "The Utilitarian Base" and "Bentham's Ends of Legislation," pp. 25–34.

64. Bentham includes within the term "psychological entity" all intellectual and volitional promptings; see *A Table of the Springs of Action* (London, 1915), pp. 27, 28.

65. Ibid., p. 13.

66. Ibid., p. 14.

67. *Deontology*, Bk. I, Ch. III, p. 42.

68. See *Deontology*, Ch. III, Bk. I, "Anti-Deontological Propositions Removed," pp. 38–58. "What does the term [summum bonum] signify? Nonsense, and nothing more." p. 39.

69. *A Table of the Springs of Action*, p. 21.

70. Ibid., p. 22.

71. *Introduction to the Principles of Morals and Legislation* (Oxford, 1892), p. 1.

72. Ibid.

73. For an attempt to put order into pleasures, see Charles W. Everett, *Jeremy Bentham* (London: Weidenfeld and Nicolson, 1966), pp. 48 ff.

74. *Introduction to the Principles of Morals and Legislation*, Pt. XVII.2.

75. *Deontology*, p. 30.

76. Ibid., p. 27.

77. Ibid., p. 29.

78. Ibid.

79. *Defence of Usury* (London, 1788), p. 3. This is restated later in Letter XII, pp. 152–53.

80. "Plan of Parliamentary Reform," *Works*, III, 470.

81. *A Fragment of Government* (London, 1776), p. 149.

82. Ibid., Ch. I, p. 31.

83. Ibid., p. 21*n*14.

84. Ibid., Preface, p. ii.

85. Ibid., Ch. I, p. 62.

86. *Deontology*, p. 156.

87. Ibid.

88. Ibid., p. 132.

89. Ibid., p. 133.

90. Ibid.

91. Ibid.

92. *Essays on Political Tactics, Essay* VI, p. 3.

93. *Deontology*, p. 22.

94. Bentham explicitly criticized the Rousseauan conception of "general will" in "Anarchial Fallacies," *Works*, Vol. III, ed. J. Bowring (London, 1843), p. 507. See also "Essay on Political Tactics," *Works*, II, 332.

95. *Codification Proposal* (London, 1822), p. 1.

96. *Fragment on Government*, p. 161.

97. *On the Liberty of the Press and Public Discussion* (London, 1821), p. 1.

98. Ibid., p. 12.

99. Ibid., p. 24.

100. Ibid.

101. Ibid.

102. Ibid.

103. See for his full account of this incident the Preface to *Church-of-Englandism* (London, 1817–1818). For a good discussion of the influence of Bentham's religious writings, see James Steintrager, "Morality and Belief: The Origin and Purpose of Bentham's Writings on Religion," *Mill Newsletter*, 6 (1971), 3–15.

104. Ibid., p. xix.

105. Ibid., pp. xix–xx.

106. Mary P. Mack, *Jeremy Bentham* (New York: Columbia University Press, 1963), p. 302.

107. *Analysis of the Influence of Natural Religion*, p. 1.

108. Ibid., p. 4.

109. Ibid., p. 10.

110. Ibid., p. 13.

111. Ibid., p. 20.

112. Ibid., Pt. II, pp. 68ff.

113. Ibid., p. 65.

114. *Deontology*, p. 269.

115. *Of Laws in General* (London: Athlone Press, 1970), p. 31.

116. Ibid.

117. For an alternative interpretation, see: J. A. W. Gunn, "Jeremy Bentham and the Public Interest," *Canadian Journal of Political Science*, 2 (Dec. 1968), 398–413.

118. *Mill on Bentham and Coleridge*, ed. with Intro. by F. R. Leavis (London: Chatto and Windus, 1950), p. 44.

119. J. S. Mill, *Nature, The Utility of Religion and Theism* (London: Longmans Green, 1874), p. 4.

120. Ibid., p. 5.

121. Ibid.

122. Ibid., p. 7.

123. Ibid., p. 8.

124. Ibid., p. 12.

125. Ibid., p. 13.

126. Ibid., pp. 15, 16.

127. Ibid., p. 17.

128. Ibid., p. 20.

129. Ibid.

130. Ibid., p. 25.

131. Ibid.

132. Ibid., pp. 28–29.

133. Ibid., p. 29.

134. Ibid., p. 35.

135. Ibid., p. 37.

136. Ibid., p. 38.

137. Ibid., p. 41.

138. Ibid., p. 46.

139. Ibid., p. 49.

140. Ibid., p. 51.

141. Ibid., p. 52.

142. Ibid., p. 53.

143. Ibid., p. 61.

144. Ibid., p. 62.

145. J. S. Mill, *Utilitarianism, Liberty and Representative Government* (London: Dent, 1910), p. 2.

146. Ibid., p. 4.

147. Ibid., p. 5.

148. Ibid., p. 6.

149. Ibid.

150. Ibid., p. 6.

151. Ibid., p. 7.

152. Ibid.

153. Ibid.

154. Ibid., p. 9. For a discussion of Mill's hedonism, see Rex Martin, "A Defence of Mill's Qualitative Hedonism," *Philosophy*, 47 (1972), 140–51; also Henry R. West's reply to Martin: "Mill's Qualitative Hedonism," ibid., 51 (1976) 97–101.

155. J. S. Mill, *Utilitarianism, Liberty and Representative Government*, p. 8.

156. Ibid., p. 10.

157. Ibid.

158. Ibid., p. 11.

159. Ibid., p. 12.

160. Ibid., p. 13.

161. Ibid., p. 15.

162. Ibid., p. 16.

163. Ibid.

164. Ibid.

165. Ibid., p. 25.

166. Ibid., p. 26.

167. Ibid., p. 29.

168. Ibid., p. 31.

169. Ibid.

170. Ibid.

171. Ibid., p. 32.

172. Ibid., p. 33.

173. Mill gives more attention to this topic than to any other in *Utilitarianism*, a total of 21 pages.

174. Ibid., pp. 47–48.

175. Ibid., p. 49.

176. Ibid., p. 55.

177. Ibid., p. 59.

178. Ibid.

179. Hilail Gildin, "Mill on Liberty," in Joseph Cropsey, *Ancients and Moderns* (New York: Basic Books, 1964), p. 299.

180. *System of Logic*, VI, 7.1. *Works*. For a discussion of Mill's individualism, see: Martin Hollis, "J. S. Mill's Political Philosophy of Mind," *Philosophy*, 47 (1972) 334–47.

181. *Representative Government*, p. 192.

182. Ibid., p. 207.

183. Ibid., p. 218.

184. J. S. Mill, *Autobiography* (New York: Liberal Arts Press, 1957), p. 46.

185. "Theism," *Works* X, 482.
186. Ibid., p. 487.
187. Ibid.
188. Ibid., p. 488.
189. Ibid.
190. Ibid.
191. Ibid., p. 434.
192. Ibid., p. 433.
193. Ibid., p. 450.

8

Plato's Dialogue *Gorgias*

IT MAY APPEAR OUT OF PLACE to invite the reader to consider
Plato's dialogue *Gorgias* at the end of a chronological account of
the development of political hedonism. But it would be a major
oversight not to consider it at this point, for the *Gorgias* is the most
penetrating critique of political hedonism ever written. And since
the primary purpose of this book is to present a critical account of
the rise and development of the tradition of political hedonism, it
should prove instructive to view the principles of that tradition
from a detached vantage point—from a philosophic perspective
remote from our time. Not being a captive of the modernist commitment, Plato's critique transcends the limitations of modernity.
From a critical perspective, he provides in this dialogue an analysis
of the dangers and limitations which flow from political hedonism.

Plato uncovers in this dialogue the fundamental weakness of the
central principle of hedonism: that the human good is identical
with pleasure. He also shows how, through the use of rhetoric
(ideology), citizens in regimes based on consent (democracies and
republics) can be manipulated by the appeal to their pleasures.

In the *Gorgias* Plato goes to the root issues of political hedonism
without losing sight of the appeal hedonism has for most men. Indeed, the inherent attractiveness of hedonism constitutes one of its
major dangers. In short, this dialogue is both incisive and sympathetic without ever being simplistic in its solutions. It is profoundly
contemporary and therefore must be considered at the conclusion
of this study. For if Plato's analysis is sound, it is as pertinent today
when political hedonism has become firmly entrenched as it was
when first written.

At first glance it would seem improbable that Plato should present an assessment of political hedonism in a dialogue concerning
rhetoric. But this is precisely what the *Gorgias*, in the final analysis,

is about. This dialogue with Socrates is divided into three unequal parts: a conversation with Gorgias, the great master of rhetoric; a conversation with a student of Gorgias' named Polus; and, by far the longest section, the conversation with the aspiring politician Callicles. We shall focus attention on the Callicles section since it contains the main elements of Plato's critique of political hedonism. The great battle between the two opposing ways of life—the just life of philosophy and the unjust life of hedonism—takes place in this important dialogue in the context of rhetoric or the art of persuading citizens as to what constitutes the public good.

It is especially significant that Callicles the politician is the one who espouses hedonism and seeks to learn the art of rhetoric from Gorgias. It is equally significant that he makes it clear that he is unwilling to learn philosophy from Socrates, as we shall see. This refusal will have dire consequences for Callicles and those regimes he might eventually rule.

ENTER CALLICLES

Callicles bursts in upon the dialogue with an angry rejection of Polus' concession that "to suffer an injustice is preferable to doing an injustice." Such a proposition offends his hard-headed common sense. He claims that Socrates wrested the concession from the youthful Polus through semantic trickery. He boastfully promises that he will not be taken in as easily. Not only does the politician emerge as stronger than the other two participants; he also emerges as more perceptive. For Callicles accuses Socrates of deceitfully moving the base of support for his argument from nature to convention whenever it suits his purpose. Callicles, on the other hand, argues that by nature the conventional is better or preferable; indeed he claims that nature shows that the stronger should rule over the weaker, that might is right, and that the conventional understanding of right recognizes and sanctions this popularly perceived understanding.

Having thus forcefully asserted his position, Callicles turns on Socrates and urges him to abandon philosophy; it is fit only for the childish minds of the young but not for a mature man. We here begin to see the battle between the politician (the city) and the philosopher move into the forefront of the dialogue, reinforcing its political importance. Callicles emerges as firmly anti-philosophical; he urges Socrates to give up philosophy and become involved in the life of commerce and politics where men achieve recognition and reputation. Callicles thus turns the tables on Socrates and urges him to abandon his way of life—i.e., to abandon the philosophic quest for that which is good for men by nature; he warns Socrates that unless he abandons the philosophic way of life he will not be able to defend himself against unjust accusers. "If someone should seize hold of you or anyone else at all of your sort, and drag you off to prison, asserting that you were guilty of an injustice you had never done, you know you would be at a loss what to do with yourself and would be all dizzy and agape without a word to say"[1] (486). In other words, he warns Socrates that forensic rhetoric is far more important to a man than philosophy; without forensic rhetoric Socrates will not be able to defend his pursuit of philosophy against unjust charges; indeed, he will not even be able to preserve his life.

Socrates replies to Callicles' urgings with the claim that he is fortunate in meeting Callicles because he knows that he (Callicles) will not agree with him out of undue respect or timidity as Gorgias and Polus allegedly did. Indeed he begs Callicles not to stop but to continue questioning him in the interest of rescuing him from his erroneous way of thinking. He insists that Callicles go back and repeat what he and Pindar hold natural justice to be. Callicles agrees with Socrates' formulation of the answer: natural justice is "that the superior should forcibly despoil the inferior, the better rule the worse, and the nobler have more than the baser" (488B).

With agreement on this understanding, Socrates proceeds to ask Callicles whether the "better" and the "superior" are the same. He reminds Callicles that he had boasted earlier that natural justice condoned the conquest of the weaker cities by the stronger cities. Socrates attempts here to have Callicles understand the full ramifications of his position by determining precisely what it is that makes the stronger better. Is it possible, he asks, for the stronger to be wicked, for the stronger to be a tyrant? Callicles persists in his reply that the stronger and the better are identical. He further concedes that the many are superior to the one as a logical extension of his belief that might is right. Socrates turns this conclusion on Callicles and reminds him of his earlier concession that to the many justice means having an equal share and that it is fouler to commit an injustice than to suffer an injustice (488E). Callicles replies, "Well, the many do think so," thereby conceding the point on behalf of the many while at the same time withholding assent himself. Callicles, the politician, here asserts his superiority over the many whose ruler he proposes to become.

Socrates takes this concession and shows that if it is true, then both nature and convention concur in holding that doing an injustice is fouler than suffering it, and that having one's equal share is just. In so doing, Socrates turns the tables back upon Callicles and shows that nature and convention cannot be opposites as Callicles had claimed earlier. Callicles contemptuously attempts to extricate himself from this dilemma by claiming that he made a slip of the tongue. He reaffirms his belief that might is right and that decisions which proceed from the majority have the force of law. Callicles thus appears to retreat from founding his basic principle in nature; he opts instead for convention with all its consequences. The implication is the same as Callicles made earlier—i.e., that by nature justice is conventional; that is to say, justice is the product of the might of numbers of physical strength.

But Callicles retreats further here by denying that the stronger are simply the better. By the better, he claims, he means the "more excellent." And when pressed he concedes that by the more excellent he means the wiser and the like. This leads Socrates to conclude that one wise man is often superior to ten thousand fools, and that he ought to rule and have more than those whom he rules. Callicles, having been forced to agree, adds: "that being better and wiser he should have both rule and advantage over the baser people" (490A). This he firmly claims is by nature just. Thus it is

Callicles who shifts from nature to convention when the convenience allows, not Socrates, whom Callicles accused earlier in the dialogue.

Socrates now attempts to explore what Callicles means when he says that the better ought to have more than the inferior. Does this apply to such things as food and clothing, he asks. No, replies Callicles, "I mean something different." He finally explains: "by the superior I mean not shoemakers and cooks, but those who are wise as regards the affairs of the city and the proper way of conducting them, not only wise men but courageous, with the ability to carry out their purpose to the full; and who will not falter through softness of soul" (491B).

Socrates charges Callicles with never saying the same thing. (Callicles had charged Socrates with always saying the same thing over and over.) Callicles has defined the better and superior as the stronger, then as the wiser, and now as the manlier or more courageous. Socrates insists that Callicles clear the air and give a more precise answer. Callicles, thus pressed, replies that he means by the better and superior "men of wisdom and courage in the affairs of the city. These are the ones who ought to rule our cities, and justice means this—that these should have more than others, the rulers than the ruled" (491D).

This leads Socrates to ask whether this definition applies also to those who rule themselves well—i.e., those who keep their passions in check and are temperate. This elicits an explosive response from Callicles, who calls the temperate "foolish"; in his view, by nature beauty and justice are achieved by letting one's desires grow as strong as possible and by satisfying each appetite with what it desires. Callicles claims that the manly look down upon those weaklings who lack the courage to pursue their passions to the full because most people are weak and unable to pursue their passions fully. This is why the weak praise temperance. It is important to note that in this speech Callicles also ridicules justice as well as temperance. In short, he claims, "luxury and licentiousness and liberty, if they have the support of force, are virtue and happiness, and the rest of these embellishments—the agreements of men which are against nature—are all mere stuff and nonsense" (492c).

Socrates replies that Callicles is indeed being frank, even to the extent of expressing openly what many people think privately but would not dream of proclaiming publicly. Only the indecent man asks why be decent or publicly ridicules decency. The immoderate character of Callicles emerges clearly as the dialogue progresses. This is important in view of the fact that for Plato the individual is a paradigm of the city. It is not difficult to understand that Callicles would preside over a city characterized by the pursuit of pleasure; a city where pleasure would be pursued to the fullest extent.

Socrates takes up a point raised by Callicles in the course of his speech. He asks Callicles: "do you say the desires are not to be moderated if a man would be such as he ought to be, but he should let them be as great as possible and provide them with satisfaction from some source or other, and this is virtue?" (492D). Callicles agrees with Socrates' summary, but denies that those who want nothing are happy. If this were true, he says, stones and corpses would be most happy. He steadfastly refuses to be impressed with Socrates' fables about how the life of the temperate man is happier. Once again we find Socrates appealing to Callicles to change his way of life; but Callicles says Socrates is wasting his time. Nevertheless, Socrates keeps trying; this time he attempts to persuade Callicles that the temperate life is preferable to the dissolute life. But Callicles is unimpressed, preferring to remain adamant in his claim that the life of hedonism is preferable because the happy life consists in experiencing the largest possible amount of pleasure. The happy life for Callicles consists in having the most desires and satisfying them—i.e., it is a life of unbridled hedonism. For Socrates, and for the tradition that emerged out of his influence, pleasure and pain cannot be the fundamental fact because it is one's nature or constitution that prompts one to experience pleasures and pains; the worth of a thing cannot be judged in terms of its ability to give pleasure. That is why an ass would prefer hay to gold; it would by nature derive more pleasure from the hay. For

Socrates that which completes or perfects the nature of the thing is its proper good and this is accompanied by pleasure; but it is pursued because it is the being's proper good and not because it gives pleasure. And since the human good for Socrates is related to the highest human faculty—i.e., reason—the highest goods and pleasures are those which pertain to the mind or wisdom. The bodily goods and pleasures are necessarily of a lower order and are to be subordinated to the higher. The important point is, however, that a knowledge of the proper good is prior to the quest for pleasure. For Callicles, the knowledge or anticipation of pleasure is the hallmark of the good.

Socrates then leads Callicles to explore whether there are good and bad pleasures. He proceeds by showing Callicles that knowledge and pleasure are not the same thing and that courage is not identical with pleasure. He wins Callicles' assent to the conclusion that knowledge and courage are different from the good as well as from each other (497). At length, Callicles concedes that all wants and desires are painful. This concession forces him to conclude, in contradiction of his earlier claim, that the pleasant is not simply identical with the good nor the painful simply identical with the bad. At this point Callicles professes once again not to understand Socrates. But Socrates insists that he does, and tests his understanding with the question "Does not each of us cease at the same moment from thirst and from the pleasure he gets by drinking?" When Callicles persists in his claims that he does not understand what Socrates means, Gorgias breaks into the conversation and reproves Callicles. He insists that Callicles answer Socrates for his benefit and the benefit of the other people present—i.e., "that the arguments may be brought to a conclusion" (497B). But Callicles protests to Gorgias that Socrates' questions are petty and irrelevant. Gorgias insists that Callicles must go along to the end with Socrates. Callicles concedes reluctantly for Gorgias' sake. Plato not only demonstrates that Gorgias has authority over Callicles here but he makes it clear that the dialogue is primarily addressed to Gorgias—it is primarily for the benefit of the teacher of rhetoric. The implication appears to be that if Socrates can get through to Gorgias he can get to all those whom he teaches. But does he get through to Gorgias?

This brief exchange between Callicles and Gorgias is characteristic of the entire Callicles portion of the dialogue: Callicles is not only an impatient participant in this kind of conversation but resolutely determined not to learn from Socrates; he is uncomfortable in exposing the basic principles of his political philosophy to the philosophic scrutiny of Socrates. In short, Callicles, the aspiring politician, has a closed mind, but he has the knowledge of what most people believe constitutes the human good. He also believes that, thanks to Gorgias' instruction in rhetoric, he has the means by which to win the support of the majority of his constituents.

Socrates repeats his question whether everyone does not cease to feel thirst and pleasure at the same time. Callicles agrees that this is also true for hunger and other such physical pleasures. Having shown Callicles that one can experience pleasure and pain at the same time, Socrates reminds him that he had agreed earlier that this is not possible with the good and the bad. This leads Socrates to conclude once again that the good is not identical with the pleasant nor the bad identical with the painful. This being so, he asks how Callicles can now claim that the pleasant is identical with the good and the painful identical with the bad. Socrates presses Callicles by showing that fools and cowards experience or enjoy pleasure as much as wise and brave men do, so that pleasure and pain must be clearly distinct from the good and the bad. Callicles concedes that fools and cowards enjoy perhaps even more pleasure at times. Socrates emphasizes the contradiction in Callicles' position by reminding him that he agreed earlier that the wise and brave were good and that they were good because of the presence of good things. How then does he claim that the coward is good? Because of the presence of what good things? For Callicles the pleasant is what makes the coward good, and he remains good only so long as the pleasures remain; the reverse holds true according to Callicles for the painful or bad. This leads Socrates to conclude that those who enjoy the most pleasure must, according to Callicles' reasoning, be the best. And, further, that the good and bad men are made good or bad by the same thing, i.e., by pleasures.

Callicles reacts impatiently at this point and claims that everybody knows that there are good and bad pleasures. This important retreat based on the appeal to mankind in general proves fatal to Callicles in the end. Socrates immediately pursues the advantage with the question whether the beneficial pleasures produce some good and the unbeneficial ones some evil. Callicles concedes that they do. Armed with this important concession, Socrates then asks Callicles whether what he said holds true for bodily pleasures, such as eating and drinking. Those pleasures which produce health are good and those which produce disease are bad. Callicles agrees. This leads Socrates to his first major victory in his conversation with Callicles. He asks Callicles whether it follows from what they have just agreed upon that one ought to choose only the beneficial pleasures and reject the base or unbeneficial ones. Callicles concedes that all things should be done with a view to what is good. This leads Socrates to conclude that "it is for the sake of what is good that we should do everything, including what is pleasant, not the good for the sake of the pleasant" (400).

What begins to emerge here unknown to Callicles is that *knowledge* of the human good must precede pursuit of the pleasant. Socrates will make much of this in the ensuing discussion. He begins by showing Callicles that not everyone can identify what is good for him—only the man who possesses knowledge of the art, such as the physician. At this point Socrates reminds Callicles that in the preceding discussions he placed cookery among those endeavors which produce pleasure without knowledge of the good; among those concerned with the good he named medicine. Callicles must surely have recalled that Socrates also placed rhetoric with cookery and those practices which produce pleasure without knowledge.

Socrates draws Callicles' attention to the fact that what is really at stake in the discussion is the most important subject of which course of life is best—the life of rhetoric and politics (to which Callicles has invited Socrates) or the life of moderation and virtue founded in philosophy. In other words, the conflict is presented as being between the life of unrestrained hedonism and the life of natural justice and moderation. Which way of life ought to be pursued by the city? It is from this point on that we begin to understand rhetoric as ideology and how philosophy and ideology are dramatically opposed to one another. Socrates views those knacks which pander or minister to pleasure without regard to the better or worse for man as pernicious; it is clear that he views rhetoric as such a knack. Callicles "agrees," but only in the interest of bringing the discussion to a close. He remains impervious to instruction.

At this point (502E) Socrates begins to show Callicles that the only kind of rhetoric worthy of man is that which does not pander to the multitude—i.e., that rhetoric Socrates employs which is designed to make the citizens better by reproving them; but "it is a rhetoric you never yet saw," he says (503B). That is, a kind of rhetoric he cannot learn from Gorgias. The kind of rhetoric Socrates says is the only legitimate kind is that designed to produce order in men's souls. When he asks Callicles to name that order Callicles is unable to do so—i.e., he does not know what is good for man. Socrates replies that that order is called by the names of *justice* and *moderation*. And rhetoric must be used to engender justice in one's fellow citizens and uproot injustices; to produce moderation and uproot licentiousness. For, says Socrates, what good is the life of a healthy man who is at the same time unjust? Furthermore, a temperate life—the life of moderation according to nature—is the only life worthy of men because it engenders health. And what is true of the body must also be true of the soul. All this leads to the conclusion that those who pursue a life of hedonism (proposed by Callicles) must be reproved or corrected; thus rhetoric must attempt to do this, but it is not pleasant. And it is clear that Gorgias' rhetoric is incapable of doing this—i.e., of leading men to the noble and the just.

Once again we see Callicles completely closed to instruction. He retorts: "Well, and not a jot do I care, either, for anything you say; I only gave you those answers to oblige Gorgias" (505c). Indeed he wants to discontinue the discussion or have Socrates finish it by himself. At this point Socrates addresses all three—Callicles, Gorgias, and Polus—urging that the truth of the matter must be pursued to its conclusion—"for it is a benefit to all alike that it be revealed."

Here Socrates is clearly engaging in that kind of rhetoric which he says is the only legitimate form; yet his audience is singularly unreceptive. Once again Gorgias intervenes, but this time agrees with Callicles that Socrates should finish the matter by himself. But Socrates insists that Callicles assist him in finishing the argument. It is important to observe that Socrates insists on continuing with Callicles—the politician—because the results of the discussion have profound practical importance. In other words, Socrates' message in this dialogue is addressed primarily to the practical political order through Callicles (but profoundly shaped by Gorgias' instruction in rhetoric).

From here on Socrates draws out the political consequences of the entire dialogue. He begins with a recapitulation of the arguments up to this point. In the course of this résumé Socrates draws out the important conclusion from the premisses established that "the virtue of each thing, whether of a body, or of a soul, or any live creature, does not arrive most properly by accident, but by an order of rightness or art that is apportioned to each" (506D). That is to say, right order is established *by nature* and not by convention. The further conclusion is inescapable: "Hence it is a certain order proper to each existent thing that by its advent in each makes it good" (506E). And since the ordered or orderly soul is at the same time moderate, the opposite of moderation (i.e., licentiousness) is the indicator of an unorderly soul. The temperate soul is thus good while the licentious one is bad—in short, the life proposed by Callicles cannot be said to be good (507A). The moderate man, on the other hand, is thus shown to be also just, brave, and pious, and hence the sum of what constitutes a good man. From here on Socrates attacks the kind of life Callicles was proposing. Says Socrates:

This, in my opinion, is the mark on which a man should fix his eyes throughout life; he should concentrate all his own and his city's efforts on this one business of providing a man who would be blessed with

the needful justice and moderation; not letting one's desires go unrestrained and in one's attempts to satisfy them—an interminable
trouble—leading the life of a robber [507E].

If all the preceding steps are true, says Socrates, then they must
explore the consequences of the indictment of that way of life, proposed by Callicles (and by implication by Gorgias and Polus) and
by the politicans, which Callicles cited as enviable. The first consequence is that the only valid use of rhetoric is to prevent one's
friends and fellow-citizens from pursuing the base life of unbridled hedonism. This clearly entails punishing (i.e., correcting)
those who pursue the dissolute life. But the major consequence is
that each man and especially each politician must acquire the art
and power by which the life of justice and temperance can be assured. This art and power is to be found in wisdom—i.e., in the
pursuit of genuine knowledge of the human good by being open
to philosophy. Philosophy is presented by Socrates as the active
and perpetual quest for knowledge or understanding of what is
good for men by nature. It is precisely this counter-invitation which
Callicles resolutely refuses to accept. Callicles does not want genuine knowledge of the human good. He merely wishes to lead the
many according to their understanding of the human good as
pleasure.

It is important to understand that, however insistent Socrates
has been that Callicles turn away from hedonism, he does not ever
counsel that Callicles abandon politics.

Socrates continues by showing that tyrannical rule is inevitably
associated with the rule of base hedonism. The tyrant will not tolerate the presence of just men because like engenders like; and the
just man stands as a constant indictment of the tyrant's injustice.
The power of such a tyrant is thus clearly base because it is exercised in the interest of injustice. Such a tyrant will go uncorrected
and hence lead a life of continual debasement and misery. But by
far the worse consequence of this kind of rule is that the citizens
will also become pursuers of base things in imitation of the ruler;
they will do this not only by choice in an effort to please the ruler
but through the laws established by the ruler. And Socrates has no

illusions about the fate of one (such as himself) who refuses to assimilate himself to the constitution of such an unjust regime; he cannot employ forensic rhetoric because he cannot defend himself; he will be like a physician tried by a jury of children on a charge brought by a pastry cook. He cannot plead that he had provided them with pleasure and no pains although the pain he might have prescribed as medicine was better for them in the long run.

Socrates does not dwell unduly on his likely fate; instead he presses the point that the politician must make it his endeavor in tending the city and its citizens to make them as good as possible. The indictment of rhetoric and hence of ideological politics is clear: the rhetorician or the ideological politician does not *know* what the true good for man is, and hence cannot lead his city and its citizens to virtue—to justice and moderation. All they can do is to pander to the pleasures of the citizens, thereby making them not better but worse. Is it any wonder that the rulers cited by Callicles earlier were brought down by their citizens? The fault lies with the rulers for not having made them better. Neither he nor the teacher of rhetoric can be exonerated of the blame due to the evil deeds of their followers.

Socrates now pointedly addresses himself to Callicles in the following words:

> And now, most excellent men, since you are yourself just entering upon a public career, and are inviting me to do the same, and reproaching me for not doing it, shall we not inquire of one another: Let us see, has Callicles ever made any of the citizens better? [515B]

Callicles obviously cannot point to such a one. But the question must also be put to Socrates. Callicles does not put the question, so impatient is he on finishing the argument. Socrates nevertheless continues to demand what it is that Callicles has by which the citizens shall be made better. In specific terms, how does Callicles propose to make the Athenians better? Callicles refuses to answer, but Socrates answers for him: Callicles can in no sense make them better but only worse. And, as if this were not shock enough to Callicles, Socrates claims that he himself is "one of the few, not to

say the only one, in Athens who attempts the true art of politics"
(521D), because the speeches he makes are aimed not at gratification but at what is best instead of what is most pleasant. But how
can Socrates' rhetoric be of use in politics if it cannot win over
aspiring politicians such as Callicles? Socrates clearly fails to persuade Callicles, and this failure must be seen as an indictment of
his kind of rhetoric as well as of his claim to practice the true political art.

The dialogue concludes with Socrates relating a story to which
no one responds; it is the last speech of the dialogue and it is primarily directed to Callicles. The story, a somewhat modified
Homeric tale, is intended to reinforce the last point that Socrates
makes in the dialogue: namely, that "no man fears the mere act of
dying, except he be utterly irrational and unmanly; doing injustice
is what one fears; for to arrive in Hades having one's soul full of
misdeeds is the uttermost of all evils" (522E). It is a tale which
Socrates says Callicles will understand as a myth ($\mu\hat{v}\theta$os), but
which he himself regards as reason ($\lambda\acute{o}\gamma$os), one which conveys
the truth. Leaving open the possibility of judgment in Hades,
Socrates claims that the only thing that really matters in this life
and in the next is the judgment of a wise judge of the soul or character of men stripped of all protective veneer of clothing and status.
Socrates concludes with a restatement of his invitation to Callicles:
"Let us therefore take as our guide the speech [$\lambda\acute{o}\gamma$os] now dis-
closed, which indicates to us that this way of life is best—to live
and die in the practice alike of justice and of all other virtue"
(527E).

The story is thus an appeal to the conventional poetic theology
of the judgment which awaits men in the next world. We have
here the curious picture of Socrates, the philosopher, employing
poetic speech in a rhetorical performance in a dialogue which pur-
ports (in the early stage, at least) to condemn rhetoric. Not only
do we thus see Socrates repudiate his early extreme view of rhetoric, but we also see him rehabilitate rhetoric by aligning it with
philosophy in the interest of the just regime. But by so doing Socrates explicitly acknowledges the indispensability of rhetoric for

politics. The initial unequivocal repudiation of rhetoric and Gorgias is, in the final analysis, seriously moderated. We learn above all that rhetoric is indispensable to the establishment of the just regime; it is the necessary mediator between philosophy and the city. Socrates (i.e., philosophy) cannot speak directly to large numbers because his speech is dialectic: it aims at conviction, but this requires time and attention, not to mention capacity. And not many men have these things. Rhetoric, on the other hand, leads to persuasion through speech, which does not require the essentials of dialectic. Furthermore, the rhetorician can speak to large numbers. It is for this reason that the dialogue is named after and addressed to Gorgias and not Callicles. Callicles is a fictitious person, but Gorgias is not. Socrates is therefore more concerned about his ability to teach Gorgias than to teach Callicles. And we know that Gorgias continued to teach his rhetoric. Socrates accordingly failed in practice to instruct Gorgias.

Whatever doubt remains as to the success or failure of Socrates in this dialogue, one thing remains certain: Socrates condemns the hedonistic character of those politics which flow from the low rhetoric taught by Gorgias and espoused by Callicles. Their kind of rhetoric is rendered particularly dangerous in regimes which depend upon popular consent, because the politician who can, through the use of rhetoric, appeal to the widest order of pleasures is likely to be successful. The philosopher cannot move nations; he speaks to only a few. In other words, since the politician–rhetorician who appeals to the pleasures of the people (i.e., their passions) is more likely to be more successful than the politician–philosopher who appeals to reason, the former is more than likely to be successful. For everyone knows what his or her pleasures are and can be readily *persuaded* that such-and-such will be pleasurable. And since ideological politics is the politics of mass movements—i.e., the appeal to the support of large numbers of people—rhetoric is the means by which mass movements are formed and directed. In short, when rhetoric and hedonism join forces in regimes based on consent, the triumph of political hedonism is virtually assured. Plato realized this in the *Gorgias* and attempts to show how the Socratic rhetoric, the accusatory rhetoric, can be of service to the city and the quest for virtue. Indeed, he shows how indispensable the accusatory rhetoric is to those regimes founded in consent.

NOTE

1. All references to the *Gorgias* are to the Loeb Classical Library ed., trans. W. R. M. Lamb (London: Heinemann; Cambridge: Harvard University Press, 1975).

CONCLUSION

Modern Political Hedonism and Accusatory Rhetoric

IT IS SURELY EVIDENT from the foregoing discussion that political hedonism has become firmly entrenched in the public philosophy of western liberalism: so entrenched that the success of any attempt to dislodge it by reasserting the primacy of the Socratic tradition of Plato and Aristotle (and their disciples) is highly improbable. In short, it is one thing to give an account of the rise of political hedonism, but quite another matter to correct its deficiencies or to replace it altogether with an alternative political philosophy. To concede this is not to forget that the philosophy of Plato and Aristotle (and their disciples) kept the philosophy of hedonism at bay for more than two millennia. Nor is it to concede that the Socratic critique of political hedonism has been rendered permanently irrelevant. If we learn anything from Plato's *Gorgias* it is that there must always be available in hedonistic regimes a certain kind of rhetoric inspired by Socrates which calls attention to the dangers and limitations of hedonism. But we must not lose sight of the fact that Socrates' failure to convince either Callicles or Gorgias constitutes a major failure of accusatory rhetoric. Nevertheless, the power and cogency of that critique remains as relevant today as ever, for the conflict between the life of base hedonism and the life of moderation is an ongoing, ever-recurring battle.

But the Socratic or accusatory rhetoric must be made to address the peculiar problems of contemporary liberal regimes. In order to do this we must understand clearly the implications of the development of ancient hedonism into modern hedonism. By so doing we come to understand more clearly why political hedonism has become so deeply ingrained in modern minds, and how difficult it is to moderate its influence.

The modern influential philosophers discussed throughout this study transformed ancient hedonism, which was essentially private and apolitical, into political hedonism, into a major public force in modern government and law. They elevated the pursuit of pleasure into public law; they made pleasure (or "commodious living," as Hobbes put it) the end of good government by affirming the human good in terms of pleasure. Modern political hedonism consolidated its hold on modern minds by virtue of the enormous support of modern technology, which emerged as the principal instrument of modern hedonism. We saw at the beginning of this study how indispensable technology was to the founders of modernity. All the world can see today how Francis Bacon's urgings have been heeded. Modern technology has "relieved man's estate" beyond even Bacon's wildest dreams. And the success of modern technology forecloses any simplistic attempt to reassert the primacy of premodern philosophy, any more than it could hope to assert the primacy of pre-modern science.

In addition, the successful extension of republican principles of government has provided institutional support for political hedonism. It would clearly be unthinkable today to appeal to a transcendent authority—in the form either of natural justice or of God—for the legitimacy of government, so far has legitimacy become identified with consent of the governed. And in those regimes where that consent is sought and obtained in the appeal to pleasure, there political hedonism becomes firmly established in legitimacy.

But are we justified in conceeding total victory to Epicurus and his modern disciples in *reason*, or philosophy, because they have succeeded in *practice*? What compounds this question is that reason or philosophy has been driven from the city, from public policy. Machiavelli and Bacon have successfully inculcated the concept of the primacy of doing over thinking, of practice over theory or philosophy. Indeed, philosophy has been replaced by science (physics): the worth and correctness of any modern proposal must meet the demands of "scientific objectivity," not philosophic truth.

In this context the old moral philosophy of Socrates, Plato, and Aristotle appears weak and unarmed. It cannot appeal to scientific or technological achievement in support of its teaching. Modern hedonism, on the other hand, is fully armed with the achievements of modern technology and modern republican or democratic institutions. Modern science and technology stand as a dual barrier preventing critics from penetrating through to the moral baseness of modern hedonism. It has become virtually immune to criticism; at least, it has become insulated from moral accountability.

As Daniel Bell has observed, "The world of hedonism is the world of fashion, photography, advertising, television, travel. . . . It is no accident that the successful new magazine of the previous decade was called *Playboy* and that its success . . . is due largely to the fact that it encourages fantasies of male sexual prowess. . . . In the 1950s and the 1960s, the cult of Orgasm succeeded the cult of Mammon as the basic passion of American life."[1] Hedonism in America has become preoccupied with the extension of ἔρως; contemporary hedonism has become more openly sensual. And the basis of extension is founded in the claim to right; the claim to an absolute right over one's body is the latest manifestation of the right to self-preservation.

For Socrates and his disciples the quest for pleasure as an end leads to baseness and self-destruction. As Montesquieu observed of republican Rome: "I believe the sect of Epicurus, which was introduced at Rome toward the end of the republic, contributed much toward tainting the heart and mind of the Romans."[2] Those regimes which pursue policies aimed at the widest gratification of pleasure pursue the base human ends and are incapable of preventing an ever-increasing baseness. For hedonism is essentially insatiable; it is inherently incapable of satisfaction and inimical to community because pleasures are radically private.

Today those who would attempt to restore at least a semblance of the standards espoused by the Socratic tradition must do so from outside the mainstream of the dominant influence, and they will be recognized as extraneous influences. But surely this tradition must continue to attempt to influence the direction of public policy through an accusatory rhetoric, through critical writing and speaking calling attention to the demeaning prospects of hedonism. For modern hedonism leads to the lowest form of moral relativism, which in turn leads to nihilism; for where there are no limits by nature on the satisfaction of wants, nothing is forbidden. Moral relativism thus constitutes the replacement by the lowest standards of the highest standards by which to judge the noble, the just, and the good.

We have seen that the great conflict in principle between the proponents of political hedonism and the proponents of the Socratic tradition (Plato, Aristotle, Aquinas, and their disciples) is that the human good is identical with pleasure, in the former; while for the Socratic tradition the pleasant is not an end in itself; however much pleasure may accompany the good, the good is what enriches the human condition according to standards prescribed by nature in prompting the development of man's higher capacities.

One of the surest signs of the victory of political hedonism is the absence of a critical literature which attempts to understand political hedonism in its broadest context and the failure to scrutinize the fundamental principles of modern liberalism. This is not to say that all modern authors are unaware of the problem. John Rawls's book on justice[3] is a good example of the attempt to set limits to the tradition of political hedonism—without, however, abandoning the principles of that tradition. Indeed, Rawls's book is written in the safety of the unawareness of the principles of the tradition of political hedonism. It does indicate, however, the urgency with which some clear-sighted members of that tradition have begun to see its limitations.

The failure of modern philosophy and social science to come to terms with the fundamental principles of modern political hedonism may be premised on the belief that the victory over the ancient Socratic tradition is secure for all times. The resolute refusal to re-open the theoretical controversy reaffirms the victory in practice. This anti-theoretical posture is in stark contrast to the willingness of Plato and Aristotle to explore and expose the baseness of hedonism.

NOTES

1. *The Cultural Contradictions of Capitalism* (New York: Basic Books, 1975), p. 70.

2. *Considerations on the Causes of the Greatness of the Romans and their Decline* (Ithaca: Cornell University Press, 1965), trans. with notes and an intro. by David Lowenthal; Chapter X, "The Corruption of the Romans," p. 97.

3. *Theory of Justice* (Cambridge: Harvard University Press, 1973).

Bibliography

Agrippa, Cornelius. *The Vanity of the Arts and Sciences* (London, 1569).

Ames, William. *Conscience* (London, 1639).

Bacon, Francis. *Works*, edd. James Spedding, Robert Leslie Ellis, and Douglas Denon Heath (Boston, 1862).

Bailey, Cyril. *Epicurus* (Oxford, 1926).

Baxter, Richard. *The Arrogancy of Reason Against Divine Revelations Repressed* (London, 1655).

———. *The Reasons of the Christian Religion* (London, 1667).

Bell, Daniel. *The Cultural Contradictions of Capitalism* (New York, 1975).

Bentham, Jeremy. *Works*, ed. John Bowring (London, 1838–1843; reprinted New York, 1962).

———. *Of Laws in General*, ed. H. L. A. Hart (London, 1970).

———. *A Table of the Springs of Action* (London, 1815).

———. *An Introduction to the Principles of Morals and Legislation* (Oxford, 1892).

———. *A Fragment of Government* (London, 1776).

———. *Defence of Usury* (Dublin, 1788).

———. *Justice and Codification Petitions* (London, 1829).

———. *Essay on Political Tactics* (London, 1791).

———. *Deontology or The Science of Morality*, ed. John Bowring (London, 1834).

———. *A Comment on the Commentaries: A Criticism of William Blackstone's Commentaries on the Laws of England* (Oxford, 1928).

Bernier, François. *Three Discourses of Happiness, Virtue and Liberty* (London, 1699).

Blackmore, Richard. *The Nature of Man* (London, 1711).

Boyle, Robert. *A Discourse of Things above Reason, Inquiring Whether a Philosopher Should Admit There Are Such* (London, 1681).

———. *A Free Enquiry into the Vulgarly Received Notion of Nature* (London, 1685/6).

———. *The Excellency of Theology, Compared with Natural Philosophy* (London, 1674).

———. *About the Excellency and Grounds of the Mechanical Hypothesis* (London, 1674).

——. *Some Considerations about the Reconcileableness of Reason and Religion* (London, 1875).

——. *Of the High Veneration Man's Intellect Owes to God* (London, 1685).

Brandt, Frithiof. *Thomas Hobbes's Mechanical Conception of Nature* (London, 1928).

Brett, G. S. *The Philosophy of Gassendi* (London, 1908).

Burnet, Gilbert. *A Sermon Preached at the Funeral of the Honourable Robert Boyle* (London, 1692).

——. *An Exposition of the Thirty-Nine Articles of the Church of England* (London, 1699).

Burnet, Thomas. *The Sacred Theory of the Earth* (London, 1697).

Burton, Robert. *The Anatomy of Melancholy* (Oxford, 1624).

Casaubon, Meric. *Of Credulity and Incredulity in Things Natural, Civil and Divine* (London, 1668).

Charleton, Walter. *Epicurus's Morals* (London, 1656; reprinted in 1926, ed. Frederick Manning).

Charleton, Walter. *Enquiries into Human Nature* (London, 1680).

——. *The Immortality of the Human Soul Demonstrated by the Light of Nature* (London, 1657).

——. *The Darkness of Atheism Dispelled by the Light of Nature* (London, 1652).

Chillingworth, William. *The Religion of Protestants: A Safe Way to Salvation* (London, 1640).

Clarke, John. *An Enquiry into the Cause and Origin of Moral Evil* (London, 1720–1721).

——. *A Demonstration of Some of the Principal Sections of Sir Isaac Newton's Principles of Natural Philosophy* (London, 1730).

Cohen, I. Bernard. *Isaac Newton's Papers and Letters of Natural Philosophy and Related Documents* (Cambridge, 1958).

Colie, Rosalie L. *Light and Enlightenment* (Cambridge, 1957).

Cox, Richard. *Locke on War and Peace* (Oxford, 1964).

Debus, A. G. (ed.). *Science and Education in the Seventeenth Century* (London, 1970).

De Santillana, Giorgio. *The Crime of Galileo* (Chicago, 1955).

Descartes, René. *A Discourse of a Method for the Well Guiding of Reason and the Discovery of Truth in the Sciences*, trans. Thomas Newcombe (London, 1649).

Digby, John. *Epicurus's Morals* [an English translation of du Rondelle's *La morale d'Epicure*] (London, 1712).

Eachard, John. *Mr. Hobbes's State of Nature Considered* (London, 1672).

Ehrard, Jean. *L'Idée de nature en France dans la première moitié du XVIII⁰ siècle*, 2 vols. (Paris, 1963).

Filmer, Robert. *Patriarch or The Natural Power of Kings* (London, 1680).

Fulton, John A. *A Bibliography of the Honourable Robert Boyle* (Oxford, 1961).

Gassendi, Pierre. *De vita et moribus Epicuri libri octo* (Lyon, 1647).

——. *Syntagma philosophiae Epicuri cum refutationibus dogmatum quae contra fidem Christianam ab eo asserta sunt* (Amsterdam, 1684).

——. *Exercitationes paradoxicae adversus Aristotelos*, etc. (Amsterdam, 1649).

Gay, Peter. *The Enlightenment* (New York, 1969).

Glavill, Joseph. *The Vanity of Dogmatizing* (London, 1660).

Goodman, Godfrey. *The Fall of Man or the Corruption of Nature, Proved by Natural Reason* (London, 1616).

Gunn, J. A. W. *Politics and Public Interest in the Seventeenth Century* (London, 1969).

Hadzsits, G. D. *Lucretius and His Influence* (New York, 1935).

Hakewill, George. *An Apologie or Declaration of the Power and Providence of God in the Government of the World* (London, 1627).

Halévy, Elie. *The Growth of Philosophic Radicalism*, trans. Mary Morris (London, 1972).

Hales, John. *Sermons Preached at Eton* (London, 1673).

Hall, J. G. *Thoughts on Holy Scripture by Francis Bacon* (London, 1862).

Harrington, James. *The Censure of the Rota Upon Mr. Milton's Book: The Ready and Easie Way to Establish a Free Commonwealth* (London, 1660).

Henry, Matthew. *An Exposition of the Historical Books of the New Testament* (London, 1715).

Hicks, R. D., trans. *Diogenes Laertius* (London, 1925).

Hill, W. S. (ed.). *Studies in Richard Hooker* (Cleveland, 1972).

Hirschman, Albert O. *The Passions and the Interests* (Princeton, 1977).

Hobbes, Thomas. *The English Works of Thomas Hobbes*, ed. William Molesworth, 11 vols. (London, 1839–1845).

——. *Leviathan*, ed. Michael Oakeshott (Oxford, 1960).

——. *The Elements of Law, Natural and Politic*, ed. Ferdinand Tönnies (Cambridge, 1928).

——. *Behemoth*, ed. Ferdinand Tönnies (Cambridge, 1928).

——. *A Dialogue Between a Philosopher and a Student of the Common Laws of England*, ed. Joseph Cropsey (Chicago, 1971).

Hood, F. C. *The Divine Politics of Hobbes* (Oxford, 1964).

Hooker, Richard. *Of the Laws of Ecclesiastical Politie* (London, 1639).

——. *His Judgment of Regal Power in Matters of Religion* (London, 1661).

Howard, Edward. *Remarks on the New Philosophy of Descartes* (London, 1770).

Hume, David. *A Treatise of Human Nature*, ed. L. H. Selby-Bigge (Oxford, 1896).

——. *Enquiry Concerning Human Understanding*, ed. L. H. Selby-Bigge (Oxford, 1894).

———. *Essays, Moral and Political* (Edinburgh, 1741).

Jones, Richard Foster. *The Seventeenth Century* (Stanford, 1951).

Kendall. Willmore. *John Locke and the Doctrine of Majority Rule* (Urbana, 1959).

Kocher, Paul H. *Science and Religion in Elizabethan England* (San Marino, 1953).

Krieger, Leonard. *The Politics of Discretion: Pufendorf and the Acceptance of Natural Law* (Chicago, 1956).

La Mettrie, Julien Offray. *Oeuvres philosophiques* (Amsterdam, 1764).

La Grand, Antoine. *An Entire Body of Philosophy According to the Principles of the Famous Renate Des Cartes* (London, 1694).

———. *Man Without Passion* (London, 1694).

Locke, John. *An Essay Concerning Human Understanding* (London, 1694; 2nd ed.).

———. *The Works of John Locke in Ten Volumes* (London, 1823).

———. *An Essay Concerning Human Understanding*, ed. A. S. Pringle-Pattison (Oxford, 1969).

———. *Essays on the Law of Nature*, ed. W. von Leyden (Oxford, 1954).

———. *Two Treatises of Government*, with introduction and notes by Peter Laslett (Cambridge, 1963).

———. *Two Tracts on Government*, ed. Philip Abrams (Cambridge, 1967).

Lowde, James. *A Discourse Concerning the Nature of Man* (London, 1694).

Lucretius, *De rerum natura*: trans. Thomas Creech, *On the Nature of Things* (London, 1714).

Lyons, David. *In the Interest of the Governed* (Oxford, 1975).

Macpherson, C. B. *The Political Theory of Possessive Individualism* (Oxford, 1962).

Mandeville, Bernard. *Free Thought on Religion, The Church and National Happiness* (London, 1720).

Marvell, Andrew. *A Short Historical Essay Touching General Counsels, Creeds and Impositions in Matters of Religion* (London, 1680).

Mayo, Thomas Franklin. *Epicurus in England 1650–1725* (Dallas, 1934).

McLachlan, Herbert. *Newton's Theological Manuscripts* (Liverpool, 1950).

———. *The Religious Opinions of Milton, Locke and Newton* (Manchester, 1941).

Merlan, Philip. *Studies in Epicurus and Aristotle* (Wiesbaden, 1960).

Midgely, Robert. *A New Treatise of Natural Philosophy* (London, 1687).

Mill, John Stuart. *System of Logic*, 4th ed. (London, 1856).

———. *Works* (Toronto, 1967).

———. *Utilitarianism, Liberty, and Representative Government* (New York, 1951).

Milton, John. *The Ready and Easy Way to Establish a Free Commonwealth* (London, 1659).

——. *Of True Religion, Heresie* (London, 1673).

——. *A Treatise of Civil Power in Ecclesiastical Causes* (London, 1659).

Nichols, James H. *Epicurean Political Philosophy* (Ithaca, 1977).

Parker, Samuel. *A Demonstration of the Divine Authority of the Law of Nature and of the Christian Religion* (London, 1681).

——. *History of His Own Time* (London, 1727).

——. *A Discourse of Ecclesiastical Politie* (London, 1670).

——. *The Case of the Church of England* (London, 1681).

Plato. *Gorgias*:

W. R. M. Lamb (trans.), *Lysis, Symposium, Gorgias*, Greek text and English translation (London & New York, 1961).

E. R. Dodds, *Plato, Gorgias: A Revised Text with Introductory Commentary* (Oxford, 1959).

du Rondelle, Jacques. *La morale d'Epicure avec des réflections* (Paris, 1695).

——. *De vita et moribus Epicuri* (Amsterdam, 1693).

Ross, Alexander. *The New Planet no Planet: or the Earth no Wandering Star, Except in the Wandering Heads of Galileans* (London, 1646).

Rousseau, Jean-Jacques. *The First and Second Discourses*, trans. Roger D. Masters and Judith R. Masters (New York, 1964).

——. *Oeuvres complètes* (Paris, 1971).

——. *Emile*, trans. Barbara Foxley (London, 1961).

——. *The Reveries of a Solitary*, trans. John G. Fletcher (London, 1927).

——. *Social Contract*, trans. Maurice Cranson (London, 1968).

——. *Confessions*, ed. R. Niklaus, 2 vols. (London, 1961).

Schofield, Robert E. *Mechanism and Materialism in British Natural Philosophy* (Princeton, 1970).

Senault, John Francis. *The Use of the Passions* (London, 1671).

——. *Man Becomes Guilty, or the Corruption of Nature by Sinne* (London, 1650).

——. *The Christian Man: or the Reparation of Nature by Grace* (London, 1650).

Shafto, J. *The Great Law of Nature or Self-Preservation, Examined, Asserted and Vindicated from Mr. Hobbes His Abuses* (London, 1673).

Sidney, Algernon. *Discourses Concerning Government* (London, 1753).

Spink, J. S. *French Free Thought from Gassendi to Voltaire* (London, 1960).

Spinoza, Baruch. *A Treatise Partly Theological and Partly Political* (London, 1689).

Spragens, Thomas A. *The Politics of Motion: The World of Thomas Hobbes* (London, 1973).

Sprat, Thomas. *History of the Royal Society* (London, 1667).

Stewart, John. *The Moral and Political Philosophy of David Hume* (New York, 1963).

Strauss, Leo. *Natural Right and History* (Chicago, 1952).

———. *The Political Philosophy of Hobbes* (Oxford, 1936).

Stubbs, Henry. *A Censure upon Certain Passages Contained in the History of the Royal Society, as Being Destructive to the Established Religion and Church of England* (London, 1670).

Stillingfleet, Edward. *Answer to Mr. Locke's Letter Concerning Some Passages Relating to his Essay of Humane Understanding* (London, 1697).

———. *Answer to Mr. Locke's Second Letter* (London, 1698).

Taylor, Jeremy. *Sermons for all Sundays of the Year* (London, 1653).

Temple, William. *An Essay Upon the Ancient and Modern Learning* (London, 1690).

Topazio, Virgil. *D'Holbach's Moral Philosophy* (Geneva, 1956).

Trevor-Roper, H. R. *Religion, The Reformation and Social Change* (London, 1967).

Tulloch, John. *Rational Theology and Christian Philosophy in England in the Seventeenth Century* (Edinburgh, 1872).

Tyrrell, James. *A Brief Disquisition of the Law of Nature* (London, 1692).

Védrine, Hélène. *La Conception de la nature chez Giordano Bruno* (Paris, 1967).

Wallace, William. *Chief Ancient Philosophers* (London, 1880).

Ward, Seth. *In Thomae Hobbii philosophiam exercitatio epistolica* (Oxford, 1656).

Webster, Charles (ed.). *The Intellectual Revolution in Seventeenth-Century England* (London, 1974).

Westfall, Richard S. *Science and Religion in Seventeenth-Century England* (New Haven, 1958).

Wilkins, John. *Of the Principles and Duties of Natural Religion* (London, 1675).

———. *A Discourse Concerning a New Planet* (London, 1640).

Winstanley, Gerrard. *The Law of Freedom in a Platform: or the True Magistracy Restored* (London, 1652).

Wollaston, William. *Religion of Nature Delineated* (London, 1722).

Wotton, William. *Reflections Upon Ancient and Modern Learning* (London, 1694.

White, Howard. *Peace Among the Willows* (The Hague, 1968).